DIGITAL RESEARCH IN THE STUDY
OF CLASSICAL ANTIQUITY

Digital Research in the Arts and Humanities

Series Editors
Marilyn Deegan, Lorna Hughes and Harold Short

Digital technologies are becoming increasingly important to arts and humanities research and are expanding the horizons of our working methods. This important series will cover a wide range of disciplines with each volume focusing on a particular area, identifying the ways in which technology impacts specific subjects. The aim is to provide an authoritative reflection of the 'state of the art' in the application of computing and technology. The series will be critical reading for experts in digital humanities and technology issues but will also be of wide interest to all scholars working in humanities and arts research.

Other titles in the series

Revisualizing Visual Culture
Edited by Chris Bailey and Hazel Gardiner
ISBN 978 0 7546 7568 6

Interfaces of Performance
Edited by Maria Chatzichristodoulou,
Janis Jefferies and Rachel Zerihan
ISBN 978 0 7546 7576 1

Digital Research in the Study of Classical Antiquity

Edited by

GABRIEL BODARD
King's College London, UK

SIMON MAHONY
University College London, UK

Routledge
Taylor & Francis Group

LONDON AND NEW YORK

First published 2010 by Ashgate Publishing

2 Park Square, Milton Park, Abingdon, Oxon OX14 4RN
711 Third Avenue, New York, NY 10017, USA

Routledge is an imprint of the Taylor & Francis Group, an informa business

First issued in paperback 2016

British Library Cataloguing in Publication Data
Digital research in the study of classical antiquity. --
   (Digital research in the arts and humanities)
   1. Civilization, Classical--Data processing.
   2. Civilization, Classical--Computer network resources.
   3. Civilization, Classical--Research--Methodology.
   I. Series II. Bodard, Gabriel. III. Mahony, Simon.
   930'.072-dc22

Library of Congress Cataloging-in-Publication Data
Digital research in the study of classical antiquity / by [edited by] Gabriel Bodard and
Simon Mahony.
      p. cm. -- (Digital research in the arts and humanities)
   Includes bibliographical references and index.
   ISBN 978-0-7546-7773-4 (hardback) -- ISBN 978-0-7546-9523-3 (ebook)
1. Civilization, Classical--Research--Methodology. 2. Civilization, Classical--Research--
Technological innovations. 3. Civilization, Classical--Study and teaching--Technological
innovations. I. Bodard, Gabriel. II. Mahony, Simon.

   DE15.D54 2010
   330.0285'57--dc22

                                                                                2010001406

ISBN 13: 978-0-7546-7773-4 (hbk)
ISBN 13: 978-1-138-25216-5 (pbk)

Contents

List of Figures and Tables

Figures

Tables

Notes on Contributors

Gabriel Bodard works at the Centre for Computing in the Humanities, King's College London. He has a doctorate in Classics and specializes in Greek religion, literature, epigraphy and papyrology. He was Research Associate at the *Thesaurus Linguae Graecae*, and has worked on Digital Humanities projects since 2001, including the Inscriptions of Aphrodisias (of which he is co-author). He is currently working on the Inscriptions of Roman Cyrenaica, and consulting on the Andrew W. Mellon-funded Integrating Digital Papyrology project. He is on the steering committee of the British Epigraphy Society and the technical council of the Text Encoding Initiative.

Alan K. Bowman is Camden Professor of Ancient History and Director of the Centre for the Study of Ancient Documents, University of Oxford, which has pioneered the development of ICT tools for the study and web delivery of ancient texts on papyrus, wood and stone. Projects with substantial ICT elements, completed or in progress, include: the Vindolanda Tablets On-Line; Script, Image and the Culture of Writing in the Ancient World; Image Processing of Ancient Documents; Building a Virtual Research Environment for the Humanities (with Dr C.V. Crowther, Dr M.A. Fraser, JISC). He is a former member of AHDS Steering Committee and member of the British Academy's IT Committee.

Hugh A. Cayless holds a PhD in Classics and a Master's of Science in Information Science, both from UNC Chapel Hill. He has contributed to a number of Digital Humanities projects and is one of the founders of the EpiDoc consortium. He currently works for the NYU Digital Library Technology Services group on a portal for papyrological research, under a grant from the National Endowment for the Humanities. He also serves as a co-investigator on an NEH-funded project at UNC Chapel Hill to develop methods for linking manuscript images, transcriptions and annotations.

Amanda Clarke has been Research Fellow at the Department of Archaeology, University of Reading since 1997, and is the Director of the Silchester Field School, the Department of Archaeology's training excavation at Silchester Roman Town. She is also involved in the excavation and post-excavation publication of other departmental fieldwork projects including that of Pompeii. She has over twenty years of professional archaeological fieldwork experience, most recently with York Archaeological Trust on many of their large urban sites. She is also a Teaching Fellow in the Department of Archaeology at Boston University on the student training excavations in Belize, Central America and in Mahon, Menorca.

Charles V. Crowther is Assistant Director of the Centre for the Study of Ancient Documents and specialist in Greek epigraphy. He has worked extensively on the development of ICT tools for the study and web delivery of ancient texts and is a long-term collaborator with Alan Bowman in pioneering new methods for the computer-based enhancement of damaged documents. Projects with substantial ICT elements, completed or in progress, include: the Vindolanda Tablets On-Line (AHRB and Mellon Foundation), Script, Image and the Culture of Writing in the Ancient World (Mellon Foundation), Monumenta Asiae Minoris Antiqua XI (CoI with PI Dr Peter Thonemann).

Stuart Dunn is a Research Fellow at the Centre for e-Research (AHESSC, <http://www.ahessc.ac.uk>). Stuart received a PhD in Aegean Bronze Age Archaeology from the University of Durham in 2002. He has published on topics in e-Science generally, on e-Science methods in archaeology, and in the fields of Minoan environmental archaeology and geospatial archaeological computing. He is a member of the Silchester Roman Town VRE Steering Committee and the JISC Geospatial Data Workgroup.

Michael G. Fulford has been Professor of Archaeology at the University of Reading since 1988. His principal research interests are in Roman archaeology, particularly in the fields of urbanism, economy, material culture, technology and trade. He directs the Silchester Roman Town Insula IX 'Town Life' Project. He is a Fellow of the British Academy and is currently a Vice-President and Chair of the Board for Academy-Sponsored Schools and Institutes. He is also President of the Society for the Promotion of Roman Studies and Chair of RAE 2008 Main Panel H (Architecture and the Built Environment, Town and Country Planning, Geography and Environmental Studies, Archaeology).

Sebastian Heath is a Research Scientist at the American Numismatic Society in New York City. He currently serves as Vice-President for Professional Responsibilities of the Archaeological Institute of America. His undergraduate degree is from Brown University and he completed his PhD in Classical Art and Archaeology at the University of Michigan. He has participated in fieldwork in many Mediterranean countries and continues to publish the results of work in France, Greece and Turkey. He is a co-editor of *Greek, Roman and Byzantine Pottery at Ilion (Troia)* and of *Pylos Regional Archaeological Project: Internet Edition*.

Ruth Kirkham joined the University of Oxford in July 2005 as the Project Manager of the Building a VRE for the Humanities project. Ruth is responsible for the day-to-day running of the project, including the conduct of the detailed user requirements survey. Ruth joined the University having worked at Ingenta Plc as a Project and Technical Manager where she oversaw the construction and day-to-day management of a wide range of bespoke websites. She has a degree in Fine Art and a Postgraduate Diploma in Publishing.

Dejan Ljubojevic is Research Fellow with the Learning Technology Research Institute (London Metropolitan University, from which he gained his PhD). He is the key developer of the GLO Maker software tool featured in Chapter 9 of this volume. His research interests lie in the area of modelling the instructional reuse of digital learning materials and learning designs.

Cary MacMahon is the HCA's e-Learning Projects Coordinator; her degree was in history and classics at Cambridge, where she went on to doctoral study. She has conducted extensive research into the uses made of e-resources by academics in the historical disciplines and has contributed her expertise in pedagogically viable applications of technology to this project.

Simon Mahony is a classicist by training with a background in Latin literature, and now works as Teaching Fellow in the UCL Centre for Digital Humanities, University College London. His current interests are in teaching and learning, and particularly the teaching of digital humanities techniques. Simon teaches undergraduate and postgraduate students, is a member of the University of London's Centre for Distance Education, and Student Support Manager on a King's College London based e-learning programme. He is a founding editor of the Digital Classicist.

Eleanor OKell gained her PhD (Exeter) for demonstrating the means by which Sophoclean tragedy teaches citizenship and is now a lecturer in Greek tragedy at Durham University where she also continues to research educational methods as the Classics Project Officer for the History, Classics and Archaeology (HCA) Subject Centre.

Emma J. O'Riordan is the Archaeological Research Assistant on the Virtual Environments for Archaeology project, based at the University of Reading. Before taking up this post, Emma worked at the Archaeology Data Service and the journal *Internet Archaeology*. She has also spent time in commercial archaeology and worked on various excavations across Scotland since graduating from the University of Glasgow in 2005. Her research interests include the use of emerging computer technologies in archaeological field recording and the electronic publication and dissemination of archaeological reports and their underlying data.

John Pybus is the Technical Officer on the BVREH project. He has a background in creating e-Science services within the biological sciences where he has worked on GRID projects, and latterly on the integration of Semantic Web tools. He also has a role in Oxford University's Phonetics Laboratory, supporting the use of cluster computing in phonetics and linguistics research.

Michael Rains has been IT Manager at York Archaeological Trust since 1996. He has a background in field archaeology and archaeological computer applications. He has specialized in the development of the Integrated Archaeological Database (IADB), a web-based application for the recording, analysis, archiving and publication of excavation databases. The IADB has been adopted by a number of UK-based archaeological organizations and projects including the Silchester 'Town Life' project and in 2005 Michael was appointed as an Honorary Research Fellow at the University of Reading. He has been a member of both the OGHAM and VERA projects within the JISC-funded Virtual Research Environments programme.

Neel Smith is Associate Professor of Classics at the College of the Holy Cross (Worcester, MA), where he teaches a wide range of courses in Greek, Latin, Classical Archaeology and Ancient Science. For more than twenty years, his research has focused on the implications of information technology for humanists. He was a founding member of the Perseus Project, hosted the conference at Holy Cross where the Stoa Consortium was founded, designed the information architecture for the Turkish–American excavations at Hacımusalar, and currently leads a technical working group to define standards for digital publication at the Center for Hellenic Studies (Washington, DC).

Melissa Terras is the Senior Lecturer in Electronic Communication in the School of Library, Archive and Information Studies at University College London (UCL), teaching Internet Technologies, Digital Resources in the Humanities, and Web Publishing. With a background in classical art and computing and engineering science, her interests include Humanities Computing, Digitization and Digital Imaging, Artificial Intelligence, Palaeography, Knowledge Elicitation, and Internet Technologies. A general editor of Digital Humanities Quarterly, she is the Secretary of the Association of Literary and Linguistic Computing, and Deputy Manager of the UCL Centre for Digital Humanities.

Notis Toufexis is a member of the Grammar of Medieval Greek project at the University of Cambridge. At his current position he is developing electronic tools that facilitate collaborative linguistic analysis and description of medieval texts and is exploring the development of literary registers in the context of medieval Greek diglossia. With a background in Classics, Notis is especially interested in exploring new ways for the edition of texts that show linguistic variation and mixing of forms from different periods of Greek.

Charlotte Tupman is a Project Research Associate at the Centre for Computing in the Humanities, King's College London. Her interests lie in archaeology and epigraphy. Having completed a PhD thesis on the barrel-shaped and semi-cylindrical tombstones of Roman Iberia, she has developed her interests in the application of digital technologies to the study and publication of inscriptions.

Whilst working at King's College London on the Inscriptions of Aphrodisias (<http://insaph.kcl.ac.uk>) and Inscriptions of Roman Cyrenaica (<http://ircyr. kcl.ac.uk/>) projects, Charlotte taught on several Epidoc Summer Schools (in London and Italy), which provided participants with the knowledge to mark up inscriptions in XML for digital publication.

Series Preface

Digital Research in the Study of Classical Antiquity is volume seven of *Digital Research in the Arts and Humanities.*

Each of the titles in this series comprises a critical examination of the application of advanced ICT methods in the arts and humanities. That is, the application of formal computationally based methods, in discrete but often interlinked areas of arts and humanities research. Usually developed from Expert Seminars, one of the key activities supported by the Methods Network, these volumes focus on the impact of new technologies in academic research and address issues of fundamental importance to researchers employing advanced methods.

Although generally concerned with particular discipline areas, tools or methods, each title in the series is intended to be broadly accessible to the arts and humanities community as a whole. Individual volumes not only stand alone as guides but collectively form a suite of textbooks reflecting the 'state of the art' in the application of advanced ICT methods within and across arts and humanities disciplines. Each is an important statement of current research at the time of publication, an authoritative voice in the field of digital arts and humanities scholarship.

These publications are the legacy of the AHRC ICT Methods Network and will serve to promote and support the ongoing and increasing recognition of the impact on and vital significance to research of advanced arts and humanities computing methods. The volumes will provide clear evidence of the value of such methods, illustrate methodologies of use and highlight current communities of practice.

Marilyn Deegan, Lorna Hughes, Harold Short
Series Editors
AHRC ICT Methods Network
Centre for Computing in the Humanities
King's College London
2010

About the AHRC ICT Methods Network

The aims of the AHRC ICT Methods Network were to promote, support and develop the use of advanced ICT methods in arts and humanities research and to support the cross-disciplinary network of practitioners from institutions around the UK. It was a multi-disciplinary partnership providing a national forum for the exchange and dissemination of expertise in the use of ICT for arts and humanities research. The Methods Network was funded under the AHRC ICT Programme from 2005 to 2008.

The Methods Network Administrative Centre was based at the Centre for Computing in the Humanities (CCH), King's College London. It coordinated and supported all Methods Network activities and publications, as well as developing outreach to, and collaboration with, other centres of excellence in the UK The Methods Network was co-directed by Harold Short, Director of CCH, and Marilyn Deegan, Director of Research Development, at CCH, in partnership with Associate Directors: Mark Greengrass, University of Sheffield; Sandra Kemp, Royal College of Art; Andrew Wathey, Royal Holloway, University of London; Sheila Anderson, Arts and Humanities Data Service (AHDS) (2006–2008); and Tony McEnery, University of Lancaster (2005–2006).

The project website (<http://www.methodsnetwork.ac.uk>) provides access to all Methods Network materials and outputs. In the final year of the project a community site, 'Digital Arts and Humanities' (http://www.arts-humanities.net>) was initiated as a means to sustain community building and outreach in the field of digital arts and humanities scholarship beyond the Methods Network's funding period.

Acknowledgements

The editors would like to thank the Institute for Classical Studies, and especially the events administrator Olga Krzyszkowska, for their support and generosity in hosting and supporting the Digital Classicist Work-in-Progress seminars. Thanks are also due to all those members of our community who have presented papers at our seminars and conference panels as well as all those who have come along to listen and support these events.

We are grateful to the following scholars for comments, criticism and advice on individual chapters in this volume: Andrew Bevan; Christopher Blackwell; Gerhard Brey; Alexandra Georgakopoulou-Nunes; Stephen Grace; Timothy Hill; Leif Isaksen; Marion Lamé; Brett Lucas; Paolo Monella; Espen Ore; Dot Porter; Julian Richards; Robert Rosselli del Turco; Charlotte Roueché; Claire Warwick.

List of Abbreviations

ABM	Agent-based Modelling
ACLS	American Council of Learned Societies
ADS	Archaeology Data Service
AHRC	Arts and Humanities Research Council
BVREH	Building a Virtual Research Environment for the Humanities
CC	Creative Commons
CFT	Cognitive Flexibility Theory
CIL	*Corpus Inscriptionum Latinarum*
CNG	Classical Numismatics Group
CQL	Common Query Language
CSAD	Centre for the Study of Ancient Documents
CTS URN	Canonical Text Services Uniform Resource Name
DNID	Domain Namespace Identifiers
DNS	Domain Name System
DOI	Digital Object Identifiers
DRM	Digital Rights Management
DTD	Document Type Definition
EDUCE	Enhanced Digital Unwrapping for Conservation and Exploration
eMI	Evaluating Multiple Interpretations
EPSRC	Engineering and Physical Sciences Research Council
eSAD	e-Science and Ancient Documents
EXIF	Exchangeable Image File format
FRBR	Functional Requirements for Bibliographic Records
GIS	Geographic Information System
GLO	Generative Learning Object
GPS	Global Positioning System
GSIV	Giant Scalable Image Viewer
HCA	Higher Education Academy's History, Classics and Archaeology
HEI	Higher Education Institution
HLF	Heritage Lottery Fund
HMP	Homer Multitext Project
HTML	Hypertext Markup Language
HTTP	Hypertext Transfer Protocol
IADB	Integrated Archaeological Database
IPTC	International Press Telecommunications Council
ISS	Interpretation Support System
JISC	Joint Information Systems Committee

KML   Keyhole Markup Language
LEAP   Linking Electronic Archives and Publication
LGPN   *Lexicon of Greek Personal Names*
MCQ   Multiple Choice Question
MFA   Museum of Fine Arts
NEH   National Endowment for the Humanities
OCR   Optical Character Recognition
OeRC   Oxford e-Research Centre
OGHAM   Online Group Historical and Archaeological Matrix
OHCO   Ordered Hierarchy of Content Modules
PDF   Portable Document Format
QAA   Quality Assurance Agency
RAE   Research Assessment Exercise
RDF   Resource Description Framework
RIC   *Roman Imperial Coins*
RLO   Reusable Learning Object
RLO-CETL   Centre for Excellence in Teaching and Learning for Reusable
             Learning Objects
RPC   *Roman Provincial Coinage*
SCORM   Shareable Content Object Reference Model
SDI   Spatial Data Infrastructure
SDL   Scaife Digital Library
TEI   Text Encoding Initiative
TIFF   Tagged Image File Format
TLG   *Thesaurus Linguae Graecae*
UCeL   Universities' Collaboration in e-Learning
UGC   User-Generated Content
VERA   Virtual Environments for Research in Archaeology
VLE   Virtual Learning Environment
VRE   Virtual Research Environment
VRE-SDM   Virtual Research Environment for the Study of Documents
             and Manuscripts
VWSAD   Virtual Workspace for the Study of Ancient Documents
WYSIWYG   What You See Is What You Get
XML   Extensible Markup Language
XSLT   Extensible Stylesheet Language: Transformations

Introduction

Simon Mahony and Gabriel Bodard

The purpose of this volume is to present a cross-section of projects performed by Classicists (archaeologists, ancient historians, philologists, etc.) using advanced digital methods and technologies, and thereby to illustrate some of the main challenges and opportunities offered to Classical scholarship by the Digital Humanities. No such volume can hope to be a comprehensive review of the current state of digital research in the area of Classics, and this is not our purpose. By presenting a representative cross-section of scholarship and focusing as much as possible on the research itself rather than a meta-discussion or history of the discipline, we hope to show some ways in which digital methods are pervading, and in some senses transforming, the study of antiquity across the board.

Collections of papers on digital Classical topics have often focused on one of two things. On the one hand Jon Solomon's 1993 collection is a history of digital resources in Classical Studies, with retrospective papers by the founders of many of the great innovative projects of the 1970s and 1980s.[1] On the other, the recent Festschrift for Ross Scaife in *Digital Humanities Quarterly* is forward looking, explicitly imagining Classical Studies in 2018, but from the point of view of a very specific technological perspective: the scale and power of cyber-infrastructure.[2] Both of these approaches to discussing the discipline of Digital Classics are of course important reflections of the present state of the art: the foundational projects influence all that come after them (and many are in fact still active and ground-breaking), and predicting the future of a discipline is clearly both a rhetorical comment upon the observed state of the present and a recommended pathway for future utopian development.

All of the chapters in this volume are research papers in their own right, which engage with and contribute to the history of scholarship both in the study of Classical Antiquity and in the Digital Humanities. Half of the papers originated as presentations made at the Digital Classicist seminar series at the Institute of Classical Studies in London in the summer of 2007 (Bowman et al., Dunn, Fulford et al., OKell et al., Smith); a few were given at conference panels we organized at the Classical Association Annual Conference held in Birmingham in the same

---

1   Jon Solomon, *Accessing Antiquity: The Computerization of Classical Studies* (Tucson: University of Arizona Press, 1993).

2   Gregory Crane and Melissa Terras, 'Changing the Center of Gravity: Transforming Classical Studies Through Cyberinfrastructure', *Digital Humanities Quarterly*, 3/1 (2009).

year (Terras, Toufexis, Tupman);[3] and a couple are new papers written specially for this volume (Cayless, Heath). This publication collects together scholarship on a wide range of Classical subjects, exemplifying multiple technical approaches, and taking a variety of forms; it shows that this diversity of scholarly activity contributes in a coherent way to the academic agenda that makes Classical Studies a leader in the use of modern and innovative methods. Collectively, this volume illustrates and explores the highly collaborative nature of research in this field, the interdisciplinarity that has always been core to Classical Studies, the importance of innovation and creativity in the study of the ancient world, and above all the fact that digital research relies just as heavily upon traditionally rigorous scholarship as mainstream Classics does.

The Digital Classicist, established in 2004, is a network, a community of users, and has become defined by what we (as a community) do. There is a website (<http://www.digitalclassicist.org/>) hosted at the Centre for Computing in the Humanities at King's College London, and a wiki (<http://wiki.digitalclassicist. org>) where, as well as sharing information about themselves and their own work, members collaboratively compile, review and comment upon articles on digital projects, tools, and research questions of particular relevance to the ancient world. They also list guides to practice, introduce the discussion forum and, most importantly, list events. It is these events that more than anything else define the Digital Classicist community by providing a showcase for our members' research and a venue for discussion, introductions and inspiration for new collaborative relationships and projects.

The most striking and successful aspect of Digital Classics is its sense of community and collaboration. Digital Classicists do not work in isolation; they develop projects in tandem with colleagues in other humanities disciplines or with experts in technical fields: engineers, computer scientists and civil engineers. They do not publish expensive monographs destined to be checked out of libraries once every few years; they collect data, conduct research, develop tools and resources, and importantly make them available electronically, often under free and open licenses such as Creative Commons,[4] for reference and for re-use by scholars, students and non-specialists alike. It is this sense of community, combining the promise of the Social Web and the infrastructures of Linked Data and e-Science, that the Digital Classicist (in collaboration with and taking the lead from the Stoa Consortium and the Perseus Project[5]) aims to encourage among scholars of the ancient world.

---

3   Digital   Classicist   Work-in-Progress   seminar   series   2007,   <http://www. digitalclassicist.org/wip/wip2007.html>. Classical Association Annual Conference 2007, <http://www.ca2007.bham.ac.uk/CAProgramme.pdf>.

4   Creative Commons, <http://www.creativecommons.org/>.

5   Stoa Consortium, <http://www.stoa.org/>; Perseus Project, <http://www.perseus. tufts.edu/>.

The important distinction between research in the Digital Humanities (whether Classics or any other humanistic discipline), and traditional research that merely makes use of digital tools or methods, is that the former by definition involves interdisciplinary work between multiple skill-sets. It may be that a given Classical scholar also has the technical skills to build and develop tools and innovative digital methodologies, but no scholar can possibly possess all of the skills and resources to perform digital research in complete isolation. To some extent this has always been true in the Classics. As Italo Gallo pointed out in a handbook on papyrology over twenty years ago:[6]

> According to its obvious etymology, 'papyrology' means 'the study of papyri', both as a writing material obtained from the papyrus plant and from the point of view of its written content. In the first ... meaning, technical knowledge is required, in botany, organic chemistry, climate geography, and the like, which is not usually part of a papyrologist's basic training, so that he will often need to consult experts in these fields: ideally, they will collaborate.

Just as no papyrologist is expected to possess all of the scientific and forensic skills to research the more technical side of their field entirely alone, so no Classicist will master all of the computational skills and research methods necessary to conduct innovative digital research in complete isolation.

Classicists are used to this situation, belonging as they do to one of the most interdisciplinary and diverse disciplines in the academy (as Melissa Terras points out in Chapter 10 of this volume). Classics departments are already filled with experts on literature, history, archaeology, ethnography, mythology, religion, philosophy, palaeography, linguistics, art, heritage and reception. In recent years we have known Classicists who have also taken higher degrees or professional training in (for example) film studies, psychology, history of medicine, Asian linguistics, politics or economics, anthropology, geology and biology, all with a view to increasing their proficiency in their own academic area. These are scholars who are not only aware of the importance of applying the expertise of multiple disciplines to the complex problem of studying an ancient culture, but also of the importance of collaboration with academics from different backgrounds and with different skills.

Equally, Classicists are now striving to learn more about the digital resources and methods available to enhance publication and research on antiquity. Computational techniques are undeniably useful, but research is not just about *using* tools so much as *mastering* them, understanding how they work, their history and social/political context. One can perhaps not collaborate with a computer scientist without learning something about their discipline, language and tools, but no individual can learn enough about these disciplinary competences to completely do away with the

---

6   Italo Gallo, *Greek and Latin Papyrology*, trans. M.R. Falivene and J.R. March (Institute of Classical Studies, Classical Handbook 1, 1986 [Italian version 1983]), 1.

need for collaboration, in one form or another. We should highlight that the use of Open Source software and Open Access publication is a form of collaboration enabling, even if the collaboration is asynchronous rather than as a conventional team.[7] Concern with issues like the use of open standards (such as the TEI, as discussed by Charlotte Tupman in Chapter 4), and the use and evaluation of Social Web and Linked Data protocols (see Sebastian Heath's discussion in Chapter 2, and Stuart Dunn's in Chapter 3) also further the needs of collaboration and open scholarship.

Digital research, or e-Research, in our view, involves the use of computational methods and theories to enable real advances in Classical research. We are not concerned merely with the convenience or speed that computers can bring to research and publication, but especially with methods and digital practices that can add to the empirical understanding of facts about the ancient world, its literature and its people, or the continuing use of that heritage in later texts and ages.

There are lessons to be learned from the different trajectories of two major Classical projects that were both founded in 1972, and are both still giants in the field.[8] The *Thesaurus Linguae Graecae* (TLG), while a technologically innovative project from the outset, and one which has changed the study of Greek literature and continues to be indispensable to it,[9] has not made a great contribution in tools, protocols or theory to the Digital Humanities as a discipline. This state of affairs is of course largely because of the closed, for-profit and self-sufficient strategy of the TLG, and is not a criticism of the project or its policies. The *Lexicon of Greek Personal Names* (LGPN), on the other hand, began life as a technologically conservative project, geared to the production of paper volumes of the *Lexicon*.[10] The LGPN has always been reactive to changes in technology rather than proactive as the TLG was. As a result of this, however, researchers there have been able to change with the times, adopt new database and web technologies as they have appeared, and are now actively contributing to the development of standards in XML, onomastics and geo-tagging, and sharing data and tools widely. It may be counter-intuitive that a reactive attitude leads to more productive digital research than a proactive one, but as Gregory Crane has pointed out, we as Classicists

---

7   Gabriel Bodard and Juan Garcés, 'Open Source Critical Editions: A Rationale', in M. Deegan and K. Sutherland (eds), *Text Editing, Print and the Digital World* (Ashgate, 2009), pp. 83–98.

8   This comparison was drawn at the Digital Classicist panel at the Digital Resources for the Humanities and Arts conference, September 2008 in Cambridge, <http://www.stoa.org/?p=833>; for the history of the LGPN we draw upon the presentation by Elaine Matthews at the International Epigraphic Congress in Oxford, September 2007, <http://www.currentepigraphy.org/2007/09/16/epigraphy-and-the-information-technology-revolution/>.

9   *Thesaurus Linguae Graecae*, <http://www.tlg.uci.edu/>.

10   *Lexicon of Greek Personal Names*, <http://www.lgpn.ox.ac.uk/>.

should not be inventing technologies when there are information professionals in better-funded disciplines whose needs overlap to a large degree with our own.[11]

The Digital Classicist therefore serves as a community of expertise centred on the application of Digital Humanities methods, cyberinfrastructure, e-Science and Computer Science research to the study of the ancient world. This field often focuses on collaborative research between Classicists and computer scientists to apply large-scale computational resources to problems across disciplines. Such collaboration pushes forward both fields – with digital tools serving Classics, ancient material validating new computational methods and the research agenda being driven forward by the needs of – and contributing to – both disciplines. Digital infrastructure, Open Access publication, re-use of freely licensed data, and Semantic Web technologies will enable Classics, archaeology, and associated disciplines fully to engage with an increasingly digital academic environment. The Digital Classicist fosters engagement with and expresses the outcomes of several related interest groups and projects; it is an inclusive forum for Classicists interested in advanced digital methods, and also presents concrete agendas and engages with the mature community of practice that combines digital and ancient studies.

The Digital Classicist works closely with and shares the concerns of several other communities; there are sufficient scholars who are members of both (or all) groups to bring together several agendas and needs. These communities include: Antiquist,[12] a community of cultural heritage professionals; the Arts and Humanities e-Science community,[13] who according to their statement 'support, co-ordinate and promote e-Science [a broad term encompassing grid technologies, distributed and high-performance computing, and the e-Infrastructure needed by "big science"] in all arts and humanities disciplines'; the Scaife Digital Library (SDL),[14] 'a distributed collection and a method whereby humanists from around the world can automatically aggregate their content'.

The sub-disciplines spanned by the chapters in this volume include archaeology and geography, text, linguistics, reception and community building; and most chapters cover more than one of these. The chapters themselves take different forms, through pedagogical questions to theoretical, disciplinary or methodological discussions. The academic content of the chapters includes resources for research and teaching, tools for the Classical scholar, international and academic standards

---

11   Gregory Crane, 'Classics and the Computer: An End of the History' in S. Schreibman, R. Siemens, J. Unsworth (eds), *A Companion to Digital Humanities* (Blackwell Publishing, 2004), pp. 46–55.

12   Antiquist, <http://www.antiquist.org>.

13   Arts and Humanities e-Science Support Centre, <http://www.ahessc.ac.uk/>.

14   On the Scaife Digital Library, see Gregory Crane, Brent Seales and Melissa Terras, 'Cyberinfrastructure for Classical Philology', in G. Crane and M. Terras (eds), *Changing the Center of Gravity: Transforming Classical Studies Through Cyberinfrastructure*, DHQ, 3/1 (2009), <http://www.digitalhumanities.org/dhq/vol/003/1/000023.html>.

and protocols, and reports on original research. The digital methods in evidence in this cross-section of scholarship are also wide-ranging: text and data markup; databases, data management and search techniques; network analysis; e-Science and cyberinfrastructure. This diversity of topics, forms, contents and methods enhances the underlying unity of the Digital Classicist community and its collaborative nature.

The chapters include historical surveys (Fulford et al.) as well as futuristic proposals (Terras, Toufexis), demonstrations of the impact of innovative methodologies on Classical research (Tupman) as well as reports of advanced tools, technology and services (Bowman et al., OKell et al., Smith), and discussion of Classical research in the Web 2.0 environment (Cayless, Dunn, Heath). The unifying agenda of this volume is not based on any particular technology, methodology, approach or philosophy, but focuses rather on the future of Classics as part of a community of expertise and practice. Together, we explore concepts of disciplinarity and interdisciplinarity; research practice and pedagogy in the age of the Internet and Social Web; digital tools and methods for publication and communication; standards and recommendations for interoperability and compatibility; strategies and resources for preservation and maintenance of fragile digital output.

The first section of this volume is comprised of three chapters that address aspects of digital practice in Classical archaeology and geography. This section includes an account of the history of informatic and technical support for field archaeology, an exploration of the implications of Internet publication for amateur and commercial contributions to numismatic and archaeological bibliography, and a discussion of the complex advances in geographic methodology brought about by the Social Web and Linked Data resources and tools. Collaboration and outreach play a large part in all three of these chapters, inasmuch as none of these advances take place in isolation, and all have implications both for the researcher and the consumer of that research, the academic audience and the wider, public audience that every scholar also needs to address.

In the opening chapter, 'Silchester Roman Town: Developing Virtual Research Practice', Michael Fulford et al. recount research from a major project run over the last decade by the Archaeology Department at the University of Reading. They examine the history of IT use at Silchester and the effects that this has had on all aspects of excavation, recording and publication at one of the largest open-area research excavations in the country. The Integrated Archaeological Database (IADB) has been key to the success of the Silchester excavations, providing access to all the digitized site data from context cards to photographs and plans. It can be accessed via the Internet, allowing the geographically dispersed research team to keep in contact with the core team at Reading and with excavators on site. The increasing amounts of excavation data being 'born digital' has led to decreased publication time; multiple authors working in a collaborative environment within the IADB; and electronic publication of the research output. This chapter shows the development of a project from largely analogue origins to the gradual adoption of cutting-edge and innovative technologies that transform the research process. It also serves both as an introduction to the volume, showing the development of many of the themes that will be explored further, and as a useful guide to archaeologists looking for the state of the art in excavation support technologies.

Sebastian Heath's chapter, 'Diversity and Reuse of Digital Resources for Ancient Mediterranean Material Culture', begins with the observation that materials relating to ancient material culture are increasingly appearing on the Internet. One source is the scholarly community (professional and academic archaeologists and art historians affiliated with universities, museums and such institutions); another is commercial dealers of unprovenanced antiquities who are making very effective use of the Internet to promote their businesses. Heath points out that the output of the 'commercial community' is often more accessible on the Internet than that of the scholarly one. Major auction houses selling ancient art, and in particular coins, regularly publish online high-quality images and descriptions of the objects they have sold. Commercial entities are relatively permissive in the reproduction rights they grant for this copyrighted material. This openness by commercial organizations is in contrast to most sources of scholarly information: academic journals are frequently unavailable except through gated and subscription sites; museums and field projects – with notable exceptions – put only a small proportion of their collections online and comprehensiveness is often curtailed in the name of protecting publication rights. Documenting the choices made by commercial and scholarly sources of information shows the practical implications of these choices. The increasing role of search engines such as Google in mediating the discovery of and access to information means that commercial and scholarly information exist side by side. There are lessons to be learned from this analysis, not only for scholars and teachers making use of online materials in their research and pedagogy, but especially for academics seeking to publish online and create rich resources for the academic community at large.

Working in complex digital environments often provides opportunities to reassess entrenched assumptions about many basic concepts in the humanities. In Chapter 3, 'Space as an Artefact: A Perspective on "Neogeography" from the Digital Humanities', Stuart Dunn shows how the emergence in the past few years of 'neogeography' – broadly speaking the application of so-called Web 2.0 methods and technologies in the visualization and analysis of geospatial information – provides opportunities for a rethink of how we understand the concept of 'space'. However, the growth of neogeography has been accompanied by relatively little consideration of that broader Web 2.0 context, particularly with regard to the implications of enabling wider user communities to access, manipulate, provide and 'mash up' geospatial data. This chapter ties together many of the issues that are important to this section: the use of emerging technologies and the way it transforms both publication and research; the grounding of digital humanities methods in the disciplines of archaeology and geography; the importance of understanding both technological and disciplinary issues for all academics moving forward.

The next section of this volume focuses on another aspect of Classical academia: scholarship around ancient texts and languages, literary, philological and linguistic studies. This section includes some reflections on the way digital research and open publication can blur some of the traditional sub-disciplinary boundaries between textual scholars and archaeologists (in epigraphy), a project report on how a virtual research environment can foster both collaboration and technological adoption by diverse scholars (in papyrology), and some thoughts on how digital methods combined with large numbers of Open Access texts could offer new opportunities for diachronic linguistic study of the history of the Greek language. The importance of open standards and open publication are core strands in this section.

Charlotte Tupman's chapter, 'Contextual Epigraphy and XML: Digital Publication and its Application to the Study of Inscribed Funerary Monuments', aims to reunite inscribed texts with the artefacts on which they sit, and their original contexts through the medium of electronic publication. She describes traditional methods of publishing inscribed funerary material, exploring both the benefits and limitations, before moving on to digital methods of publication and considering how these might contribute to original research questions, as well as making materials available for further use via widely adopted open standards. Tupman's chapter draws on the work of the highly active EpiDoc community,[15] and applies the lessons learned from several recent and ongoing projects to her own forthcoming work, demonstrating that digital research (and indeed all scientific research) is both collaborative and cumulative.

How might collaborating scholars in different physical locations be brought together along with a disparate range of resources so that they might work more effectively? 'A Virtual Research Environment for the Study of Documents and Manuscripts' by Alan Bowman et al. describes the background to such a project and outlines the need for these tools in document and manuscript studies. This chapter focuses on the development of technologies and methods to address concrete user requirements, with data drawn from studying the process and methodology of the research conducted in the area of ancient documents, consultation and a continuous dialogue with both discipline specialists and technical and infrastructure developers. Bowman's chapter shares with the first chapter in this volume the theme of the needs of the target discipline. Again open standards are highlighted here, with access to rich digital materials essential for such enhanced collaborative work, and also the importance of building innovative methods on the firm foundation of established academic practice.

In 'One Era's Nonsense, Another's Norm: Diachronic Study of Greek and the Computer', Notis Toufexis considers the study of Greek, a linguistic label that covers a span of almost three millennia (from about the eighth century BC until the present day), and the ways in which new methodologies and resources can contribute to and transform our investigations into its development and evolution. In particular, he proposes a detailed, digitally enabled analysis of the textual and

---

15   EpiDoc Collaborative, <http://epidoc.sourceforge.net/>.

linguistic multiplicity in 'diplomatic' editions of literary manuscripts, texts whose scribal variants are almost universally normalized in traditional textual criticism to Classical or Koine forms. The existence of large numbers of freely available texts in open standards, and of high-powered digital approaches such as computational linguistics and text-mining, make such work both possible and essential to the study of language development from Antiquity and beyond.

The final and most diverse section of this volume considers infrastructural and disciplinary issues, including digital citation and reference; the preservation of texts in a digital medium that feels far more fragile than the papyrus and parchment that have survived since Antiquity; the possibilities of digitally disseminated resources to be packaged for a powerful pedagogical environment; and finally the question of how digital research and resources affect the very definition and understanding of our academic discipline.

Neel Smith's chapter, 'Digital Infrastructure and the Homer Multitext Project', introduces an innovative online resource that takes advantage of many of the possibilities opened up by digital research and publication. The Homer Multitext Project (HMP) views different versions of the *Iliad* not as sources for reconstruction of an 'original' text, but rather as evidence for the fluidity of the textual tradition that developed from the oral origins of the *Iliad*. HMP already includes digital editions of six *Iliad* manuscripts, and has begun work on digital texts of the scholiastic comments. Smith summarizes the long-term archival plans including data warehousing supported by Google, and the importance of supporting flexible scholarly reuse of materials. This chapter then explores the details of an architecture allowing distinct components (digital images, texts of the *Iliad*, scholiastic texts, *inter alia*) to be used independently, combined in various ways and cited, via the robust Canonical Text Services protocols. Smith brings together many of the key themes in this volume; open standards for publication and Open Access distribution are here seen not merely as desirable means for improving interoperability and enabling further research, but they are the essential underpinnings of this kind of project.

How does the claim of the Greek historian Thucydides that his work is designed to be a 'possession for all time', and his apparent success, give us a model for digital archiving today? This is the starting point for Hugh Cayless's chapter '*Ktêma es aiei*: Digital Permanence from an Ancient Perspective'. We cannot predict how future generations will view or use the works in our care and since the things a culture values can change radically over the course of several generations, there is no guarantee that the intrinsic value of a work will be estimated in the same way a hundred or a thousand years from now. Therefore, while due care must be taken in preserving digital resources in our archives, their long-term survival, Cayless argues, may best be ensured by releasing copies from our control and thus developing a self-sustaining community of interest. The use of open standards and Open Access licences, as we have argued throughout this volume, will highly increase the possibility of our publications being duplicated, repurposed, circulated and therefore preserved.

Based on research and data gathering, Eleanor OKell et al., from the History, Classics and Archaeology Subject Centre in the UK, give us, 'Creating a Generative Learning Object: Working in an "Ill-Structured" Environment and Getting Students to Think'. How might we model the teaching process focusing on disciplinary concerns and our students' critical thinking skills to create reusable learning objects? Using a case study of the Altar of Zeus at Pergamum the team exteriorize a disciplinary teaching process and render it electronically. At the same time, they demonstrate that innovative learning technologies need not be imposed upon disciplines from outside but rather that they should be constructed to suit these disciplines' own pedagogical requirements and allow practitioners to maintain control over their teaching materials. Again we see that interdisciplinary collaboration is essential to fulfil the most promising potentialities of digital research.

Finally, Melissa Terras draws together many of the central themes of this volume in Chapter 10, 'The Digital Classicist: Disciplinary Focus and Interdisciplinary Vision'. She sketches out issues of disciplinarity and the benefits of interdisciplinary research, observing that Classicists have always been at the forefront of innovation and collaborative thinking. There are potential problem areas, including disciplinary identity, skill sets and expectations for publication, which need to be negotiated at the outset of any project. What are the benefits of utilizing computational technologies to undertake research on Classical Antiquity? Important case studies (including projects described in Chapters 1 and 5) are used to tease out and highlight the need for effective communication and collaboration between competing academic disciplines. By understanding interdisciplinarity (which has always been part of Classical scholarship due to the disparate subjects and methods routinely utilized) those undertaking Digital Classics research should be ideally placed to undertake collaborative and digitally innovative projects.

As we noted above, this volume does not seek comprehensively to cover all aspects of innovative digital research in the study of the ancient world, but rather to create a snapshot of the research activities of Digital Classicist members as represented by a selection of the papers given at our Summer seminars and conference panels in one particular year, 2007. Most notably, none of the chapters in this volume deals with image processing and visualization and its importance in our field of academic research. The following Summer's seminar series saw two major imaging projects reported and discussed: the Codex Sinaiticus project at the British Library,[16] which features the oldest almost complete copy of the New Testament, and EDUCE: Enhanced Digital Unwrapping for Conservation and Exploration at the University of Kentucky,[17] which is using non-invasive volumetric scanning techniques to virtually unroll inaccessible manuscripts such as the carbonized papyri of Herculaneum.

16   Codex Sinaiticus, <http://www.codexsinaiticus.org/>.
17   EDUCE: Enhanced Digital Unwrapping for Conservation and Exploration, <http://www.stoa.org/educe/>.

The natural delay between the delivery of papers at a work-in-progress seminar and the appearance of chapters in a published volume means that things have moved on since many of the ideas in this volume were presented in 2007. This book, almost every word of which has been a collaborative endeavour between the authors, editors and reviewers, is very different from how we might have imagined it then. The Digital Classicist has moved on in the intervening period, with our seminars and other occasional talks now being podcast as Open Access audio recordings along with accompanying slides and published on our seminar web page.[18] Events such as these are still the focus of the community and provide our members with a venue to showcase what is innovative and important in the areas where Classics, technology, and e-Science intersect. The 2009 summer seminars in London were specifically selected for the way they demonstrated collaborative projects at the cutting edge between Classics and Computer Science, and half of the speakers came from outside of the UK. Conference panels are planned for future Classical Association (UK) and American Philological Association annual conferences. The summer seminars at the Institute for Classical Studies in London will continue to provide a focus; we have envisaged small summative conferences at the end of future seasons. The Digital Practice seminars being hosted at the Institute for the Study of the Ancient World, New York University,[19] will give a wider international dimension to our events.

As rich as are the chapters that make up this volume, and as important as are some of the themes we have highlighted here, this record barely scratches the surface of the huge range of research that Digital Classicists are carrying out around the world. There will be many more seminars, and volumes of papers as well as monographs before anything like a comprehensive account of the digital development of Classical Studies can be proposed.

---

18 Digital Classicist Seminars, <http://www.digitalclassicist.org/wip>.
19 ISAW Events Calendar: <http://www.nyu.edu/isaw/events.htm>.

PART I
Archaeology and Geography

Chapter 1

Silchester Roman Town: Developing Virtual Research Practice 1997–2008

Michael G. Fulford, Emma J. O'Riordan,
Amanda Clarke and Michael Rains

Introduction

In 1997 a major new excavation was launched within the walled area of the Late Iron Age and Roman town of *Calleva Atrebatum* (Silchester, Hampshire) in Insula IX, to the north-west of the forum basilica. The excavation was major in two senses: one, that the area under excavation was, at 55 x 55 m (3,025 m²), large in any urban context; second, even though we had no real insight into the extent and quality of the surviving stratigraphy, the expectation was that the project would last at least five seasons in the field, and probably as many as ten. The objective of the project was to complement research undertaken in the 1970s and 1980s into the public buildings and defences of the Roman town with an investigation of a residential Insula. Although the Roman town had been subjected to major excavation in the later nineteenth and early twentieth centuries which had revealed a plan of most of the masonry buildings within the walls, research in the 1980s on the forum basilica indicated that this work had been superficial, leaving the underlying stratigraphy very largely untouched.[1]

A major aim in the Silchester Roman Town Life Project, as, perhaps, might be the case in any comparable urban archaeological project, is to achieve as fine-grained an understanding of the change in urban conditions through the whole life of the settlement as is possible. An essential prerequisite for this is the putting back together of all the relationships of the individual contexts or layers which make up the site in their correct stratigraphical, hence chronological order. Although excavation methodology assumes one starts with the latest layer and works backwards in time and sequence to the earliest, in practice this is not so easy to achieve over a large area where the presence of, for example, later interventions (in our case in Insula IX trenches dug by the Victorian excavators

---

1 Michael G. Fulford and Jane Timby, *Late Iron Age and Roman Silchester: Excavations on the Site of the Forum-Basilica, 1977, 1980–86* (London, Society for the Promotion of Roman Studies, Britannia Monogr. 15, 2000).

in 1893–1894[2]), or of major Roman building events, may isolate or truncate blocks of stratigraphy. Those stratigraphic relationships are usually represented graphically in the form of a matrix diagram and the construction of the latter is an essential building block in reporting the development of the area under investigation. The reconstructed stratigraphy, simply displayed in diagrammatic form, can then be tested against the evidence of dated artefacts such as coins, ceramics and other independently dated finds or radiocarbon dates. With a tested, dated chronology of the excavated sequence it is then possible to refine the significant periods and phases in its development, which were first observed in the field and reported on in interim fashion. To those phases, with their structures and other archaeological features, can then be associated the relevant material and biological evidence whose study illuminates the changing character of urban life: occupations, social and economic relations. From this introduction, it will be becoming clear that the development of a complex and often deep stratigraphy is a correlate of urban life. In rural settlements, by contrast, it is rare for deep, complex stratigraphic sequences to develop, let alone be preserved from the ravages of later cultivation. Silchester was abandoned between the fifth and seventh centuries and, unlike most major Roman towns, did not re-emerge in the late Saxon period as an urban centre. Consequently it and its environs are extremely well preserved.

At what point, then, does a computerized database become a useful investment for a project, such as the Silchester Roman Town Life Project? If we set aside for the moment the fundamental desirability of developing a digital record for all archaeological interventions, one criterion, admittedly subjective, might be the point where memory fails to be able to hold together all the excavated contexts and their relationships, and the periodization of occupation which follows from them, such that it is not possible to analyse and report the stratigraphic sequence *without* recourse to computerized databases. The excavations of the amphitheatre and forum basilica at Silchester in the 1980s were both substantial, but the total number of recorded layers or contexts from each site was a little less than 1,000. In comparison, there are, to date, just under 9,000 context records from the current excavations in Insula IX. However, in the case of the forum basilica in particular, where four major Roman periods were identified following on a complex Iron Age occupation, itself sub-divided into three phases, the reconstruction of the stratigraphic sequence and the associated establishment of the matrix diagram was complex and hard. And, with hindsight, post-excavation research would undoubtedly have been aided by a computerized database.

---

2   Amanda Clarke, Michael G. Fulford, et al., *Silchester Insula IX: The Town Life Project: The First Six Years 1997–2002* (Reading, University of Reading Department of Archaeology, 2002); Amanda Clarke and Michael G. Fulford, 'The Excavation of Insula IX, Silchester: The First Five Years of the "Town Life" Project, 1997–2001' *Britannia*, 33 (2002): 129–66.

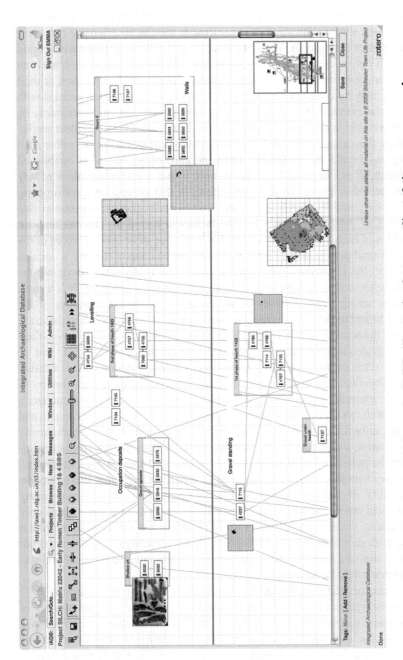

Figure 1.1 Screenshot of a matrix from the IADB, illustrating how complicated the sequence can be

Source: © University of Reading.

Thus far we have focused on the layer and its stratigraphic relationships without considering the spatial dimension. In a settlement, such as an extensive rural one, without complex stratigraphy, it may be possible to develop comprehensive period plans which derive closely from drawings made in the field. However, such an approach cannot be assured in an urban context, since individual periods, or their sub-phases, may be composed of very many individual layers, each perhaps with limited spatial extent, and the boundaries between periods may not necessarily be clearly observable in the field. Indeed the periods may well be a complete artifice imposed by the excavator to facilitate diachronological comparisons, rather than reflecting any breaks in occupation. Until the chronology has been established it is difficult, if not impossible, to know how to put together the plans of any particular period or phase. To assist, therefore, in that process of reconstructing the stratigraphy and its significant phases and periodization, it is essential that a computerized database not only has the facility to record the descriptions and relationships of each layer or context, but that it also has an integrated record of the two-dimensional plan made of each context. As the phasing of the site is decided in relation to the emerging stratigraphic matrix, so it is absolutely desirable for the database to be able to represent that plan information graphically. It is a short step then to seeing the desirability of associating a photographic archive of the excavation linked to individual contexts. Equally, it is incredibly helpful to have the evidence of the accessioned, individual finds, such as coins or metalwork, with their photos, integrated into the database; and indeed to have the contribution of 'spot' or preliminary dates from the ceramics, themselves a potential major source of dating evidence. Together, this material provides key information for the attribution of dates to the emerging periodization or phasing of the sequence. To summarize, a database which can capture the written and plan record of each layer or context, and display that information as well as stratigraphic relationships in both diagrammatic form, as a matrix, and as a multi-context phase or period plan, provides the necessary means for the post-excavation analysis of a complex settlement, such as a town.

A further benefit of capturing these data electronically is that there remains the possibility of making them available online. A problem with very many archaeological reports which are derived from the analysis of paper records only is that, because the data are so numerous, it is impossible to reconcile their total reporting with economic printed publication. Hence for many excavations it is not possible to reassess results without recourse to examining the physical archive, wherever that might be located.

In the case of Silchester Insula IX it was evident from the first season in 1997 that the preservation of the stratigraphy was very good and that the number of contexts would certainly lie in the high hundreds, if not the thousands. While the director (Michael Fulford) had had no previous experience of using computerized databases in the field he was fortunate in having been able to recruit a field director (Amanda Clarke) who had had just this experience in previous employment at the York Archaeological Trust. This background was crucial in the decision to adopt the Integrated Archaeological Database (IADB), developed by Michael Rains, also in post at the York Archaeological Trust, from the outset of the Silchester Insula IX project in 1997.[3] The IADB was also an ideal system for working with single-context planning, a methodology widely practised in urban archaeology and adopted at the outset for the Insula project. It has continued to host the data from the project throughout its thirteen years of existence. Providing it can continue to be maintained and developed during and beyond the anticipated 20–25-year life of the excavation and publication programme of the Silchester Roman Town Life Project, it will remain a permanent major resource for Romano-British urban archaeology.

In reviewing the development of the digital aspects of Silchester, we could take an integrated approach, reviewing all aspects simultaneously through time from 1997 onwards. Alternatively, a thematic approach which explores individual strands, such as the excavation itself and the associated recording in the field, or the post-excavation process leading to publication, allows for focus on the development of these very distinct components of the project. The latter approach is adopted here, even though the IADB is core to all aspects. Thus Silchester represents a case study of the integration of digital methodologies with a complex, stratified (urban) excavation project. The challenges that this kind of excavation presents are being addressed by similar projects elsewhere and are by no means confined to Roman or Classical archaeology. The work of the York Archaeological Trust, for example, whose work ranges up to the modern period and where Michael Rains continues to develop the IADB, is typical of that of the larger professional archaeological organizations of the UK where digital methodologies are embedded in their practice.[4] The distinctiveness of Silchester is its longevity, which has provided an opportunity for experimentation and development rarely possible at the level of an individual project in the context of time-limited, developer-funded or, indeed, university-based, research-funded archaeology.

The aim of this chapter, then, is to describe the digital experience of a single, complex excavation project, but all the issues which it has addressed, or tried to address, are generic to such excavation projects. Where Silchester is, of course, unique is in its archaeological *content*. This contribution is not intended to be technical but has in mind the archaeologist intent on setting up a major, long-term project. An important message is that whatever digital systems and approaches are adopted at the outset, they will require continual refinement, re-evaluation and investment to sustain them throughout the lifetime of the project.

---

3   The larger context for the project in archaeological computing can be reviewed through, e.g. Harrison Eiteljorg, *Archaeological Computing*, 2nd edn (CSA, 2008), <http://archcomp.csanet.org/>; G. Lock and K. Brown (eds), *On the Theory And practice of Archaeological Computing* (Oxford University Committee for Archaeology/Oxbow Books, 2000); P. Reilly and S. Rahtz (eds), *Archaeology and the Information Age: A Global Perspective* (Routledge, One World Archaeology 21, 1992); S. Ross, J. Moffett and J. Henderson (eds), *Computing for Archaeologists* (Oxford University Committee for Archaeology Monograph No.18, 1991).

4   York Archaeology, <http://www.yorkarchaeology.co.uk>.

The Integrated Archaeological Database (IADB) and Silchester: The field perspective

The IADB was first developed by Rains in Perth for the Scottish Urban Archaeological Trust[5] in 1989. Early versions of the IADB used MS-DOS and were written in Clipper, using the dBase database format. The migration to Windows and MS Access database occurred when Visual Basic arrived. The project moved with Rains to the York Archaeological Trust in 1997, where it has remained ever since. The system no longer uses an Access database but is a fully web-based application using MySQL and PHP. Essentially, the IADB hosts the excavation and finds record: context descriptions with their plans and associated images, and records of the finds and their associated images. The unique context or layer number links all these categories of records. Crucial to the interpretation of the archaeological record is the IADB's capacity to build the hierarchical relationships (archaeological matrix) which mirror the stratigraphic sequence and enable the capture of composite, spatial plans of the individual context record to demonstrate the changing character of occupation over time. The data can be viewed through individual records, through 2D matrices, or through groups or sets of objects. As well as the field data, post-excavation notes and interpretation can be created and stored in the IADB either as HTML documents or imported from external applications such as PDF or Microsoft Word formats. Besides the York Archaeological Trust and the University of Reading, the IADB is used by a number of professional organizations such as the Canterbury Archaeological Trust and the Cotswold Archaeological Trust[6] as well as other Universities such as the University of East Anglia, the University of Southampton and University College London.

At the time of the start of the Silchester Insula IX project there was no tradition of using databases with the kind of functionality associated with IADB in either academic or professional archaeology. Bespoke solutions were adopted for individual projects, and there was no track record of the continuous development of one system. Indeed, in a survey carried out of user needs and digital data in archaeology in 1998 only 75 per cent of field archaeologists had access to a computer.[7] The figure for academics in a better resourced environment of higher education was somewhat higher at 90 per cent. Electronic publishing was in its infancy with the refereed journal *Internet Archaeology* only having been established in 1995.[8] Indeed, the York-based Archaeology Data Service (ADS) was only set up in 1997.[9]

---

5   Scottish Urban Archaeology Trust, <http://www.suat.co.uk/>.

6   Canterbury Archaeological Trust, <http://www.canterburytrust.co.uk/>; Cotswold Archaeological Trust, <http://www.cotswoldarch.org.uk/>.

7   F.J. Condron, J. Richards, D. Robinson and A. Wise, 'Strategies for Digital Data: A Survey of User Needs' (ADS, York, 1999), <http://ads.ahds.ac.uk/project/strategies/>.

8   *Internet Archaeology*, York: Council for British Archaeology, <http://intarch.ac.uk/>.

9   Archaeology Data Service, <http://ads.ahds.ac.uk/>.

A continuing preoccupation throughout the thirteen years of the project to date has been how to stream the field records into the database most effectively and efficiently. There are several possibilities, all of which have been carried out during the Insula IX project. First, all field records and photographs can be entered between field seasons. In this situation context records can be entered manually, while the associated plans need to be digitized. In the early years of the project, with digital technology in its infancy, conventional colour and black-and-white photography were used in the field and those images needed to be scanned into the IADB. Accessioned finds and their images, as well as the basic context-by-context record of the various categories of bulk finds – pottery, animal bone, building material, etc. – also required entering. For this to happen an appropriate level of staffing, or a combination of staff and volunteer(s), and computer, digitizing tablet and scanner and University office accommodation are required and have to be allowed for in the budget. After the first season in 1997–1998 the context and plan record was digitized by Amanda Clarke.

Second, these processes can take place in the course of the field season, preferably on site, and thus drawing on student and volunteer assistance. For this to happen on a site such as Silchester Insula IX, without mains electricity at the location of the excavation, it is necessary to have a portable generator, or to negotiate access to mains electricity from the nearest available source. Security demanded that a copy of the database be made to be used on site for the duration of the excavation; the new data being reunited with the master database in Reading at the end of the season. This approach was adopted in 1998 with one on-site computer, printer, and digitizing tablet. In 1999, however, this work was undertaken at the university and there were no computers on site. Even by the end of the second season it was becoming clear that it would not be possible to match the data entry with the duration of the field season. This was partly a reflection of the growing volume of data and partly of the flow of completed records from the trench. These tended to bunch in the closing days of the season. To increase the volume of data entry on site required more hardware – computers, scanners and, if the finds team were also to enter data on site, a further generator. Oversight of the process and of quality assurance demanded dedicated staff time. Fortunately, it was also possible to make an appointment, with support from 2000 from the Arts and Humanities Research Board (AHRB) funding (see further below) of a full-time database manager (R. Shaffrey, replaced by K. Tootell in 2002) as a third member of the Silchester Town Life Project team. As well as overseeing the entry of data on site, working in close collaboration with the trench supervisors, and ensuring the completion of the process for all categories of excavation and finds records between seasons, her role included the management of the storage of the finds and liaison between conservators, specialists reporting on the finds, illustrators, etc., as the work of publishing the excavation began (see further below). In 2000 there were three networked computers on site, one functioning as the server and all powered by a generator with surge protectors. Most of the field records were entered before the end of the season. The 2000 season was also the first to make extensive use of digital photography and the first 2,000 images were uploaded by the end of the year. The mixed approach of some data entry on site during the season and completion of the process off-site between seasons continued in this way until 2005, with daily back-up and transfer of data to the master server at the university.

A major development took place in 2005 when, with funding from the JISC (Joint Information Systems Committee) as an integral part of the OGHAM (On-line Group Historical and Archaeological Matrix)[10] project with its over-arching aim of establishing a Virtual Research Environment (VRE) for Silchester, the excavation was linked to the broadband network via a wireless connection between an aerial fixed to one of the site cabins and one on a barn, approximately 600m distant, in which was housed the ADSL connection. This meant that data could be streamed directly to the server in the University and the issue of ensuring data integrity between the on-site server and the master in the university could be overcome. At the same time this facility could provide a platform for testing and experimenting with other digital approaches to site recording. One of the fundamental issues of archaeological site and finds recording, and not just confined to Silchester, is that it involves the double-handling of data, all records being written or drawn in the first instance, then subsequently digitized during and after the excavation season. Such an approach has obvious resource implications. Would it be possible to enter all the field and finds data without first hand-writing or drawing them? To address this problem the JISC-funded OGHAM project provided resources for two seasons of experimentation using hand-held devices (PDAs) in the trench to record accessioned finds in the first instance and also to provide access to the records of previous seasons stored in the IADB, while a ruggedized tablet PC was deployed to record context plans, with the aim of replacing the use of pencil plans on permatrace which subsequently require digitization. The PDAs could also be used to enter context records. These devices would operate using a local wireless network established to function across the area of the trench. While issues emerged over the reliability of the wireless network in the trench, the problem of using the tablet PC in bright daylight, and the general usefulness of the small PDAs, having direct access to the network proved invaluable. The benefit was not just in terms of data entry via a web interface for the excavation database, but also that the larger issues associated with the day-to-day management of the ever-growing field project, involving a staff of forty and over a hundred trainee archaeologists, could be addressed via email and access to the Internet. It also offered the possibility of real-time broadcasting of the progress of the excavation season using webcams. Such aims had been envisaged back in 1999 when an unsuccessful application was made to British Telecom Awards to establish a Silchester website and a live site presence during the excavation season.

---

10   JISC, 'Silchester Roman Town: A Virtual Research Environment for Archaeology', <http://www.jisc.ac.uk/whatwedo/programmes/vre1/silchester.aspx>.

Project Name:	Site code:	Plan Zone(s):	Context No.
Context type (tick) Deposit Cut Structure	Deposit type:	Cut type:	Structure type:

Deposit description: 1.Colour 2.Consistency 3.Texture 4.Inclusions (<50%) 5.Thickness & extent 6.Other comments 7.Method & conditions
Cut description: 1.Shape in plan (**sketch overleaf**) 2.Corners 3.Dimensions/depth 4.Break of slope – top 5.Sides 6.Break of slope – base 7.Base 8.Orientation 9.Shape in profile (**sketch overleaf**) 10.Fill nos. 11. Other comments
Masonry description: 1. Materials 2. Size of materials (brick;BTL in mm) 3 Finish of stones 4. Coursing /bond 5. Form 6. Direction of face(s) 7. Bonding material (brick: height of 4 courses and 4 bed joints in mm). 8. Dimensions of masonry as found 9. Other comments

Description:	Inclusions:
	Stones: Number <1 1-5 5-15 15-35 35-70 >70% Shape (A) (S-A) (S-R) (R) Size: (2-6mm) (6-20mm) (2-6cm) (6-20cm) (20-60cm) (60cm+)
Edge definition:	

Stratigraphic Matrix

This context is [   ]

This context is stratified below:	Contemporary with:
This context is stratified above:	Butts/butted by:

Cuts:	Cut by:	Same as:
Contains:	Fill of/Part of:	**Context is:** (tick and date) Completely removed Partially removed Not excavated

Interpretation:

UNIVERSITY OF READING, DEPARTMENT OF ARCHAEOLOGY

Figure 1.2   A typical context recording card

Source: © University of Reading.

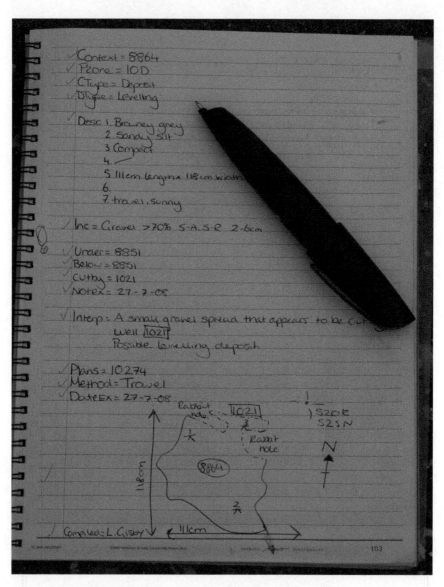

Figure 1.3   Digital pen counterpart to the recording card

Source: © University of Reading.

The JISC continued to invest in the development of a generic VRE for Archaeology with a second project (VERA – Virtual Environments for Research in Archaeology) funded 2007–2009.[11] Whereas OGHAM had involved a collaboration between

---

    11   Virtual Environments for Research in Archaeology, <http://vera.rdg.ac.uk>.

HE and professional archaeology – the University of Reading and the York Archaeological Trust – with VERA the collaboration was extended to include computer scientists – the School of Systems Engineering at the University of Reading and information scientists from the School of Library Archive and Information Studies at University College London. Amongst other aims, which will be discussed further below, an important component of the project has included further experimentation with devices to be used in the trench to capture the field data digitally directly into the IADB and so bypass cumbersome post-excavation digitization. These new field trials have also involved a strengthening of the reliability and capacity of the broadband signal received on site. At the same time, while still maintaining a wireless network in part of the trench, the emphasis has shifted to using devices, particularly digital pens and notebooks, but also digital clipboards, which do not depend on a wireless network within the trench. The results of these experiments can be seen on the VERA project blog.[12]

The digital pens function just like normal ballpoints. The user writes on digital paper using the digital pen. Since the pen uses normal ink the writer can see the text which is also being recorded digitally. The pen contains a miniature camera which records the strokes and their place on the page, using a series of map coordinates. The pen is then docked with the computer via the USB port and the software uploads all the stored information. The user is then able to view an image on the screen that matches the digital notebook. The software then performs optical character recognition (OCR) on the page and displays as editable text what it identifies as having been written in the notebook. The user is able to make corrections to the text at this stage and the software can learn any new words. Any sketches or images drawn in the notebook can be selected and saved as an image file in either a JPEG or TIFF format. The text can be saved as a text file or exported into Microsoft Word.

Following preliminary testing in 2007 extensive trials were undertaken in 2008 using the digital pens and notebooks, but without sufficient resources in terms of the numbers of pens and staff time required to download and check entries in order to record all the contexts digitally. Altogether some 43 per cent of the 2008 season's 1652 recorded contexts were captured digitally and downloaded onto the IADB. The volume of recording varied through the season, but with a significant increase in the last two weeks when the excavation and recording of contexts started earlier in the season were completed and checked. The pens were robust and functioned in wet weather conditions and the system as a whole was shown to work, but the ideal of capturing the whole of the season's data into the IADB by the end of the season was not achieved.[13] Nevertheless there is clear potential for developing further the use of digital pens in the trench and overcoming the bottlenecks, such as the number of available pens and the number of personnel

---

12   VERA project blog, <http://vera.rdg.ac.uk/blog/>.

13   Claire Warwick, Melissa Terras, C. Fisher et al., 'iTrench: A Study of the Use of IT in Field Archaeology', *Literary and Linguistic Computing*, 24:2 (2009): 211–23.

trained in their use. Training and support for the new and inexperienced user are critical, but, with such resource in place, further roll-out is planned in 2009 and beyond.

Since the award of the JISC grant in 2004, the experimentation with improving the flow of information arising from the eight-week field season into the IADB (and thereby cutting the cost of the process) has become an integral part of the Silchester Town Life Project. While the emphasis has been on trying to speed the flow of written, mostly contextual information into the IADB, some initial work has also been done on using a tracking Global Positioning System (GPS) as an alternative to conventional planning using measured grids, or to the use of tablet PCs where visibility of the screen is a major concern (see above). If GPS systems can be shown to be effective at the micro-recording level, their deployment will facilitate the development of an instantaneous 3D record of the excavation. Webcams were also trialled in 2008 to give an overview of the excavation throughout the season. Used in conjunction with digital camcorders these do offer the possibility of getting information about the progress of the season via the website into the public domain more rapidly. However, as with the digital pens, the management and editing of moving images of the excavation require dedicated time which introduces a further cost on the project.

The OGHAM and VERA projects have unquestionably strengthened and improved the flow of data, both field and finds records, from the trench to the database, where they can be immediately accessed by the research team. The greater the speed by which these data have become available, the faster the research manipulation of those data can be undertaken, and the faster the consequent presentation of the interpreted field record to the wider research team. The challenge now is to determine whether the same speed can be achieved with the research team of specialist analysts. It is customary practice in the UK for the specialist contributors – ceramicists, faunal analysts and other finds specialists – to write up their material months or years after the excavation. With appropriate advanced planning it should now be possible to assemble the full research team alongside the excavation and to have it work simultaneously in order to achieve rapid reporting, synthesis and interpretation of results of the entire output, both field and finds data. While the IADB remains the heart of the VRE, the *sine qua non* research resource of the project, we can now envisage a VRE for archaeology which also embraces both the digital capture and manipulation of field and finds records during the excavation and, realistically, the post-excavation analysis too.

Silchester and the IADB: Post-excavation and publication perspectives

Another *sine qua non* of the Silchester Roman Town Life Project is publication to meet the needs of both academic and public audiences. First, we need to consider the academic requirements of 'full' scholarly publication which gives as much attention to the description and analysis of the stratigraphic sequence

Figure 1.4   One of the digital pens from the VERA project in use on site
Source: © University of Reading.

and its associated buildings and other significant structures and features as it does to the finds, whether material – coins and other accessioned finds, pottery, etc. – or biological and environmental – faunal, plant remains, etc. We have already described the importance of the IADB to the construction of the period-by-period development of the site in question, in this case Insula IX, and of the role of the matrix in testing and displaying the spatial and chronological relationships between individual contexts. Indeed, development of the matrix function through, for example, extending its capacity at visualizing relationships, has been a major strand of work throughout the life of the Silchester project. Through the web, however, the IADB has the capacity to publish all the underlying stratigraphic data which underpin the interpretation of the stratigraphic sequence, as well as supporting images, etc. As we have observed above, such a potential provides the possibility of resolving the tension between the partial, summary disclosure of results of a complex archaeological excavation such as an urban project like Silchester, and the total exposure of all relevant data. Nevertheless, despite the potential of web-based publication, lack of confidence in the medium- or the longer-term sustainability of the web-based resource has meant a continued and significant reliance on traditional printed media. This is as much true of Silchester as it is of archaeology in general.

Nevertheless, the securing of a major research grant from the Arts and Humanities Research Board in 1999 to develop on-line publication of the Silchester Insula IX archive was instrumental in the project developing an enduring strand of on-line publication. One crucial step in this project was making the IADB available on-line to all potential users and researchers, particularly those closely involved with the publication of the results, but also, for example, to student users. To this end in 2001 the IADB was set up on a server at the university with a registered domain name www.silchester.reading. ac.uk. This allowed both for remote management by Rains from York, and, more importantly, it enabled those involved with the publication process to access the records from any location, providing they had access to the Internet. Up to then use of the IADB had only been possible for those sharing access at the university. Although Silchester had a web presence on the university's website, the establishment of a separate domain name allowed for much more imaginative and extensive use of the web for public communication.

In enabling remote members of the research team to access directly the field record and the interpretative structure expressed through the excavation's stratigraphic matrices, the web interface has been of inestimable value. In particular it has enabled the specialist contributor, ceramicist, numismatist, faunal analyst, etc., to become more integrated with the context of their material. In the past such integration has tended to take place only towards the closing stages of publishing an excavation, at a point where it becomes more difficult (and expensive) to correct errors and misunderstandings which could have been eliminated at an earlier stage. The next step is for individual specialist contributors, each traditionally working independently of the other, to be able to explore the interrelationships of their material and its interpretation with other colleagues, as well as with the stratigraphic record.

Given that the underlying data resource is unique and the cost of its acquisition has a token value of some millions of pounds, linking to the web also requires appropriate security against hackers. The continual enhancement of security in response to developing technologies represents a responsibility and cost on the project unforeseen at the outset.

A first aim as part of the AHRB-funded project, mentioned above, was to publish the first, discrete phase of results from the excavation. These concerned the Victorian excavations of Insula IX in 1893–4 which had used a methodology of trial-trenching that had not been documented. The network of Victorian trenches was published for the first time,[14] as was a remarkable pit full of both Victorian-era finds such as mineral water bottles and china, but also a large cache of Roman material which had been clearly discarded by the excavators after initially being retained from the excavation. Extensive use of colour photography was an obvious attribute of this publication compared with what might have been feasible in printed format. More importantly, however, the visitor to the website could follow links through to the underlying database down to the level of individual, accessioned finds as well as context records and plans. Users can explore the stratigraphic matrix and use it as an index into related elements of the project archive. The Victorian project was published in 2001, with a printed version following a year later.[15] The aims and methodology leading to the development and publication of the website were published in the proceedings of the CAA 2002 conference.[16] The website was 'Highly Commended' in the Channel 4 category of the British Archaeological Awards of November 2002.

By this time, with funding from the British Academy, work was well advanced on the analysis of the archaeology and finds associated with the late Roman occupation of Insula IX of which the last remaining contexts were excavated in 2001. Following the model set by the Victorian website a parallel publication of printed monograph and website was envisaged. Each was designed to be self-standing, but with emphasis on different aspects. Thus the monograph is text-rich, containing detailed academic discussion of the archaeology and all the finds, but with limited, monochrome illustrations, 125 in total. The only image in colour is the reconstruction on the front cover of the principal buildings and their context in the fourth century. Appendices provide the basic tables of data for each of the finds reports. The website, on the other hand, takes the user to hundreds of images of the archaeology and of the finds (there is at least one image of each of the several hundreds of accessioned finds) as well as the underlying evidential basis of accessioned finds' identifications and context records and the matrix which presents the stratigraphic relationships of all the contexts, but broken down into smaller,

---

14 The Victorian Excavations of 1893, <http://www.silchester.reading.ac.uk/victorians/clickmap.php>.

15 Michael Fulford and Amanda Clarke, 'Victorian Excavation Methodology: The Society of Antiquaries at Silchester in 1893', *Antiquaries Journal*, 82 (2002): 285–306.

16 Amanda Clarke, Michael Fulford, and R. Rains, 'Nothing to Hide: Online Database Publication and the Silchester Town Life Project', in M. Doerr and A. Sarris. (eds), *CAA 2002. The Digital Heritage of Archaeology. Computer Applications and Quantitative Methods in Archaeology. Proceedings of the 30th Conference, Heraklion, Crete, April 2002.* (Archive of Monuments and Publications Hellenic Ministry of Culture, Greece, 2003), pp. 401–404.

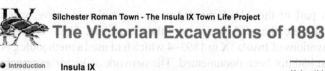

Silchester Roman Town - The Insula IX Town Life Project

The Victorian Excavations of 1893

- Introduction
- Excavation Techniques
- Trench Plan
- House 1 & Block 1
- Ogham Stone
- Rubbish Pit
- Wells, Pits & Hearths
- Matrix Browser
- Bibliography
- Home

Insula IX

Insula IX was first excavated in 1893, the fourth season of a twenty year project by the Society of Antiquaries of London to excavate the entire Roman city of Calleva Atrebatum (Silchester).

The University of Reading's excavation of approximately one-third of Insula IX (see above) began in 1997. Each year since then an enormous amount of data has been gathered, data which is managed by means of an Integrated Archaeological Database. Manipulation of these data will result in a programme of both conventional printed and on-line publication of which the Victorian excavations of 1893 is part.

About this Web Site

Within a period of twenty years (1890-1909) a programme of excavations under the auspices of the Society of Antiquaries of London revealed a plan of all the stone buildings within the walled area of the Roman town. Up until now little has been known about the methodology by which the Victorian and

Using this Web Site

▶ At the left side of this page and all main pages in this site is the main menu bar. This provides quick access to all parts of the site. Several menu items have sub-menus which will appear when you click on the menu item.

▶ Throughout this site, this right-hand column contains links to other related parts of the site, callouts providing additional information on items in the main text, and thumbnail views of images (click on a thumbnail to view the full size image).

▶ Throughout the text, Context numbers and other references are live links to the IADB. By following these links you are logged into the IADB as a guest user and can explore all aspects of the excavation archive database.

▶ The IADB Matrix Browser provides another way in which

Figure 1.5   Screenshot of the Victorian section of <http://www.silchester. rdg.ac.uk>

Source: © University of Reading.

focused groups (defined as Objects), such as groups of pits or the stratigraphy associated with a single building, etc. The summary written description of the excavation is on the website, as are summaries of the individual finds' reports and their associated tables of data. In addition to facilitating access to the mass of underlying data, a key attribute of the late Roman website was the ease with which cross-referencing could be made between context and plan, context and accessioned finds, stratigraphic group of contexts (=Object) and plan, etc. Finally, it was possible to produce the website much more quickly than the printed book; the late Roman website was launched in 2005, whereas the monograph was not published until the following year.[17] The publication of the former saw the final fruition of the AHRB project to develop an on-line archive for Silchester.

---

17   Late Roman Insula IX, <http://www.silchester.reading.ac.uk/later>; Michael Fulford, Amanda Clarke and H. Eckardt, *Life and Labour in Late Roman Silchester: Excavations in Insula IX Since 1997* (London: Society for the Promotion of Roman Studies, Britannia Monograph 22, 2006).

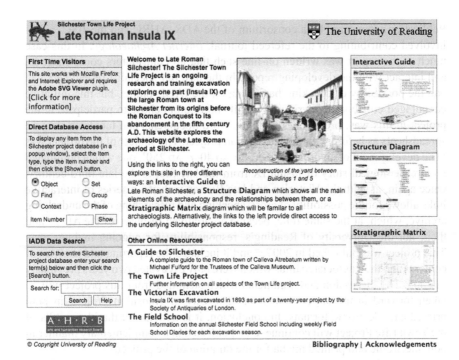

Figure 1.6   Screenshot of the Late Roman section of <http://www. silchester.rdg.ac.uk>

Source: © University of Reading.

An issue with both the 'Victorian' and 'Late Roman' website is their sustainability and reliability for the user. Interruptions of service such as migration to a new server can have significant and unforeseen impacts on the service, typically breaking links. Some users report problems but the responsibility lies with the providers of the service to ensure continuing full functionality. Deep checking of the website links and fixing of 'bugs' needs to be undertaken on a regular basis and this requires appropriate resourcing, a need, like that of maintaining the security of the website, unforeseen at the outset.

Following hard on the heels of the publication of the late Roman archaeology came plans to publish the archaeology of Insula IX of the middle Roman period, the second and third centuries, a project christened 'Silchester: City in Transition'. Further funding was obtained from the Arts and Humanities Research Council to secure reports from a range of researchers on all categories of finds and environmental data, but a further dimension was added when Silchester was invited to contribute to the LEAP project (Linking Electronic Archives and

Publication) sponsored by a consortium of the ADS, AHRC and the JISC.[18] This involved contributing to the refereed journal, *Internet Archaeology*. In this case much of the report was written on-line such that all contributors could share in, and interact with the developing report. In the past our specialist researchers had had the possibility of checking basic data on the IADB online, but this initiative encouraged collaborative writing. Not all contributors chose to participate in the project in this way, preferring to submit Word documents and tabulated data on spreadsheets as before with the late Roman project. The subject of the project was 'The development of an urban property *c.* AD 40–*c.* AD 250', one which dominated the archaeological story of Insula IX from the late first to the late third century. Once again, as with the Victorian and late Roman website, a series of interactive links allows for the possibility of cross-checking and researching of the underlying archive, which, at the same time, became an archived resource of the ADS[19] and their, not the University of Reading's, responsibility for ongoing maintenance. This project was published in 2007,[20] and it included the reporting and analysis of contexts and their associated finds which were only excavated two years previously in 2005. The discussion and arguments which stemmed from this project will be taken forward in the larger context of 'The City in Transition Project' in both printed and electronic formats. In conclusion, it is anticipated that the results of the Town Life Project will continue to be published in a complementary manner in both electronic and printed media for the duration of the project.

Silchester, the IADB and VERA

The JISC-funded VERA project (2007–2009) has used Silchester and the IADB as a model for developing a generic Virtual Research Environment for Archaeology. In addition to developing approaches to enhance the digital capture of field data in the context of the excavation, the project has also looked more widely at the various needs which are emerging as the Silchester project continues to evolve. On the one hand, there is the need to integrate further the work of specialist contributors into the VRE so that all members of the team have a greater share in, and ownership of a project which was initially set up with a view to facilitating the processing of the field data, including the stratigraphic data, arising from excavation. On the other there are several strategic objectives which need to be addressed, the first of which is to ensure the ongoing security of the database in a web context.

---

18   Linking Electronic Archives and Publication, <http://ads.ahds.ac.uk/project/leap>.

19   Amanda Clarke, Michael Fulford and Michael Rains, 'Silchester Roman Town Insula IX: The Development of an Urban Property c. AD 40–50–c. AD 250' (Archaeology Data Service, 2007), <http://ads.ahds.ac.uk/catalogue/archive/silchester_ahrc_2007>.

20   Amanda Clarke, Michael Fulford, Michael Rains and Klare Tootell, 'Silchester Roman Town Insula <http://intarch.ac.uk/journal/issue21/silchester_index.html>.

Second, there is the need to develop interoperability with other databases to enable complex cross-database searches. The OGHAM project addressed interoperability between IADBs, which use the same system, while VERA is tackling databases using different systems, in this case the Oxford Ancient Texts database,[21] whereby it will be possible to search for texts across both systems. The third area is in 3D visualization where there are two pressing needs: on the one hand to develop the 3D representation of the stratigraphic sequence, in this case of the Insula IX excavation, so that it will enhance the researcher's ability to interrogate different strands of data, and the interrelationships of those data, in their stratigraphic context, rather than through context numbers represented in a matrix diagram. The second need is to help address the requirements of both the academic and the public in the development of 3D visualization which can address such questions as 'what did Insula IX look like in the third century,' or 'how can we visualize the exterior or interior of Late Roman Building 1.' Integral to this is the need to link the evidence used to build the reconstruction with data stored in the IADB. This question of representation and interpretation takes us to the public presence of Silchester, particularly as visualized through the web.

The Silchester Website: <http://www.silchester.reading.ac.uk>

Although, as we have noted above, the Insula IX Town Life Project had an early web presence in the context of the University of Reading's website, 2001 was the year when the Victorian website was launched on a standalone Silchester website. The focus of this publication did not, however, address either the larger Silchester Town Life Project and the Insula IX excavation, nor did it have any information to set that project in the context of previous work at and finds from the Roman town. In 2003 Silchester was awarded a grant from the Heritage Lottery Fund (HLF) to develop better educational provision and public access to the project. A major part of this project was the development of the Silchester website so that it did include more about what was known about the Roman town in general, as well as more information about Insula IX and the Town Life Project. Just as visitors required better information about access to the excavation and the town site, so potential participants in the increasingly popular Silchester Field School needed more information about the Field School and the nature of training provision as well as about access to the excavations. The website continues to be updated, most recently undergoing a major facelift in summer 2008.

---

21   VRE for the Study of Documents and Manuscripts, <http://bvreh.humanities.ox.ac.uk/VRE-SDM>.

Conclusions

The above summarizes for the first time the development of the engagement of the Silchester Town Life Project with ICT over the thirteen years since its inception in 1997. It is clear that there is always more to improve in all areas: the capture of field-generated data on site; the development of tools to exploit and manipulate that data; the development of tools, such as for 3D visualization, to enable the larger research team of specialists researching the finds and environmental data of the project to make better use of and also enhance the capacity of the Silchester IADB. The pivotal role of the latter is demonstrated by the number of interrelated records which it is holding at the end of 2008: 8,354 context records, 32,290 finds records, 193 matrices and 6,186 photos. These underpin both academic and public web publication, which demand continuous investment and both media have become a *sine qua non* of the Silchester Town Life Project. All of these strands of development and support demand resources and the project is extremely grateful to organizations such as AHRB/C, HLF and the JISC, which have all invested specifically in the ICT. Without a range of other funding bodies and individuals, however, there would be no archaeology and post-excavation research to disseminate! Looking ahead towards the end of the project and beyond, a key issue will be the long-term preservation of the digital archive. Here, with uncertainty about the longer-term funding of ADS, the obvious national host for the archive, we must look to a dual approach that utilizes both the University of Reading's institutional repository and the national archive, hopefully a permanently maintained ADS.

Chapter 2

Diversity and Reuse of Digital Resources for Ancient Mediterranean Material Culture[1]

Sebastian Heath

Introduction

I open with the simple observation that large amounts of information about the material culture of the ancient Mediterranean world are becoming available online. While grounded in specific examples, this chapter is interested in the sources of that information and how diverse entities contribute to, link to, copy or otherwise reuse resources that are discoverable on the public Internet. The main goal is to document that museums, private individuals, publicly funded repositories, commercial enterprises and academic publishers are contributors to this ongoing process. Again, that may seem a well-known fact. Nonetheless, the role of commercial and private initiative in the development of the 'ancient world web' is not always acknowledged.

For example, the site *Archnet* sponsored by Arizona State University has long collected links to archaeological websites, including those relevant to the ancient Mediterranean.[2] Its editorial policy states that 'In keeping with our mission goals, we have decided not to link commercial sites (with the exception of publishing companies).' 'Artefact dealers' are explicitly included in the definition of commercial sites. Similarly, the Council on Library and Information Resources sponsored a 2003 survey of 33 digital cultural heritage initiatives that included no commercial businesses.[3] More recently, a 2006 American Council of Learned Societies (ACLS) report addressed its call to 'develop public and institutional policies that foster openness and access' to 'university presidents, boards of trustees, provosts, and counsels; funding agencies; libraries; scholarly societies;

---

1   Elements of this chapter were presented in talks given at the Institute for the Study of the Ancient World, New York University; The University of Pennsylvania; and the 2009 Computer Applications and Quantitative Methods in Archaeology (CAA) conference. I am grateful to the reviewers for their comments. The opinions and shortcomings are my own.

2   *Archnet*, Arizona State University, available: <http://archnet.asu.edu/>. All URLs in this chapter were accessed in early 2009.

3   Diane Zorich, *A Survey of Digital Cultural Heritage Initiatives and Their Sustainability Concerns* (Washington, DC: Council on Library and Information Resources, 2003), 41.

[and] Congress'.[4] While the same report does call for cooperation between the public and private sectors in order to 'explore new models for commercial/nonprofit partnerships,' it is not clear that dealer sites are included.[5] The work of private individuals is ignored. I cite these examples to say that there is a general bias within academic and not-for-profit communities against direct engagement with commercial entities that profit from the sale of antiquities, as well as a tendency by the same communities to overlook the personal efforts of individuals.

For its part, this chapter puts diversity of sources at the centre of its analysis and therefore includes digitized information that comes from commercial entities and individuals. I do so not because of any blanket claims about the relative merits of private work and professional research, nor because I wish to judge the ethics of commerce and scholarship. Instead, I hope to examine digitization and reuse as they are currently occurring in publicly accessible digital arenas. In short, I will show that commercial and private initiative is combining with academic efforts in ways that often achieve the 'openness and access' for which the ACLS has called.

Having indicated that I will discuss digitization resulting from the commercial sale of antiquities that may not have well-established provenances, it is important to reveal a personal bias. I am an archaeologist with an active programme of field research and I believe that the trade in undocumented antiquities encourages looting of ancient sites and the loss of irreplaceable information. This is not an essay about the implications of such trade and I will not press that point here.[6]

What follows should be understood as a commentary on the state of affairs resulting from the cumulative effect of academic, private and commercial efforts to digitize the material culture of the ancient Mediterranean. My approach is resolutely grounded in examination of current resources, meaning specific HTML pages and search-form accessible databases. I am not therefore writing about abstract best practices or future standards and technologies. Rather, I am interested in engaging with digital resources as they exist now. I hope that the explicit reliance on practice as it actually is, rather than how we would like it to be, explains the obvious gaps in the citations that I will make. Taking time to look at individual sites means that only a small proportion of all the relevant digital information can be considered.

My approach is also intentionally anecdotal in that I will rely on my experience using specific features of specific sites. It will also be clear that my conclusions reflect personal opinion. At times I will point out what seem to be obvious areas for improvement in the implementation of the resources I cite, but such criticism should be taken within the context of my opening observation. I take its corollary to be that the net effect of the various efforts pursuing digitization is unprecedented

---

4   American Council of Learned Societies, *Our Cultural Commonwealth* (New York: American Council of Learned Societies, 2006), p. 2.

5   Ibid., p. 3.

6   For further discussion see Neil Brodie et al., *Stealing History: The Illicit Trade in Cultural Material* (Cambridge, 2000).

and useful access to digital materials for the study of the physical remains of antiquity. This is to the benefit of both scholarly research and the public interest.

Most of my examples come from two fields of study within the broader discipline of ancient studies: numismatics and Roman pottery. For full disclosure, let me say these are my two areas of publication and research, meaning that I am very familiar with the digital resources relevant to each. To the extent that these are well-established disciplines with long histories, the choice does not need justification. But it is the case that neither sits at the very centre of ancient studies, as compared to, for example, Greek and Roman sculpture or architecture.[7] As will be seen below, however, both the study of ancient coins and of Roman period ceramics are fields for which a rich variety of digital information is currently available. It is particularly the case that each has both hobbyists and commercial dealers as content creators. Linking and reuse between the resources created by these actors and more frequently recognized members of the academic and not-for-profit establishments is a focus of this chapter.

As noted, the study of ancient numismatics is well established in the academic world, with roots stretching back to the Renaissance.[8] There is a vast bibliography that continues to expand, often through the continuing publication of specialized journals. In addition to these trappings of modern scholarship, there is an active community of collectors and dealers that has made substantial contributions to the current state of knowledge about the coinage of the ancient Mediterranean world. This community has adopted the Internet with considerable enthusiasm. For example, the email list Moneta-L, hosted on Yahoo Groups and 'dedicated to the joys of ancient coin collecting', saw 3,784 posts in 2008, more than ten per day.[9] In addition, dealer sites, whose primary purpose is the sale of coins or the facilitation of such sales, are generating large volumes of digitized information, mainly in the form of descriptions of items for sale. Some of these descriptions, though by no means all, are archived and made available to the browsing public.[10] All users of numismatic information, including those in the academic establishment, derive benefit from these activities. Accordingly, any attempt to discuss the current state of numismatic information on the Internet should take account of these commercial sites and of the sites that reuse their content.

---

7   American Council of Learned Societies, *Report of the Commission on the Humanities* (New York: American Council of Learned Societies, 1964), p. 171, where numismatics is defined as an ancillary discipline. Stephen Willis, *National Research Framework Document* (Study Group for Roman Pottery, 1997), <http://www.sgrp.org.uk/07/Doc/2.htm>, had to stress that the same term wasn't appropriate for the study of Roman pottery, an indication that some might disagree.

8   Guillaume Budé's *De asse et partibus eius* published in 1514 is recognized as the first printed book in the field of numismatics.

9   *Moneta-L*, <http://groups.yahoo.com/group/Moneta-L/>.

10   *Coin Archives*, <http://coinarchives.com/>, is currently the most comprehensive site for auction records of ancient coins.

Roman pottery, as a field of study, does not have the advantage of a similar level of online activity. There is no active Internet discussion group devoted solely to its results and methods and, while Roman pottery is bought and sold on the Internet, the dealer sites are not nearly as useful as those for numismatics.[11] Accordingly, it is my subjective assessment that the digital resources that originate from within the academic establishment make up a higher percentage of the useful information available for Roman pottery than is the case for ancient numismatics.

Having said that I will include personal and commercial sites, I do want to stress that I am not holding these up as models for future efforts to digitize the ancient world. Many of the resources I cite do not meet best practices of the emerging fields of digital humanities or digital archiving. To take one example of expectations current in these communities, the National Endowment for the Humanities (NEH) asks that the following considerations be taken into account when applying for funds from its 'Preservation and Access: Humanities Collections and Resources' programme:

> All applicants employing digital technology should follow standards and best practices that ensure longevity of digital products and facilitate interoperability with other resources and related materials.

And:

> Describe the institution's plans for storing, maintaining, and protecting the data, and, where applicable, for the preservation or other disposition of the original source material. Explain how the data will be archived (independent of the processing or delivery software and interface) to migrate them to future media and formats.[12]

The principles implicit in these requirements could be used to criticize, even exclude, many of the websites that I use as illustration here. To put the matter more bluntly, many of the sites discussed below offer no information at all on how they would meet the NEH's requirements. But exclusion is not my goal; understanding the current state of affairs is. I do not, however, mean to suggest that these requirements are inappropriate. In the context of a publicly funded grant, it is self-evidently important that recipients address issues of interoperability and long-term access. Nonetheless, this chapter recognizes that digitization is happening in communities that do not explicitly adhere to principles increasingly acknowledged as central to the success of publicly funded efforts.

---

11   Cf. *Ancient Touch*, <http://ancienttouch.com/>, for an example of a site offering a variety of Roman period ceramics.

12   National Endowment for the Humanities, *Preservation and Access: Humanities Collections and Resources*, <http://www.neh.gov/grants/guidelines/Collections_and_resources.html>.

In this chapter I observe that some commercial enterprises are far more open with their data than are many initiatives originating within the academy or not-for-profit institutions such as museums and digital repositories. This should not be taken as a blanket statement given that initiatives such as the Perseus Project and OpenContext are actively pursuing the distribution of freely licensed digital content.[13] But where it is true, the fact should be demonstrated and the implications should be explored. Before doing so, I acknowledge that commercial enterprises likely hope to gain from the exposure that reuse of their content brings, that museums fear loss of revenue from the paid reproduction of copyrighted images, and that academic initiatives hope to keep their content from being inappropriately commercialized with no benefit to themselves. This chapter does not intend to explore these motives in depth nor to pass judgment on them. Instead, I intend first to describe how data appears, is found, and also reused via linking and copying. While describing these processes, I also identify aspects of implementation and presentation that may influence the reuse and linking, or the lack thereof, that I see.

One last point of methodology: throughout this chapter I use the search engine Google to illustrate the discoverability of information and Wikipedia, and its companion site Wikimedia Commons, to illustrate processes of communal linking and reuse.[14] Neither is perfectly suited to how I use them, but both are, at the time of writing, the leading illustrations of these two concepts. Even when not welcomed, the effect of both sites on practice is widely acknowledged. For example, a recent call for greater training of students opened by declaring it to be common opinion among professors 'that superficial searches on the Internet and facts gleaned from Wikipedia are the extent – or a significant portion – of far too many of their students' investigations.'[15] The quantitative dominance of Wikipedia is indicated by recent reports that the site receives 97 per cent of the visits to five popular websites that can generically be called encyclopedias.[16] Google's reported market share for all search is over 60 per cent, and a 2005 survey of student practice in the United Kingdom indicated that 45 per cent begin their research with a Google search.[17] This high market share has had direct effect on providers of digitized scholarly resources. In 2006 JSTOR, the widely used provider of access

---

13   Gregory   Crane,   *The   Perseus   Project*,   <http://www.perseus.tufts.edu>; *OpenContext*, <http://opencontext.org>.

14   Wikimedia Foundation, Inc. *Wikipedia*, <http://wikipedia.org>; this chapter makes use of the English-language version. Wikimedia Foundation, Inc., *Wikimedia Commons*, <http://commons.wikimedia.org/>.

15   Andrew Guess, 'Research Methods "Beyond Google"', *Inside Higher Ed*, 17 June 2008, <http://www.insidehighered.com/news/2008/06/17/institute>.

16   Heather Hopkins, 'Britannica 2.0: Wikipedia Gets 97% of Encyclopedia Visits', *Hitwise Intelligence* (1/2009), <http://weblogs.hitwise.com/us-heather-hopkins/2009/01/britannica_20_wikipedia_gets_9.html>.

17   Thomas Claburn, 'Google Search Share Slips', in *Information Week*, 14 January 2009, <http://www.informationweek.com/news/internet/reporting/showArticle.jhtml?articl

to archived academic journals, opened itself to indexing by Google. The context for this agreement has been recently explained as follows:

> JSTOR began to enable indexing by public search engines at the request of many librarians at participating institutions who were seeing more of their users, particularly students, begin their search with Google. Not surprisingly, this opening of JSTOR to broad public search has enhanced discovery of scholarly materials not only among scholars, but also among a broader audience.[18]

I will look more closely at the role of JSTOR as a digitizer of information about the material culture of the ancient Mediterranean, so this quotation, with its explicit reference to Google, appears now only as explanation for using its search engine as a proxy for the discoverability of a resource. More examples of the current relevance of both Google and Wikipedia could be introduced but it seems evident that examination of current practice is well served by reference to these two sites.

Simple keyword search for numismatic resources

Although my discussion will be driven by use of specific resources, I begin this section with a summary table (Table 2.1) that categorizes and counts the sources of information that appear in the first five positions of five Google searches that stand in for mainstream topics in the field of ancient numismatics. In this table, 'Commercial' means sites that list coins for sale at the URL shown in the results; 'Personal/Collector' means sites that are written and hosted by individuals, groups or clubs that have generated or collected numismatic information or

Table 2.1   Google results for numismatic keywords

Search Term	Commercial	Personal/ Collector	Academic/ Museum	Wikipedia
'Augustan coinage'	1	3	1	
'Roman coinage'		4		1
'denarius'	1	3		1
'Athenian tetradrachm'	3		1	1
'Alexander great coinage'	3	2		
Totals	**8**	**12**	**1**	**3**

eID=212900619>. Jillian Griffiths and Peter Brophy, 'Student Searching Behavior and the Web: Use of Academic Resources and Google', *Library Trends* (Spring 2005).

18   Michael Spinella, 'JSTOR and the Changing Digital Landscape', *Interlending and Document Supply*, 36:2 (2009): 81. The author of the quoted article is an employee of the organization so I take this description as authoritative.

images; 'Academic/Museum' are resources originating within the professional establishment of not-for-profit institutionally affiliated scholarship; and 'Wikipedia' indicates the appearance of a Wikipedia article in the results. These categories are broad, but I maintain them throughout this chapter and their relevance will become clear as much by usage as by these brief definitions.

Even accounting for the considerable imprecision of this approach, the numbers seem clear. Comprising 20 out of 25 sites, or 80 per cent, commercial and personal sources dominate the discipline of ancient numismatics as presented by Google.[19]

Considering the results of the search for 'Augustan coinage' shows the mix of resources summarized in Table 2.1. When initiated at the time of writing, they were:

1. The commercial site *Forum Ancient coins* showing a list of coins for sale;[20]
2. Page 104 in the chapter 'The Augustan Coinage, 30 B.C.–A.D. 235' of K. Harl's (1996) book *Coinage in the Roman Economy, 300 B.C. to A.D. 700*, as found in Google Books;[21]
3. Coins of Augustus from the site Wildwinds.com, which is mainly an aggregator of auction records;[22]
4. Keith Emmett's 'An Unpublished Alexandrian Coin of Augustus', a specialized discussion of an Alexandrian coin hosted on the site *Coins of Roman Egypt*;[23]
5. The 'Coinage of Augustus' set on Flickr as assembled by the user Joe Geranio.[24]

Even with Wikipedia missing from this list, it illustrates both the diversity of sources and the over-representation of commercial and personal information.

Moving to the content of these sites, the results of this search ought to be judged a success, as none of the sites is of obviously low quality. It is true that somebody entirely unfamiliar with the topic would almost certainly feel dumped into a sea of information, but it would be ungenerous not to see this list of resources as indicative of collective achievement in the ongoing effort to digitize both the primary evidence and secondary sources of ancient numismatics.

---

19   I am grateful to Leif Isaksen for drawing my attention to his paper, 'Pandora's Box: The Future of Cultural Heritage on the World Wide Web', <http://leifuss.files.wordpress. com/2009/04/pandorasboxrev1.pdf>. This is an unpublished conference paper that makes a similar argument using search results for 'Mona Lisa' as its example.

20   Forum Ancient Coins, <http://www.forumancientcoins.com/catalog/roman-and-greek-coins.asp?vpar=383>.

21   Google Books, <http://books.google.com/books?id=5yPDL0EykeAC&pg=PA104>.

22   WildWinds.com, *Browsing Roman Imperial Coins of Augustus*, <http://www. wildwinds.com/coins/ric/augustus/i.html>.

23   Keith Emmett, 'An Unpublished Alexandrian Coin of Augustus', *The Celator* 17/8 (2003), <http://www.coinsofromanegypt.org/html/library/emmett/emmett_aug.htm>.

24   Flickr, *The Coinage of Augustus*, <http://www.flickr.com/photos/julio-claudians/ sets/72157594346513871/>.

Because the Harl book is of a very different nature from the other sites, I start there. As a recently published and fully referenced overview and analysis of Roman coinage, it is entirely appropriate that this conventionally published work be shown to a user interested in the broad topic of Augustan coinage. The specific chapter offered ranges in date far past the early imperial period, but that is not a fault. A reader will eventually come up against the limits of Google Books's limited preview, by which publishers set the percentage of a work that can be read by one person, but the same reader has recourse to finding the work in a library or purchasing it from an online bookseller.

The first site listed above, Forum Ancient Coins, is a commercial site. While it does host materials for the study of ancient coinage, half of its front page is given over to links into a sale catalogue, with 4,672 items available at the time of writing.

The first coin offered for sale on the illustrated page is a bronze *diobol* struck at Alexandria and issued under Augustus. Adapting numismatic convention, I will refer to this piece as FAC 33447 on the basis of its item number in the virtual sale catalogue. The coin is correctly identified as an example of *Roman Provincial Coinage (RPC) I* type 5001.[25] The colour photograph is a more than adequate representation of the piece, which like many Alexandrian bronzes is quite worn from extended circulation in the closed monetary system of Roman Egypt. Clicking on the 'magnifying glass' icon leads to a slightly enlarged version. All of this is to say that the documentation of FAC 33447 meets any reasonable standard of usefulness and is as good as one would find in many scholarly catalogues. The illustration is in fact superior to the black and white 1:1 scale images found in many paper-based publications.

The immediate fate of the coin itself is clear: it is available for sale on eBay, as indicated by text and icon at the lower right of the page. There is no reason to think that the object itself could be tracked down for subsequent study without some element of good luck. The fate of the information about this piece is slightly more encouraging. Many of the pages on the site have a link to a 'search' page. Here one can type in '33447' and select 'sold' from the 'Status' menu to find the record for the piece in question. This is far from a perfect solution. The most immediate complaint is that that there is no semantically clear and potentially stable URL by which to access the information about this coin.[26] Therefore, when judged by the criteria of the digital humanities community, concern has to be expressed about the long-term accessibility of this information. Similarly, there is also concern for its current discoverability. Using Google to search for 'site:http:// www.forumancientcoins.com/33447' returns no useful results. These observations

---

25   A. Burnet, M. Amandry and P. Ripollès, *Roman Provincial Coinage, Volume 1. From the Death of Caesar to the Death of Vitellius (44 BC–AD 69)*, 2 vols (London, 1998).

26   Timothy Berners-Lee, *Cool URIs Don't Change* (W3.org, 1998), <http://www.w3.org/Provider/Style/URI>.

suggest that this information is accessible only if a user knows its item number, exactly where to look, and how to use the FAC search form.

The site WildWinds, number two in the list of Google results, represents a partial response to the problem of archiving commercially generated records of coins for sale on the Internet. Following the link above and perusing the information shows that the page offers abbreviated descriptions of coins sold on eBay and other commercial sites. There are also coins submitted by individual collectors. That is, the site serves as an aggregator and preserver of information generated by its user community. As with many of the pages on this site, the coins of Augustus issued by imperial mints are listed first and identified by their type numbers in the second edition of *Roman Imperial Coins Volume 1* (*RIC*); the coins issued by civic mints are listed by their *RPC* numbers, with some variation at the end. These are the standard works in the field, and while neither is replaced by the many similar listings at WildWinds.com, the information that is available on the site is useful. The image quality is variable, but that is a function of the source material not a matter of choice by the organizer of the site.

For the purposes of this discussion, the interest in WildWinds lies in the fact that it leverages an existing scholarly infrastructure, the typologies in *RIC* and *RPC*, to organize and preserve information generated by commercial activity. The results of this effort are exposed on the Internet and access to them is facilitated by search engines such as Google. This is an optimistic view of the effort. Taken on its own terms, however, WildWinds.com successfully presents one segment of numismatic information in a way that has proved useful to the numismatic community. This is shown by its inclusion in lists of well-regarded numismatic sites and its appearance in Wikipedia articles. For example, the page 'Helvetica's Identification Help Page,' an entirely personal effort, says of WildWinds.com:

> The best! If you use the website a lot, make a donation, as Wildwinds requires a tremendous amount of work and the traffic and server space probably costs a fortune.[27]

On Wikipedia, there are links to the site in the articles entitled *Ancient Greek coinage*, *As (Roman coin)*, *Nabataean coinage* and many others.[28] While these are informal indications, they illuminate the typical processes by which numismatic information is generated, reused, and linked on the Internet.

The private site *Coins of Roman Egypt* provides access to K. Emmet's discussion of a recently identified issue of Augustus from the mint of Alexandria. The text is a reprint from a 2003 article in the *Celator*, a print-based magazine

---

27   Helvetica's Identification Help Page, <http://www.catbikes.ch/coinstuff/coinlinks. htm>.

28   A review of the editing history of each of these articles suggests that third parties made the links from Wikipedia to WildWinds, which I take to indicate that they are not a result of self-promotion.

whose main readership is collectors of ancient coins.[29] In terms of the quality of the material, it is worth noting that the author of the article has also published a catalogue of Alexandrian coin types that is widely used in the field.[30] There is no reason to doubt that this article is intended as a serious contribution.

It is also worthwhile taking note of the *Coins of Roman Egypt* site itself. This resource is the personal effort of Michael Covill, an otherwise unaffiliated collector. In addition to a catalogue describing his collection, the site includes overviews of the denominational structure of Alexandrian coinage, an introduction to the dating system found on Alexandrian coins of the Roman period, a bibliography, a set of links, and a library of hosted resources relevant to the topic. Emmett's article that led this discussion to the site appears in this last section. The site's editor also offers an explanation of why he has made this resource available:

> One of the things that I enjoy most about the hobby of ancient coin collecting is the willingness of others to share their knowledge along with insight they have received from the coins in their collection. This website is my attempt to aid and encourage the discussion of Alexandrian coinage under the Romans, and to hopefully give something back. If I can be of help to you, or you have found an error on my site, please do not hesitate to email me.

The breadth and generally good quality of the information on the site gives substance to this idealistic statement.

The last site appearing in the first five sites of our example Google search is the appropriately titled Flickr set, 'The Coinage of Augustus'. Consisting of 985 photographs, this set is at first glance useful as an aggregation of attractive photos of iconographically interesting coins.

On closer inspection, however, it appears that almost all of the images in this set are taken from the site of the dealer Classical Numismatics Group (CNG) at <http://cngcoins.com/>. For example, the first image in the set, issued in the name of Augustus' adopted grandson Gaius, also appears at <http://cngcoins.com/Coin. aspx?CoinID=56516>. The CNG site provides a more complete description of the piece that includes the standard references to RPC and the catalogue of the British Museum. The Flickr set has stripped out this information and presents only the coin with a brief title. Other coins, such as no. 702 in the Flickr set, do retain both the image and the informative text, copied in this instance from item 115218 on the CNG site.

While there is perhaps a lack of courtesy in the failure to directly acknowledge the source of each of these images, such reuse may actually be consistent with the spirit by which CNG has made this material available. The FAQ on the CNG site contains the following question and response:

---

29   Keith Emmett, 'An Unpublished Alexandrian Coin of Augustus', *The Celator*, 17:8 (2003).

30   Keith Emmett, *Alexandrian Coins* (Lodi, 2001).

Can I use a photograph from CNG's website?

Any of our photographs may be reproduced as long as credit is given to CNG as the source of the photographs. Please include our site's URL, www.cngcoins. com, in any citation.[31]

Although this requirement seems to be clearly stated, I am not a lawyer so I cannot offer an opinion as to whether or not language found in a FAQ is legally binding. It does suggest a willingness to see these images reused in a wide variety of settings.

More explicit is the legal infrastructure by which digital images of CNG coins are duplicated in the Wikimedia Commons, an important source of openly licensed content. Looking at the Wiki source for the page <http://commons.wikimedia.org/wiki/File:Solidus_Julian.jpg> shows that it includes a {{{CNG}}} tag, a reference to the template at <http://commons.wikimedia.org/wiki/Template:CNG>. While an explanation of such templates lies beyond this discussion, the practical result is that inclusion of the characters {{{CNG}}} is sufficient to invoke documentation establishing that the duplications and redistribution of CNG's images is legal. The specific rights invoked are those of the Creative Commons Attribution-Share Alike 2.5 licence and of the GNU Free Documentation Licence. This simple approach has made the dealer a prominent source of Wikipedia's numismatic content: at the time of writing over 950 pages link to the CNG template, a minimal indicator of the number of its coins that have been uploaded to the Commons. I was not able to find a similarly convenient arrangement for another source of equivalent imagery.

Returning to the Flickr set, while the failure to acknowledge the source of its images would be unacceptable in an academic context, the end result shows that the publication of reusable data, which CNG's images certainly are, leads to incremental improvement of Internet resources. CNG does not group the records in its database of sold coins under thematic headings, so the existence of an 'Augustan Coinage' Flickr set fills a gap in the functionality of that site. A Flickr set is not a perfect presentation tool, but its appearance in the Google search that initiated this discussion has made this set part of the public resources available for the study of its well-defined subject matter.

The purpose of this section has been to sample actual current practices in the creation and reuse of numismatic content on the Internet. Following the examples suggested by Google searches leads to an emphasis on commercial and personal sources of information. I hope it has been clear that it is not my goal to say whether such sources are good or bad as compared to information originating within academic contexts. They exist; they are being read and their content is being reused, and to the extent that such reuse enriches the materials available for the study of the ancient world as a whole, this benefits all users.

---

31   Classical Numismatics Group, *Frequently Asked Questions,* <http://www.cngcoins. com/Frequently+Asked+Questions.aspx>.

Search form accessible data

The previous discussion took the dominant search engine metaphor for accessing information on the Internet on its own terms and focused on the results of simple keyword searches. I now shift my focus to information accessible through search forms, a body of knowledge sometimes referred to as the 'deep web'.[32] It is well understood that these forms, while enabling users to find specific items within large datasets, can present a problem for search engines that 'crawl' the Internet. Progress has certainly been made, with search engines now showing results from sites such as JSTOR as well as from museum catalogues such as that of the Museum of Fine Arts in Boston. These two resources are well established and I use them as my first two examples of the academic and professional contributions to the digitization of the ancient Mediterranean material culture.

A centralized repository: JSTOR

The site JSTOR describes itself as:

> a not-for-profit organization dedicated to helping the scholarly community discover, use, and build upon a wide range of intellectual content in a trusted digital archive.[33]

The concept of a 'trusted digital archive' distinguishes JSTOR from the majority of possibly ephemeral information accessible through Google, as does its focus on the 'scholarly community'. In practice, and I write the following as a user, JSTOR provides access to peer-reviewed scholarship, much of it previously published in academic journals or otherwise sourced from the academic community. As with Google, the primary means of accessing the archive is full-text search via user selected keywords. One sees this on the front page, which presents visitors with a simple box for entering terms, along with a link to 'Advanced Search'.

Initiating the search 'athenian tetradrachm' shows that JSTOR is a repository of information on this particular coinage, which in the Classical and Hellenistic periods was one of the most widely circulated issues in the Mediterranean world. This is not a surprise and it is not necessary to give a detailed review of the 442 articles that were listed at the time of writing. Instead, I wish to look at how the information in JSTOR appears when accessed from the public web. I do this because there are instructive comparisons to be made with the sites discussed in the previous section, and then with the museum and academic resources introduced below.

---

32   Michael Bergman, *The Deep Web: Surfacing Hidden Value* (2001), <http://dx.doi.org/10.3998/3336451.0007.104>.

33   JSTOR, *Mission and History*, <http://www.jstor.org/page/info/about/organization/missionHistory.jsp>.

I have already noted that JSTOR allows Google and other search engines directly to index its content. This effectively enables the discovery of relevant articles. Searching for 'site:jstor.org athenian tetradrachm' at Google again offers a list of highly relevant articles. I cite this search not to compare the relative quality of the results, but instead to look for indications that JSTOR is reaching the 'broader audience' it hopes to reach by opening itself to Google. As with WildWinds and CNG, I take as an indication of success the fact that links to articles in JSTOR appear in Wikipedia entries. At the time of writing, a search for 'link:jstor.org site:en.wikipedia.org roman greek archaeology' showed that titles in JSTOR are linked from the Wikipedia articles such as *Greek mythology*, *Roman art*, *Kourion*, *Archaeology of Israel*, and *History of Roman Egypt* – to name only the first five.

Such linking occurs because JSTOR has long promoted the use of stable URLs to refer to articles in its collection. While early efforts relied on the SICI system and resulted in very long strings of characters, since April 2008, JSTOR has established URLs similar in form to <http://jstor.org/stable/297385>.[34] In addition, JSTOR also publishes Digital Object Identifiers for articles so that the URL <http://dx.doi.org/10.2307/297385> will also work. As it stands now, there are four forms of stable JSTOR URLs and all appear in Wikipedia articles.

But there is a limit to JSTOR reusability. While not a for-profit commercial enterprise, JSTOR does charge for access to its content. Consequently, most users reading the Wikipedia article *Symmachi–Nicomachi diptych* will not be able to follow the links to K. Dale's 1994 *American Journal of Archaeology* article 'A Late Antique Ivory Plaque and Modern Response' or to E. Simon's 1992 'The Diptych of the Symmachi and Nicomachi: An Interpretation' from *Greece and Rome*, without payment of $10.00 or $19.00 respectively. It is good that any gaps in Wikipedia's text are mitigated by reference to peer-reviewed scholarship. The efficacy of such a link is lessened by JSTOR's need to fund its current and long-term operations. I understand that these revenues help ensure the long-term stability of the URLs linked, but the contrast with CNG's approach to sharing its content is clear.

Museums

A distinguishing feature of museums is their direct ownership of ancient objects and the intention to maintain that ownership over the long term. It is also the case that museums usually acknowledge that the fact and right of ownership comes with a responsibility to share information about their collections. This responsibility is acknowledged in individual mission statements. For example, the Museum of Fine Arts (MFA) in Boston states that:

---

34 In practice these addresses often redirect to URLs of the form <http://jstor.org/pss/297385>, though for practical purposes either form serves the same purpose.

Through exhibitions, programs, research and publications, the Museum documents and interprets its own collections.[35]

Digital technologies are an increasingly important component of achieving the mission of the modern museum and the MFA has been a leader in providing access to its curatorial database via a search form accessible from the main page.[36] According to the Internet Archive, a link to this functionality first appeared on the opening page of the museum's website in early 2004.[37] As of this writing, 346,000 artworks are documented, including thousands drawn from the more than 70,000 objects in the museum's Greek, Roman and Near Eastern collections. The form defaults to requiring that all search terms be found in a record, so that entering 'african red slip' should be adequate to return objects said to be of this common Roman period fine tableware. Of the fourteen objects listed in response to this search, twelve are in fact African red slip vessels, most from the fourth century. The quality of the documentation is very good. While there are no references to Hayes's standard typology for the ware and no profile drawings as would be found in an expert catalogue, details such as the diameter of the vessels are given and the photographic documentation is excellent.[38]

Despite the high quality of this resource, I was not able to find any reuse of this material on the public Internet. That there is no direct copying of these images is not surprising given the language controlling the reuse of materials on the MFA website. All search results on the site include the following text:

> We are pleased to share images of objects on this Web site with the public as an educational resource. While these images are not permitted to be used for reproduction, we encourage you to do so by visiting our image rights page to submit a request.[39]

The text 'image rights page' links to a page on 'Web Use and Gallery Photography,' which reads in part:

> The reproduction, redistribution, and/or exploitation of any materials and/ or content (data, text, images, marks, or logos) for personal or commercial gain is not permitted. Provided the source is cited, personal, educational, and noncommercial use (as defined by fair use in US copyright law) is permitted.[40]

---

35   Museum of Fine Arts, *Mission Statement*, <www.mfa.org/about/index.asp?key=53>.

36   Museum of Fine Arts, *Collection Search Results*, <http://mfa.org/collections/search_art.asp>.

37   Cf. <http://web.archive.org/web/20040410214702/>, <http://www.mfa.org/>.

38   John Hayes, *Late Roman Pottery* (London, 1972).

39   Museum of Fine Arts, *Collections Search Results*, <http://www.mfa.org/collections/>.

40   Museum of Fine Arts, *Web Use and Gallery Photography*, <http://www.mfa.org/about/sub.asp?key=50&subkey=1082&topkey=50>.

Additionally, images on the individual object pages appear above a link with the text 'license this image'. This leads to a page asking the user to describe the specific use being requested and with fields for providing credit card information, though actual prices are not given. Taking the combined language of the relevant MFA pages, one does not need to be a lawyer to recognize that there are legal obstacles to integrating this material into third-party resources such as Wikipedia and Wikimedia Commons.

But what about citation of and linking to records in the MFA database along the lines of what JSTOR has promoted with its stable URLs? Unfortunately, the idea of a permanent digital reference for objects in the MFA database is not currently implemented. For example, the late Roman ceramic bowl with the accession number 1981.658 appears in the list of ARS vessels generated above. Clicking from that list to the individual record brings one to a page with the URL:

```
http://mfa.org/collections/search_art.asp?recview=true&id=4
59660&coll_keywords=&coll_accession=2005%2E102&co
ll_name=&coll_artist=&coll_place=&coll_medium=&coll_
culture=&coll_classification=&coll_credit=&coll_provenance=&coll_
location=&coll_has_images=&coll_on_view=&coll_sort=2&coll_sort_
order=0&coll_view=0&coll_package=0&coll_start=1
```

While a technically sophisticated user can shorten this string to <http://www. mfa.org/collections/search_art.asp?recview=true&id=459660>, no indication of this is offered. The MFA website, despite the high quality of its content, is not then amenable to reuse by legal duplication or by linking on the basis of well-formed addresses. Accordingly, references to the MFA ancient collection are rare on Wikipedia, nor could I find links to this material through Google.

I do note that the prohibition against copying is not always followed. The same Flickr user, Joe Geranio, who constructed the Augustan Coinage photo set, has included MFA material in his 'Julio-Claudian Women' set. For example, the image and some of the documentation for MFA 88.642, a Julio-Claudian portrait of a young woman, appears in this set.[41] There is an implication, though not a direct assertion, that the intent of this reuse is personal and educational, but there is no explicit reference to permission from the MFA to include its images in Flickr. In the absence of such permission, it may be that this reuse is in violation of the terms of the MFA's image right page as quoted above. A definitive statement on that issue lies beyond the scope of this discussion.

---

41 Flickr, *Julio Claudian Girl MFA*, available <http://www.flickr.com/photos/julio-claudians/2303095903/>.

Scholarly content

The site *Roman Amphoras: A Digital Resource*, hosted by the UK's Archaeological Data Service (ADS) describes itself as an 'online and introductory resource for the study of Roman amphorae, rather than a definitive study of all amphorae for specialists'.[42] This is correct to the extent that it acknowledges the potential enormity of trying to describe all variants of all known Roman amphora forms. The content that is on the site is, nonetheless, certainly expert, up to date, and useful to anyone working in the field. Indeed, by publishing a catalogue of amphora forms online and by deploying high-resolution colour images of amphora fabrics, the site surpasses the utility of many printed reference works. As with the MFA site, it is interesting to look for aspects of the interaction between this resource and the public Internet.

As noted, *Roman Amphorae* is part of the UK's ADS. Because of this relationship, all users coming to the site are presented with a page that asks them to confirm that they accept the terms and conditions of two documents: a Copyright and Liability Statement, and a Common Access Agreement.[43] The terms are not onerous. The Copyright and Liability Statement states that:

> A non-exclusive, non-transferable licence is hereby granted to those using or reproducing, in whole or in part, the material for valid not-for-profit teaching and research purposes.

The Common Access Agreement also invokes 'research use or educational purposes' and 'asks that users be fair and reasonable in their use of the data supplied through the ADS'. In general, many of the terms are unexceptional within the genre of end-user licences that govern use of many sites on the Internet. There does seem to be encouragement of reuse and this is welcome.

It is unusual, however, that users are required to indicate their agreement with these documents each time they come to use *Roman Amphorae*. This requirement is implemented by showing an intermediate page that appears whenever one accesses ADS data as part of a new session.[44] A further distinctive feature of *Roman Amphorae* is the suggestion that references point only to the front page of this publication. The text '*Cite only*: http://ads.ahds.ac.uk/catalogue/resources. html?amphora2005 for this page' appears at the bottom of each page (with my

---

42   Simon Keay and David Williams, *Roman Amphorae: A Digital Resource* (ADS, 2005), <http://ads.ahds.ac.uk/catalogue/resources.html?amphora2005>.

43   Archaeology Data Service, *Copyright and Liability Statements*, <http://ads.ahds. ac.uk/copy.html>; Archaeology Data Service, *Common Access Agreement*, <http://ads. ahds.ac.uk/cap.html>.

44   The authentication page is at <http://ads.ahds.ac.uk/catalogue/terms.cfm>. The site tests for http cookies that only require new agreement with terms after an unspecified period of no usage.

emphasis indicating use of red text in the online version). The intent of this notice is to promote the use of a stable URL that will continue to work for the foreseeable future.[45] It may have the outcome of reducing the reuse and discoverability of the separate components of the publication.

I note these two features of *Roman Amphorae* because they provide context for the observation that its pages are invisible to search engines. Looking at the entry for the common late Roman amphora form Keay 62, manufactured in what is now Tunisia, one sees the sentence 'Keay (1984) subdivides this type into five variants (A–E)'.[46] Searching for this quoted string at Google does not lead to this page. The same is true when searching at AskJeeves.com, Microsoft's Live.com and Yahoo.com. Searching without the quotes returns a long list of URLs but no links to *Roman Amphorae*. A search just on 'Keay 62' also does not include *Roman Amphorae* in its results. This page, then, does not seem to exist from the perspective of search engines, and it falls beyond the scope of this chapter to explain this fact beyond making the observations already offered.

Conclusion

In my introduction I made clear that personal opinion played a role in my selection and presentation of particular sites. When not guided by the results of Google searches, I have selected sites whose evident utility and high profile make them suitable for consideration. My presentation has certainly been influenced by my strong opinion that information ought to be deployed in such a way that it can be easily found and be part of public reuse and reinterpretation. As I said, I took Google to be one indicator of discoverability and Wikipedia of reuse. I am interested in the cumulative effect of small decisions by authors and distributors of digital resources; and I believe that one consequence of the choices made by academic sources is the ceding of important territory in some of the most dynamic and visible parts of the Internet. Commercial entities and private individuals are engaging in practices that are open and that do promote access, and they are reaping the benefit of their decisions. I of course do not mean to suggest that academics are not exploring new forms of scholarship that are likewise open. I have already mentioned the Perseus Project, which itself does have a coin catalogue, and OpenContext, which includes Roman pottery. Recently, the Suda Online, long a model of open scholarship, established permanent and short URLs for all its entries.[47] In my research, I have ensured that the American Numismatic Society's collection publishes a stable URL for every piece catalogued in its collection, and the overview of pottery at Troy

---

45   I thank Julian Richards for this information.
46   I respect the text quoted above and do not offer the direct URL for this entry.
47   E-mail from Raphael Finkel republished at <http://www.stoa.org/?p=853>.

that I co-edit is available under a Creative Commons licence.[48] Other projects that I work on are in different stages of implementing sustainable links and allowing meaningful reuse, so I understand that digital publication is an ongoing process that can respond to developing best practices.

It is important to repeat that visibility in Google and Wikipedia is not a sufficient basis for judging the success or viability of digital information. Nonetheless, I do believe that if museums are going to restrict the copying of their information, they should make it easy to link to individual records; that offering some version that can be reused in Wikipedia, or other contexts, is a service that will increase the impact of digital assets; and that discoverability via search engines for high-quality scholarly information means that students and others starting their research with these tools are more likely to find materials that increase their understanding of the ancient Mediterranean world.

Finally, let me say that I understand that citation of specific websites means that my primary sources will probably not be available for any great length of time after the publication of the preceding observations and critiques. The underlying data may be preserved, but appearances and policies change over time. As an extreme example, the results of the Google searches I use will certainly be different even before publication. It is also the case that standards and best practices are evolving. Many researchers look to the development of the 'Semantic Web', which allows linking between concepts and not just spans of text within documents, to enable new forms of interaction between digital resources.[49] To the extent that these tools for publication will be available to the same diversity of sources that I have invoked throughout this chapter, it may be the case that my comments remain relevant.

---

48   Items in the American Numismatic Society database are accessible using URLs of the form <http://numismatics.org/collection/1858.1.1>. Sebastian Heath and Billur Tekkök, *Greek, Roman and Byzantine Pottery at Ilion (Troia)* (2006–2009), <http://classics.uc.edu/troy/grbpottery/>.

49   Leo Sauerman and Richard Cyaniak, *Cool URIs for the Semantic Web* (2008), <http://www.w3.org/TR/cooluris/>.

Chapter 3

Space as an Artefact: A Perspective on 'Neogeography' from the Digital Humanities

Stuart Dunn

That was how I saw it then, and how I continue to see it; along with the five senses. A child of my background had a sixth sense in those days, the geographic sense. The sharp sense of where he lived and who and what surrounded him.

Philip Roth, *The Plot Against America*[1]

Introduction

A recurring issue in the digital humanities in general, and in digital classics in particular, is the problem of identifying and articulating 'grand challenges'. One such challenge however, in whichever way it is articulated, must surely fall within the realm of geographic information, and in how geographic information can be used to understand the human past. There is a mass of evidence at all levels which attests to the importance of geography as a means for organizing and communicating information: from the UK government's 2008 report 'Place Matters',[2] which discusses the critical role of information about location in the contemporary policy-making process, to the formalization of geographic metadata elements by such initiatives as the Alexandria Digital Library project;[3] in long-standing bibliographic and bibliometric metadata which records aspects of location in library records; technical refinements in the field of Geographic Information Systems (GIS);[4] and, perhaps most importantly of all, to the development of the 'Geospatial Web' from around 2005.[5] Although former Vice-President Al Gore's vision of 'a multi-

---

1   Philip Roth, *The Plot Against America* (Vintage, 2005), p. 212.

2   UK Government 2008: The Location Strategy for the United Kingdom. Geographic Information Panel <http://www.communities.gov.uk/publications/communities/location strategy>.

3   Alexandria Digital Library project, <http://alexandria.sdc.ucsb.edu>.

4   E.g. David Wheatley and Matt Gillings, *Spatial Technology and Archaeology: Archaeological Applications of GIS* (London, 2002).

5   The Geospatial Web remains a loose concept, but it may be broadly characterized as the heterogeneous mass of information that describes, or refers to, location on the Internet, and the tools used to connect, explore, visualize and manipulate it. These can be placenames

resolution, three-dimensional representation of the planet, into which we can embed vast quantities of geo-referenced data'[6] may still be some way away, web-mapping applications such as Google Earth have unquestionably changed for ever the way in which classicists and archaeologists are able to perceive and use geospatial data. Keyhole Markup Language (KML), computer language for expressing three-dimensional geographic data used by platforms such as Google Earth, is already widely taken up in the social and earth sciences.[7] Its recent adoption as an open standard by the Open Geospatial Consortium[8] (the international industry/academic body which oversees geospatial data standards), its flexibility as a means of encoding geodata and rendering it downloadable and easily transportable in the zipped KMZ format, has ensured this. But deeper questions about the relationship between so-called 'neogeography' and the digital classics (and humanities generally) remain.

The practical benefits for archaeological research were recognized in an early stage of Google Earth's life.[9] The capacity for intuitive retrieval of satellite imagery of any part of the globe, for encoding and/or downloading features in KML, for associating any hyperlinked information on the web with that imagery must not be underestimated. Likewise, relatively more advanced functions for overlaying images, incorporating websites (such as Wikipedia pages), and the ability to visualize present-day terrain in 3D, significantly lessen the resources and technical skills needed to achieve outcomes that would otherwise require relatively sophisticated archaeological illustration practice and methods to produce. Elliott and Gillies describe in eloquent terms the 'rich and profitable dialogue' between computing, classics and geography,[10] a vision not dissimilar to Gore's, where the conventional distinctions between browse and search, processing, thematic layers and geospatial datasets are effectively broken down. Against this background, it is difficult, if not impossible, to divorce the emergence of the wider Geospatial Web from the discipline-specific needs of archaeologists and classicists working with geospatial data.

---

in ordinary webpages, online gazetteers, databases with geographic components, images showing places. See Arno Scharl and Klaus Tochtermann (eds), *The Geospatial Web* (Springer, 2007).

6   Al Gore, 'The Digital Earth: Understanding our Planet in the 21st century'. Speech given at the California Science Center, Los Angeles, California, 31 January 1998, <http://www.isde5.org/al_gore_speech.htm>.

7   E.g. Maurizio Gibin, Alex Singleton, Richard Milton, Pablo Mateos and Paul Longley, 'An Exploratory Cartographic Visualisation of London through the Google Maps API', *Applied Spatial Analysis and Policy*, 1/2 (July 2008): 85–97.

8   Open Geospatial Consortium, <http://www.opengeospatial.org/>.

9   Lee Ullmann and Yuri Gorokhovich, 'Google Earth and Some Practical Applications for the Field of Archaeology', *CSA Newsletter*, 18:3 (2006), <http://csanet.org/newsletter/winter06/nlw0604.html>.

10   Tom Elliott and Sean Gillies, 'Digital Geography and Classics', Digital Humanities Quarterly 3.1 (2009), <http://www.digitalhumanities.org/dhq/vol/3/1/000031.html>. My thanks to Tom Elliott for supplying a pre-publication copy of this paper.

A comprehensive discussion of the democratizing effect of mapping platforms has accompanied the emergence of the Geospatial Web. In a short paper entitled 'Participating in the Geospatial Web', Rousse et al. link this with the more established practice of 'participatory GIS', which allows users to access and analyse geospatial information on the Internet, rather than with locally hosted GIS programmes, whether proprietary or open source.[11] From the point of view of an academic community, the human element is critical to this. Alongside data which, in traditional archaeological discourse, comes from the trench, the library or the museum (data which contains both spatial and chronological significance), there now exists an abundance of digital information created by other specialists, and the wider public, so-called 'user-generated content' (UGC). As Goodchild has noted in a recent review, the ubiquitous global spatial data infrastructure (SDI) effectively connects together 'six billion sensors', i.e. the planet's total human population, whose constituents have accumulated highly developed aggregations of spatial data about the landscapes they inhabit on a daily basis, supplemented in some cases by electronic devices which can capture and/or use georeferenced data, including mobile phones, cameras with GPS, SatNav devices and so on.[12] As Goodchild notes, only a very small amount of this has ever been gathered systematically, much less analysed or interpreted. The inhabitants of past societies must have been similarly 'spatially aware' (minus the spatially sensitive hardware devices of course), and one does not need to adhere to a rigidly uniformitarian or processual view of archaeology to recognize that their decision-making processes must have followed some comparable set of mental functions, even if they operated without the mapping technologies available today. Furthermore, few archaeological theorists would argue with the premise that space (at least in human-occupied environments) is an *artefact*, something that is created, manipulated, changed and used by humans for their own purposes. Indeed the methodological leaching between archaeology and geography has been recognized for more than twenty years: in 1983, the archaeologist Colin Renfrew noted that

> In a number of ways the methods of the geographer both at the hard (i.e. physical) and softer (i.e. social or political) ends have already proved of great value to the archaeologist ... But when the geographer seeks to look more closely at the role of human action in the past, he or she must set that action in a context that is more than simply spatial.[13]

11   L. Jesse Rouse, Susan J. Bergeron and Trevor M. Harris, 'Participating the Geospatial Web: Collaborative Mapping, Social Software and Participatory GIS', in Scharl and Tochtermann (eds), *The Geospatial Web*, pp. 153–8.

12   Michael F. Goodchild, 'Citizens as Voluntary Sensors: Spatial Data Infrastructure in the World of Web 2.0', *International Journal of Spatial Data Infrastructures Research*, 2 (2007): 24–32.

13   Colin Renfrew, 'Geography, Archaeology, Environment: 1. Archaeology', *Geographical Journal*, 149:3 (November 1983): 316–33.

The 'grand challenge' for collaborative digital geography therefore, with its vast user base, and its capacity for generating new data from across the specialist and non-specialist communities, is to establish how its various methods can be used to *understand* better the construction of the spatial artefact, rather than simply to *represent* it.

The deluge of complex digital information is not confined to archaeology or classics. In a forthcoming article, Steve Anderson examines the impact of pervasive digital technologies on the writing and reception of history.[14] He identifies two divergent corollaries from the 'proliferation of digital information systems', in the historical domain, as represented by database and search engine technologies – the two tool types most widely used in the field, for conventional historiographies. Firstly, there is that of a 'total history', in which an all-encompassing digital knowledge base contains and makes available a comprehensive view of the past; and a 'recombinant history', in which artificial intelligence and related types of system provide a means for 'reconfiguring the categories of knowledge and understanding on which history is based'.[15] This distinction is an appropriate background for considering the nexus between neogeography, archaeology and classics: as more and more data relating to the human record is digitized or 'born digital',[16] and there is a key distinction to be made between a comprehensive platform from which to explore all digital information about the past, and a nuanced and semantic treatment of select elements of the existing body of digital information. But a further dimension of complexity is added by the fact that neogeography is more – much more – than simply a set of tools and technologies for digital research; it is also a set of recognized methods for using tools and technologies *collaboratively*, whether that collaborating be synchronous or asynchronous. Neogeographic applications are not typically executed on the user's local desktop; they are conducted in 'the cloud' on remote Internet servers,[17] and with many – potentially limitless – people contributing content, analysis and interpretation. There is a need to shift the focus away from the capabilities of the technology, and towards the outcomes of such work; and its intellectual context in the archaeological and historical tradition.

---

14   Steve Anderson, 'Past Indiscretions: Digital Archives and Recombinant History', in Marsha Kinder and Tara McPherson (eds), *Interactive Frictions* (University of California Press, forthcoming).

15   Anderson, 'Past Indiscretions'.

16   There is an extensive body of research on the so-called data deluge, and its impact on the arts and humanities disciplines. For a recent UK perspective, see Stuart Dunn and Tobias Blanke, 'Next Steps for e-Science, the Textual Humanities and VREs', *D-Lib Magazine*, 14:12 (January/February 2008), <http://www.dlib.org/dlib/january08/dunn/01dunn.html>. The vocabularies and emphases differ for North America: see, for example, John M. Unsworth, *Our Cultural Commonwealth: The Report of the ACLS Commission on Cyberinfrastructure for the Humanities and Social Sciences* (American Council of Learned Societies, 2006), p. ii.

17   See, for example, Brian Hayes, 'Cloud Computing', *Communications of the ACM*, 51:7 (July 2008): 90–11.

Despite (or perhaps because of) the benefits of the Geospatial Web for exploring and retrieving archaeological information, most treatments of the subject have focused on the technical and/or application side, without delving into the conceptual context of space and time. Most applications of digital geography in classics and archaeology fall into one of three categories: *representation* (including visualization), *resource discovery* and *geospatial semantics*. Although the utility of geospatial computing in these areas is impossible to doubt, the extent to which they facilitate existing research rather than enabling new research, is a more open question. Indeed, the wide availability of such digital cartographic resources, and the consequent focus of many proprietary platforms on non-scholarly uses such as tourism and travel directions, has led to criticisms that the global corpus of digital data is being devalued intellectually: in summer 2008, for example, the president of the British Cartographic Society declared that digital mapping is 'demolishing thousands of years of history' because historic landmarks such as churches and ancient sites are typically not included in databases designed (for example) to assist dashboard SatNav devices.[18] Such criticisms should not be dismissed out of hand simply because they deal with generalist rather than specialist communities. It must also be recognized that representing data in innovative ways that improve its clarity, making it easily discoverable, and describing it comprehensively, does not necessarily lead to new understanding of that data.

The aim of this chapter is not to find fault with neogeographic techniques in the representation of the past. On the contrary, I take as read Elliott and Gillies's thesis of the 'fruitful relationship between computing, classics and geography,'[19] and do not seek to question the value of the support that neogeographic tools lend to the archaeological and classical research processes. From there on, however, a high-level synthesis of the utility of such methods in *understanding* past constructions of space (both theoretical and applied) is attempted, as opposed to *representing* and *describing* them. In other words, can neogeography offer new approaches to reconstructing the 'geographic sense', as felt by the young Philip Roth in the United States of the 1930s, but from the material evidence left to us from history and prehistory?

Location and the human experience

As noted above, the facility of applications such as Google Earth to 'fly to' any area of the globe allows instant access to often, but not always, good-quality satellite imagery of archaeological sites. Beyond the purely illustrative (and, of course, setting aside intellectual property issues, an aspect I do not intend to discuss in this chapter), one valuable application of this approach is in the field of landscape

---

18 BBC News article, 'Online maps "wiping out history"', <http://news.bbc.co.uk/1/hi/uk/7586789.stm> (accessed March 2009).

19 Elliott and Gillies, 'Digital Geography and Classics'.

archaeology. Theories of what Crumley has described as 'the cultural elaboration of landscapes'[20] can be developed in this area. Key to such a process of 'elaboration' is how the landscape, and its natural and man-made features, are documented in the archaeological research cycle; and how the archaeologist responds to (and interprets) both the landscape and the documentation. The interaction exists at a number of levels: although nothing can, of course, replace the direct personal experience of *visiting* a landscape, certain computational tools and methods can undoubtedly support the process of elaboration off-site. Consider, for example, the case of the Minoan Peak Sanctuary cult. It has been argued that this network of mountain-top shrines, one of the key characteristics of prehistoric Cretan religion which flourished in the Middle Bronze and early Late Bronze Ages in the early second millennium BC, was intimately associated with the rise of political elites within the palatial centres of the island's New Palace Period.[21] A fairly sophisticated typology of what constitutes a peak sanctuary has been developed from conventional archaeological survey and excavation.[22] In essence this includes presence of votive offerings (a general feature of cult practice in this time), evidence of burning, and the most fundamental feature, a commanding view of the adjoining region, which was also most likely the area 'served' by the sanctuary, and from whose settlements the cult participants were probably drawn. The implied relationship between cult leadership and political leadership can be further explored by plotting a selection of peak sanctuary data – in this case, five peak sanctuary sites in the north-east tip of Crete, from the authoritative map of Peatfield (1983)[23] – which can then be placed in the present-day landscape (Figure 3.1) in Google Earth. Given the relative positions of the sanctuaries within the terrain, it can indeed be seen that intervisibility between the peaks and the palatial centres and significant areas certainly existed. Although this does not prove an intentional link, it provides us with an additional perspective that suggests that there might have been, and allows a more intuitive visualization than a 'conventional' GIS could provide. Google Earth is not, of course, a direct proxy for how the landscape would have looked in the Bronze Age; but it can provide a three dimensional framework for considering relative locations of natural and man-made features in a purely quantitative manner. As such, it does not necessarily *create* understanding of past environments; it is a useful tool for *augmenting* such understanding, as part of the broader process of 'cultural elaboration'. The significance of this qualitative/quantitative distinction is explored further below.

---

20   Carol Crumley, 'Sacred Landscapes, Constructed and Conceptualized', in B.A. Knapp and W. Ashmore (eds), *Archaeology of Landscape: Contemporary Perspectives* (Oxford, 1999), pp. 269–76.

21   Oliver T.P.K. Dickinson, 'Comments on a Popular Model of Minoan Religion', *Oxford Journal of Archaeology*, 13: (1994): 173–84; B. Rutkowski, *The Minoan Peak Sanctuaries: The Topography and Architecture* (Liège, 1988), p. 10.

22   Alan Peatfield, 'The Topography of Minoan Peak Sanctuaries', *Annual of the British School at Athens* (1983): 78, 273–80.

23   Peatfield, 'The Topography of Minoan Peak Sanctuaries'.

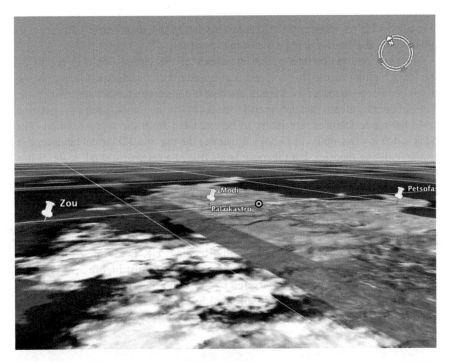

Figure 3.1   Google Earth-based visualization of Minoan peak sanctuary sites in north-eastern Crete

Source: © Google Earth.

There is also a parallel between the kind of direct terrain visualization of virtual representations of the world such as Google Earth, and the method of interpolation. In their discussion of interpolation, Robinson and Zubrow describe it as 'a method of inferring what surrounds a point or region by looking at its neighbours'.[24] This method of 'spatial averaging' is particularly useful for expressing the results of surface survey, where one is presented with datasets which cannot blanket cover the whole area surveyed, such as surface findspots on field walking projects.[25] While a review of the debate of broad and comprehensive versus small and intensive archaeological survey is beyond the scope of this chapter, interpolation is an essential tool for the interpretation of material culture at all scales, and it lies at the heart of many GIS applications, especially those which take the binary single-cell (raster) approach. Direct terrain visualization of the kind provided in

24   Jennifer M. Robinson and Ezra B. Zubrow, 'Between Spaces: Interpolation in Archaeology', in Mark Gilling, David Mattingly and Jim Van Dalen (eds), *Geographic Information Systems and Landscape Archaeology* (Oxford, 2000), pp. 65–84.

25   See Gary Lock, *Using Computers in Archaeology: Towards Virtual Pasts* (London, Routledge), pp. 69–77.

'virtual worlds' is, in effect, a 1:1 representation of the actual earth's surface – in other words the diametric opposite of interpolation.

There is one major interpretive drawback of the virtual world in retrieving the 'geographic sense'. This is that a real-time terrain visualization is, by nature, disembodied; a 'snapshot' of a landscape that is constant in neither space nor time. This, of course, means that ephemeral features of the landscape, such as vegetation and man-made features, are likely to be excluded from the representation. The peak sanctuary example cited above illustrates the use of a 3D virtual landscape in testing existing theories, but this only holds true at a relatively small scale. When one goes down to the scale of a human individual's experience, more significant problems arise. For example, Figure 3.2a shows the Google Earth view from a spot on the earth's surface with which the author is personally familiar (Arborfield Church in Berkshire). The geographic position is triangulated with two further points of familiarity: a wind turbine which is frequently used for giving driving directions to motorists travelling towards Reading, UK (and, due to its size, a well-known local landmark); and the author's home. Whilst Figure 3.2a is useful for reconstructing the sense of place felt by the author in relation to three familiar localities, the actual view from the original location is shown in Figure 3.2b. In

Figure 3.2a   Known position looking north from Arborfield Church, Berkshire, UK in Google Earth

Source: © Google Earth.

this case, the line of sight between the two triangulating points is blocked by trees, and a man-made feature, a graveyard, is visible in the foreground. These, along with intangible considerations such as the viewer's personal history, previous experience of the place, relationship with other familiar but unmarked features, is lost. In the case of this location, there is a significant distinction to be drawn between the author's *knowledge* of the place in relation to other landmarks, which can be explored and visualized within the actual terrain so long as the three points are known, and his *experience* of the place, which, in most cases, cannot. However, future notions involving the relationship between neogeographic methods, agency theory, and agent-based modelling, which might go some way to addressing such factors in the future, are discussed below.

Although this distinction between (quantitative) human knowledge and (qualitative) human experience in landscapes is significant in terms of reconstructing the human experience of space, the accuracy of any model of the former kind is based on an assumption that the features within that landscape are correctly located with relation to the virtual terrain – that they are correctly *georeferenced*. Georeferencing is a well-established set of methods for associating non-geographic information with geography. The great complexity of the material renders

Figure 3.2b   Actual view from the same location

georeferencing of archaeological information a non-trivial matter for a number of reasons. It extends beyond simply assigning x/y coordinates to excavations, or conceptualizing maps and plans as points, lines and polygons: the neogeographic methods discussed here raise the question of how information created, elaborated and annotated by third parties can be incorporated within a GIS. Elsewhere, this has been referred to as the 'rehumanising' of GIS.[26] Information comprising of, containing or referring to geographical material is everywhere.[27] But this takes on a more literal meaning if one is seeking to recreate or represent information in a virtual world such as Google Earth, or even immersive environments such as Second Life. Although this can facilitate richer and more visual exploration of data, it can also lead to the transmission of inaccurate or false geographic associations of information in the database behind the virtual terrain in question. For example, such a flaw exists in the quantitative understanding of the landscape near Reading just cited: if one takes a perpendicular view of the first feature (the wind turbine) referred to here, it appears some distance to the west of its actual position. The problems with, and criticisms of, using user-generated or user-contributed web resources such as Wikipedia in research and teaching are well documented.[28] And an appreciation of the fact that many of the same limitations apply in neogeographic applications is essential. Practical approaches to dealing with this vary, but the best example in the field of classics is the Pleiades project. Pleiades is a collection of data about place in the ancient world, and is described in detail by Elliott and Gillies.[29] It adapts pre-existing (and largely analogue) geographic concepts, such as coordinate and toponym systems, by defining its data ingest simply in terms of *place*. Place is defined loosely, as a collection of open-ended attributes of features which share some kind of concrete geographic consistency. A discreet editorial policy is applied to the collection of user-contributed geographical data, to create a body of information which can be 'reused and remixed by others'.[30]

The appropriateness or otherwise of the open 'Wikipedia model' in archaeology has been a subject of vigorous debate. One might question whether the risk of errors in spatial identifications (or any other kind of user-generated content) which have been created online with little or no editorial oversight really matters: even if the content is 'wrong', it should be possible to rely on the reader/user's critical judgement to select what they use for their own interpretations. However, opening that discourse up to the possibility of false, misleading or even malicious

---

26   Paul Rivett, 'Conceptual Data Modelling in an Archaeological GIS', in *Proceedings of GeoComputation '97 & SIRC '97* (1997), pp. 15–26.

27   Linda L. Hill, *Georeferencing: The Geographic Associations of Information* (Cambridge, MA, 2006), pp. 5, 215.

28   G.E. Gorman, 'Editorial: Is the Wiki Concept Really so Wonderful?', *Online Information Review*, 29:3 (2005): 225–6.

29   For the Pleiades Project see <http://pleiades.stoa.org/> (accessed March 2009); Elliott and Gillies, 'Digital Geography and Classics'.

30   Elliott and Gillies, 'Digital Geography and Classics'.

information certainly carries interpretive risk, and a very real risk in volatile areas such as the Middle East.[31] The open content model contrasts with hybrid approaches of the kind used by the Pleiades project. This rejects a purely semantic (toponym) or quantitative (coordinate) basis for organizing geodata, and instead relies on multifaceted instances of 'place', which can include names, locations, areas; all of which have a looser and more flexible geographic association. This harnesses the advantages of a broad knowledge base of many contributors, with the rigour of expert editorial process, and at the same time allows 'multivocal' views of the data in a way that single-point ascription based on toponyms or coordinates does not.[32]

Aside from the questions of trust, authenticity and accuracy, collaborative neogeography actually brings opportunities to view afresh methodologies such as georeferencing. If multiple users are adding georeferenced content – even if it is of only approximate accuracy and/or precision – to a photorealistic representation of the earth's surface (e.g. photographs from GPS-enabled cameras and other mobile devices), then this is certain to include content about archaeological features in that landscape. The so-called 'long tail effect', where a large number of users contribute volumes of data which, individually, are trivial (uploading a photo to a site such as Panoramio or Flickr is an excellent example), means that the datapoints, however imperfectly georeferenced, will cluster in a consistently visual manner around their subjects. Two examples which illustrate this are the views of Hadrian's Wall and Stonehenge, Wiltshire in the Google Maps satellite terrain mashup[33] with the Panoramio photo-sharing community[34] (Figures 3.3a and 3.3b). In both cases, the uploaded photos plot the lines of the features, and thus provide the viewer with a consistent and collective interpretation of which sections of the feature are of greatest interest (of course this is limited to areas of terrain which are publicly accessible). Although these examples are fairly crude, they illustrate what we might think of as neogeography's version of georeferencing: mass quasi-collaborative annotation of digital terrains with georeferenced digital objects. This leads to an accurate, if not necessarily precise, abstraction of a feature's location, even where the feature is itself too small to be visible in the terrain imagery. This accords directly with the Pleiades project's aggregation approach (see above).

31   Stuart Dunn and Leif Isaksen, 'Space and Time: Methods in Geospatial Computing for Mapping the Past' (AHRC ICT Methods Network workshop report, 2007, <http://www.methodsnetwork.ac.uk/redist/pdf/act24report.pdf>), p. 5.

32   Elliott and Gillies, 'Digital Geography and Classics'.

33   A 'mashup' is a website which aggregates different streams of data and/or web services together from different sources. Usually the user can use an interface to define which services and data are displayed.

34   Panoramio <http://www.panoramio.com> (accessed March 2009).

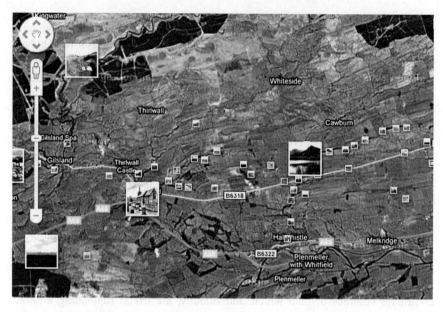

Figure 3.3a   Aggregation of georeferenced photos from multiple sources showing the line of Hadrian's Wall, Northumberland, UK

Source: © Google.

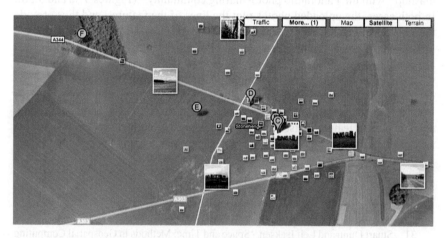

Figure 3.3b   Similar aggregation effect over Stonehenge

Source: © Google.

Structure and agency

If one follows the Pleiades project's approach, and lays aside a rigid notion of location based on toponym and/or coordinates, and instead adopts a more fluid concept of 'place' – an approach which makes excellent sense in any neogeographic context – then it follows that there are theoretical questions regarding how one reconstructs human interaction with 'place'. One possible such method is Agent-based Modelling (ABM). ABM is a computational methodology with its roots in the social science domain, whose purpose is to abstract the behaviours of large populations from the behaviour of individuals. Individuals are represented by software 'agents', acting out behaviour patterns according to predetermined parameters.[35] This effectively negates analogue concepts of 'scale' in much the same way that virtual worlds do. Just as one can work at whichever scale one wishes in Google Earth, or at many scales at once, so a high-performance computing-based ABM simulation can work at any scale. In most cases, the agents' predefined parameters will include (but are certainly not limited to) factors relating to their spatial environment, whether at a macro or micro scale. One important recent application of ABM in archaeology is the Medieval Warfare on the Grid project at the University of Birmingham's Institute of Archaeology and Antiquity.[36] This ground-breaking project is seeking to reconstruct the logistical operation undertaken by the Byzantine army as it crossed Anatolia prior to the battle of Manzikert in 1071 AD. This involves identifying classes of agents, from the emperor and his retinue at the top to mercenary units at the bottom, and defining variable attributes for the agents, which include the material, such as hunger, hunger tolerance, speed, health, and the non-material, such as religion and morale. The project will use this network of variables to reconstruct (or perhaps rather to 'postdict', as opposed to predict) the massively complex historical process of moving the Byzantine army.

Typically, the ABM methodology is employed in large-scale social science experiments such as GENeSIS, the 'Generative e-Social Science' node of the UK's National centre for e-Social Science, which is seeking to model various scenarios affecting the entire population of the UK at the level of the individual human 'actor', and visualize the results. There have been some applications of ABM as a method for reconstructing the historical development of past populations, including the Manzikert project, but in general, it has been open to some criticism in that it seeks to make 'strong' claims about the development of complex societies, and that it promotes a falsely empirical view of human development.[37] Discussions

---

35   E.g. Charles M. Macal and Michael J. North, 'Tutorial on Agent-Based Modeling and Simulation', in *Proceedings of the 37th conference on Winter Simulation*, Orlando, Florida (2005), pp. 1–15.

36   University of Birmingham, Institute of Archaeology and Antiquity <http://www.cs.bham.ac.uk/research/projects/mwgrid/> (accessed March 2009).

37   Jennifer L. Dornan, 'Agency in Archaeology: Past, Present and Future Directions', *Journal of Archaeological Method and Theory*, 9:4 (2002): 303–29.

of agency theory in the study of the past have focused on the degree to which macro-scale human action is determined by individual will, versus determination by external social and environmental factors, or rather *structures*. One might quote John Bintliff's useful summary of the problem: 'What insights follow ... as regards our initial search for the ways in which individuals and societies, places and regions, events and trends in the medium and long term, come together to make specific pasts?'[38] A major problem of course is determining the nature of the parameters that will govern the agents' activity. Frequently, these themselves will be influenced, whether consciously or not, by the spatial, temporal and cultural context of the modeller. As Jennifer Dornan states in a recent review of the subject, '[M]uch of current agency theory has in fact injected western, modern notions about human action into our attempts to address the ongoing uncertainty surrounding the relationship(s) between the individual and society in the past.'[39] In this sense, agency theory – and in particular agency theory as expressed in relation to the application of ABM technologies in the study of the past – sits well with postprocessual archaeological thought, which rejects the notion that the past can be objectively and absolutely reconstructed. In other words, because there are no tight social structures above the level of the agent which can be reconstructed by the archaeologist, we must look instead to reconstruction at the level of the individual agent. The principal interpretive advantage of the 'postdiction' approach that ABM adopts is that it bases itself on the individual-level decisions made within historic populations. It does not require abstraction from the material record, as 'conventional' interpretive approaches do; rather it augments such processes, in much the same quantitative way that Google Earth can 'augment' the study of ancient landscapes (see above).

Given neogeography's relatively short history, it is not surprising that there has been relatively little exploration in the literature of the link between collaborative digital geography and agency theory. Such a link might be articulated as follows: neogeography offers numerous ways for collaborative reconstruction and visualization of the past using disparate and (potentially) uncoordinated user-generated data sources, which become coordinated as a result of common sharing, annotation and visualization. Each user-generated addition to a web-based repository of information about the past, be it a photo, a drawing, or a descriptive tag, reflects user/archaeologist's experience of archaeological data. It has an individual significance, as well as a collective one, a point that has been touched on with regards to the distinction between the reconstruction of quantitative knowledge versus qualitative experience in Google Earth. But if the past is being reconstructed by many people in real time, by different people with different processes and different assumptions, this means that the process of reconstruction

---

38   John Bintliff, 'Time, Structure and Agency: The Annales, Emergent Complexity, and Archaeology', in John Bintliff (ed.), *A Companion to Archaeology* (Oxford, 2004), pp. 174–94.

39   Jennifer L. Dornan, 'Agency in Archaeology'.

is itself an agentive process. In their analysis of the epistemic relationship between performance and archaeology, Pearson and Shanks note that 'both performance and archaeology are modes of cultural production which work with resources to create contemporary meaning.'[40]

If one accepts this last point, then it follows that in order to derive any kind of 'rich' theoretical understanding of the past from neogeographic user-generated content, one must first gain an appreciation of the process by which that content was created, and why. It is possible to gain a high-level overview that tells us that Hadrian's Wall is significant from the line of user-added photos in Panoramio/Google Maps, and from that which sections of the wall have been photographed the most. But it does not allow us to understand why the photographers (agents) took the photographs in the first place. Of course there could in theory be as many reasons as there are photographers; but we lack the material evidence to recover that significance, just as we lack the material evidence to recover the Wall's full ancient significance.

This is related to a broader problem: the process of capturing archaeological data in the field is in itself a spatial exercise. Our reconstructions of the past are produced by individuals and groups moving through, and interacting with, landscapes, in a wide variety of roles (as excavators, surveyors, analysts, etc.) – Shanks and Pearson's 'modes of cultural production'.[41] A more complete analysis of those actions could, logically, tell us more about the reconstructions. One method of approaching this at a theoretical level is to examine how practitioners in the visual and performative arts capture, record and analyse choreographic entities such as dance movements and choreographic performances. There is a large and well-developed body of theory, literature and practice in this area.[42] Motion capture for example, and ways in which digital records resulting from motion capture can be (re)used and analysed and disseminated, have been explored by two recent e-science projects in the UK.[43] This is a conceptual reversal of the more established practice of reconstructing/re-embodying historic dance practices from iconographic and textual evidence; and leveraging archaeological material to 're-embody' ancient dance practice. In a paper entitled 'The Present Past: Towards an Archaeology of Dance', Alessandra Iyer notes that 'There is room for developing an archaeology of dance, through a study of iconography and/or textual evidence,

40   Mike Pearson and Michael Shanks, *Theatre/Archaeology* (London, 2001), p. 54.

41   Jennifer L. Dornan, 'Agency in Archaeology'.

42   Helen Bailey, James Hewison and Martin Turner, 'Choreographic Morphologies: Digital Visualization and Spatio-Temporal Structure in Dance and the Implications for Performance and Documentation', in Stuart Dunn, Suzanne Keene, George Mallen and Jonathan Bowen (eds), *EVA London 2008: Conference Proceedings* (London, 2008), pp. 9–18.

43   The e-Dance project <http://www.ahessc.ac.uk/e-dance>; and the Associated Motion Capture User Categories project <http://culturelab.ncl.ac.uk/amuc/>.

in which dance reconstruction is a means of historical enquiry'.[44] The emergence of neogeography, and of digital site-based infrastructure projects such as Virtual Research Environments for Archaeology (see Chapter 1 of this volume), gives us an opportunity to apply these same methods of 'historical enquiry' to the process of reconstructing the past from raw data. An excellent example of this is the Remediated Places project. This enterprise is employing a variety of multimedia devices, including podcasts, interviews with excavators, videos, audio recordings, as well as archaeological databases and GIS, etc., to bring to a wider audience the 'multi-dimensional experience' of the site of Çatalhöyük, Turkey. It is 'multi-dimensional in that it incorporates multiple voices, multiple viewpoints, multiple scales of meaning and view, multiple databases, multiple media formats, and so on',[45] and articulates an explicit ambition to realize the postprocessual vision articulated by Hodder for 'multivocality' at the site of Çatalhöyük.[46]

Conclusion

Archaeology has a decades-old tradition of blurring its disciplinary boundary with geography, and in self-critiquing the way in which it conceptualizes the processes that led to the creation of the material record we see today above, and below, the ground. This context has shaped thinking about space, and consequently the development of neogeography in archaeology and classics. In his analysis of this area, in the direct context of a discussion of the contrasting importance of place in the study of sedentary versus mobile populations (which mirrors the importance of place highlighted above), Lesure notes that 'a unifying theme in archaeology is surely the attempt to think creatively beyond the apparently obvious material facts we recover … and the attempt by an archaeology of mobility to think beyond The Site is a good example'.[47] This chapter set out to identify ways in which Web 2.0-type methods in general, and neogeography in particular, can contribute to our understanding of the past by thinking creatively beyond the material evidence. There is a widespread perception that such tools are useful only for representation or, perhaps at best, information storage, and information retrieval and/or resource

44   Alessandra Iyer, 'The Present Past: Towards an Archaeology of Dance', in Stephanie Jordan (ed.), *Preservation Politics: Dance Revived, Reconstructed, Remade* (London 2000), pp. 141–5.
45   Ruth Tringham, Michael Ashley and Steve Mills, 'Senses of Places: Remediations from Text to Digital Performance' (California 2008), <http://chimeraspider.wordpress.com/2007/03/01/beyond-etext-remediated-places-draft-1/>.
46   Ian Hodder, '"Always Momentary, Fluid and Flexible": Towards a Reflexive Excavation Methodology', *Antiquity* 71 (1997): 691–700.
47   Richard G. Lesure, 'Archaeologists and the Site', in John K. Papadopoulos and Richard M. Levanthal (eds), *Theory and Practice in Mediterranean Archaeology: Old World and New Perspectives* (Los Angeles 2003), pp. 199–202.

discovery.[48] However it is clear from the examples given above that the emergent 'Geospatial Web' provides a platform, and a suite of tools and methods for reconstructing the past, that sit in a tradition going back four decades or more. As a discipline, archaeology has a robust and well-established tradition of self-examination and theoretical construction. On this have been founded a number of theoretical attempts, sometimes evolving and sometimes competing, to provide a unifying and internally consistent view of how human culture develops. Whether agentive or structuralist, processual or postprocessual, these have, of course, all centred on the methods by which humans change the physical world around them, and the resulting traces left in the material record. The potential of neogeography for combining masses of user-generated content around such interpretations is not transformative in the same way as, for example, the discovery of radiocarbon dating techniques; but it is nonetheless a 'digital dimension' beyond the purely material, which has already stimulated new forms of the fundamentally creative process of historical reconstruction.

---

48   Vincent Gaffney and R.P. Fletcher, 'Always the Bridesmaid and Never the Bride! Arts, Archaeology and the e-Science Agenda', in P. Clarke, C. Davenhall, C. Greenwood and M. Strong (eds), *Proceedings of Lighting the Blue Touchpaper for UK e-Science – Closing Conference of ESLEA Project* (Edinburgh, 2007), <http://adsabs.harvard.edu/abs/2007lbtu.conf...31G>.

PART II
Text and Language

Chapter 4

Contextual Epigraphy and XML:
Digital Publication and its Application to
the Study of Inscribed Funerary Monuments

Charlotte Tupman

This chapter examines traditional methods of publishing inscribed funerary material and explores both the benefits and the limitations of such approaches. It considers whether digital methods of publication can assist with the research questions that Classicists ask of this type of material, and specifically how inscribed monuments might be integrated with other types of funerary material evidence. It assesses the current circumstances of digital publication, and examines how digital resources for inscriptions and their associated materials could develop in the coming decade.

The material evidence that results from ancient funerary customs is abundant and varied. It encompasses skeletal remains; grave goods of pottery, glass, metal and other substances; cinerary containers; coffins; commemorative inscriptions; paintings; and an enormous array of tomb constructions of stone, brick, tile and other materials. It is inevitable, and absolutely necessary, that specialists should work on very particular aspects of these funerary remains, in order to understand most comprehensively each kind of evidence that exists for burial practices; to ascertain the circumstances and extent of the use of that type of material amongst ancient societies; and in some cases to produce theories about its significance within those societies. It is equally necessary that our understanding is informed by the bringing together of different categories of archaeological evidence, as we cannot make sense of a particular practice based on only one or two of its aspects. To study the epitaph without its monument, or the skeleton without its surrounding grave goods, limits our ability to understand the reasons and processes by which the customs resulting in these artefacts came into being.

The assembling and association of related funerary materials is a fine ideal, but various difficulties lie in its way. The most significant of these is a lack of contextual evidence for a monument or item that was originally deposited in a grave, but which is now in a museum collection or has otherwise been removed from its archaeological environment. If details of that environment have not been recorded, there is no possibility of reconstructing the other materials that would have been associated with the object. However where a grave or cemetery has been excavated that has experienced little or no interference from subsequent eras, there exists a wealth of contextual information that can be compiled and analysed. In this case, there is only one main difficulty: how to present such varied evidence in a way that can be absorbed and processed usefully by scholars. This is the question that confronts all who seek to publish archaeological materials, and the abundance of interrelated evidence that the funerary sphere presents creates particularly formidable circumstances in which to find an answer.[1]

Inscribed epitaphs bring with them their own particular publication issues, the foremost of which is how to link the text with the monument on which it has been inscribed. Recent attempts to present the epigraphic and the archaeological analysis in a more balanced way[2] have recognized that there is a need to move away from the traditional prioritisation of the text.[3] As Bodel notes, '... this means trying to combine the skills of an archaeologist with those of a philologist in order to understand the physical context in which a document was produced and the significance of the monument that carried the text as well as the message of the text itself'.[4] There remains, however, the question of how best to present texts and their monuments in a way that provides the researcher with an effective means of discovering parallels between inscribed content and sculpted motifs, or investigating connections between visual display on the monument and the commemorative relationships that are revealed through the inscriptions. In the case of a cemetery excavation, the publication ought also to provide the researcher with a detailed picture of how individual monuments or groups of monuments feature in the landscape of the cemetery. These are the key issues that inscribed funerary materials present to their publishers: this chapter investigates whether digital publication is a medium that can help to resolve them.

---

1   The question of how to contextualize funerary evidence from the Roman period has been given much attention in recent years: see in particular J. Pearce, M. Millett and M. Struck (eds), *Burial, Society and Context in the Roman World* (Oxford, 2000), and I. Morris, *Death-Ritual and Social Structure in Classical Antiquity* (Cambridge, 1992). Archaeological theory has produced a number of studies specific to the importance of context, the arguments for which are discussed in H. Johnsen and B. Olsen, 'Hermeneutics and Archaeology: On the Philosophy of Contextual Archaeology', in J. Thomas (ed.), *Interpretive Archaeology* (London, 2000), pp. 97–117.

2   Z. Newby and R. Leader-Newby (eds), *Art and Inscriptions in the Ancient World* (Cambridge, 2007), p. 6, note the 'false distinction [between "art" and "inscription"] which makes little sense when applied to the monuments themselves'.

3   This issue is explored in further detail in the following section. Addressing this question in the funerary sphere are M. Koortbojian, 'In commemorationem mortuorum: Text and Image along the "Streets of Tombs"', in J. Elsner (ed.), *Art and Text in Roman Culture* (Cambridge, 1996), pp. 210–33, and G.J. Oliver (ed.), *The Epigraphy of Death* (Liverpool, 2000), throughout but particularly pp. 4–9.

4   J. Bodel, 'Epigraphy and the Ancient Historian', in J. Bodel (ed.), *Epigraphic Evidence: Ancient History from Inscriptions* (London, 2001), pp. 1–56, 5.

Traditional epigraphic publications

Inscriptions are most commonly published in collections based on location.[5] They can also be published according to the content of the inscriptions themselves[6] or they can be arranged in volumes based on the type or function of the monument.[7] The text of the inscription in majuscule (i.e. what can be seen on the stone) is followed where necessary by the editor's interpreted and expanded version, and is often accompanied by a translation of the text into a modern language. Supplementary information about the text is usually given, such as a description of letter forms and measurements of the letter heights. The majority of print publications now include information about the object onto which the inscription was cut: this includes the type of monument, its measurements, and its present condition. They are also likely to include information (where known) about the circumstances and date of its discovery, along with any changes of location or condition that the monument has undergone, including reuse in antiquity or in modern times. The written description concludes with editorial comments, dating criteria, and bibliography.

Along with this written descriptive data, a photograph or drawing of the text and its monument is sometimes included. This is much more common in today's printed publications, but, due to the expense of including photographs, books are almost always limited to one photograph per inscribed object.[8] In older printed publications, photographs and drawings were often not included at all, which is illustrative of the traditional prioritization of text over image. For example, the vast majority of inscriptions in the original volumes of *CIL* have no accompanying illustration. Occasionally, the outline of the stone is shown but only where a broken or damaged stone has interfered with the reading of the text. Rare contradictions to this rule do exist, for instance the tombstone *CIL* VI: 3177, whose decorative elements the editors clearly considered sufficiently worthy of note to include: to

---

5   The major collection *Corpus Inscriptionum Latinarum (CIL)* (Berlin, 1863–) is published according to province of the Roman Empire; within each volume the province is divided into smaller geographical areas, and the inscriptions of each area are divided according to the content of the inscription. Numerous publications use ancient or modern regions as boundaries for collecting together inscribed materials.

6   E.g. N.M. Dimitrova, *Theoroi and Initiates in Samothrace: The Epigraphical Evidence* (Princeton, 2008).

7   E.g. J. Edmondson, T. Nogales Basarrate and W. Trillmich, *Imagen y Memoria: Monumentos Funerarios con Retratos en la Colonia Augusta Emerita* (Madrid, 2001), which includes a number of inscribed monuments within its study of funerary monuments with portraits.

8   The corpus of inscriptions from *Barcino* (modern Barcelona), for instance, provides a photograph of each extant inscription, but only illustrates more than one side of a monument if the extra side is also inscribed: G. Fabre, M. Mayer and I. Rodà, *Inscriptions Romaines de Catalogne IV. Barcino* (Paris, 1997). No. 45, inscribed on two faces (pp. 114–17), is illustrated with two photographs and a drawing (Pl. XXIV).

the left of the text there is a brief description of the items represented on the stone: 'cassius et gladius', and to the right 'scutum et hasta', then above and below the text, various individuals are described within the sculpted scenes ('iuvenus tunicatus' and so forth). The modern editions of *CIL* do incorporate photographs, but not all the texts that could apparently have been photographed are included: *CIL* II 5 (Berlin, 1998) contains good quality illustrations, but these are limited to around one-sixth, or fewer, of the inscriptions within the volume. On occasion the nature of the inscribed stone prevents adequate visual representation: the publication of the Law Code of Gortyn,[9] for instance, includes large photographs, but, due to the size of the monument itself, each column of text has to be printed on a separate page so it is not possible to place the photographs next to one another to gain an overall picture of the monument. A fold-out drawing attempts to resolve this problem, but clearly it would be preferable to have a photograph of the whole monument as well as a drawing.

Funerary texts are rarely published in the same printed volumes or even by the same people as other material evidence of burial practices such as pottery or skeletal remains. This is partly due to the scarcity of inscribed tombstones in context, and partly to the different specializations of those who work in this field. A perhaps inevitable result of this situation is that epitaphs and their monuments have tended not to be thought of as archaeological material, but rather as the preserve of historians and literary scholars: they have been considered as texts rather than artefacts. Although it is relatively rare to find inscribed monuments in their original contexts, it is by no means unknown, and where possible it is desirable to be able to link these monuments to other objects found in the same archaeological contexts. Even if an inscribed funerary object is not in its original context, it can often be ascribed with some certainty to a particular cemetery or site, in which case it can be studied in its local, if not its specific, context. Lack of immediate context should not prevent consideration of material associated with the object on a wider scale; the data yielded from a local contextual approach can still give us valuable information about the nature and development of the burial practices of particular settlements, cities or areas.

To take an example, we might have an instance where tombstones are known to belong to one of the cemeteries of a town, but we no longer have information about their specific findspots.[10] Despite the lack of specific contextual information

---

9   R.F. Willetts, *The Law Code of Gortyn* (Berlin, 1967).

10   An example of this is a funerary monument from Mérida (Augusta Emerita, the provincial capital of Lusitania) that was re-used as a grave cover for a fourth-century burial in the eastern necropolis of the Roman colony. The monument itself dated from the second century AD and was almost certainly set up in the same cemetery: J. Edmondson et al., *Imagen y Memoria*, pp. 126–9. Mérida has a large and varied monumental record, including many examples of reuse in antiquity and in modern times. Some of its monuments have been found in context; others are known to belong to specific cemeteries; and others have no known findspot.

we can nevertheless study as a group the monuments known to have been set up in that cemetery. These can be compared with those found in other cemeteries of the town or with those of nearby settlements, to ascertain whether there are differences in commemorative themes from site to site, either iconographically or epigraphically. Other material evidence from those cemeteries can also be included in the study in order to provide the most complete picture we can, under less than ideal circumstances, of commemorative behaviour. If our reason for studying inscribed epitaphs is that we are seeking to understand ancient funerary behaviour and the cultural processes that underlie it, we should be looking for ways of bringing together all the possible evidence that is available to us, even if circumstances place some limitations on that aspiration.

It makes perfect sense for inscriptions to be published by different people from those who publish pottery catalogues or bone analysis. It is unlikely that one person would acquire sufficient knowledge of each type of material evidence to be able to analyse and publish all of it with equal depth and understanding. Indeed the sheer amount of time that this would require probably renders it unattainable. Specialists, therefore, need to work to make their material available to others in a way that permits their various forms of data to be combined meaningfully. This will be most effective if undertaken collaboratively, so that shared aims and standards can be established. This does not imply that there should be any diminution of expert knowledge or information in any of these fields for the sake of making it easier for others to digest; to do so would entirely miss the point of the exercise. Rather, we should be seeking ways of linking these different types of information in a rational and useful manner that not only increases our own understanding of the data, but also enhances the way in which computers can process that data.[11] We now have so much data and so many ways of storing, linking and delivering it that we should be using this to our advantage to move scholarship forward.

When considering digital alternatives to print publication, three important points must be taken into account. Firstly, any digital publication must provide everything that a book does, and more besides. There is little point in publishing digitally if it does not improve our knowledge and allow research to be conducted in ways that would not otherwise be possible. Secondly, digital publication does not necessarily exclude print publication: there may well be a case for producing a print publication alongside a digital publication, or producing the digital one in a way that allows sections of it to be printed. Digital publication can stand alone or alongside a print one, depending upon the types of material included and the

---

11 In other words, enabling computers to handle the structure and semantics of information so that they can perform data integration in a more effective manner. It has been proposed that ultimately this could lead to a Semantic Web: 'The semantic theory provides an account of "meaning" in which the logical connection of terms establishes interoperability between systems', N. Shadbolt, W. Hall and T. Berners-Lee, 'The Semantic Web Revisited', *IEEE Intelligent Systems* (2006), <http://eprints.ecs.soton.ac.uk/12614/1/Semantic_Web_Revisted.pdf>, p. 96 (accessed May 2009).

specific aims of the editors. Thirdly, there is a common anxiety that publishing online is something that anyone can do, regardless of their expertise (or lack of it), whereas a print publication from one of the university presses, for example, provides some indication of quality. Mechanisms to ensure that the same high standards of publication are achieved and are signalled clearly online are essential, and the procedures which are already in place to do this will be detailed herein.

What digital publication involves

Before we discuss the application of digital publication to inscribed funerary material, it will be helpful to set out what the production of a basic digital corpus of inscribed monuments entails. Further development of this type of publication and ways in which it might help us link our data with other types of material can then be explored. The three main choices as to how material can be published online are as follows: content can be marked up directly in HTML; raw data can be entered into a database and then views of it delivered via HTML; or, as I will discuss, it can be marked up in XML (Extensible Markup Language: a system of tagging data semantically) and then transformed for display in HTML. The time taken to digitize the data will depend upon the method chosen, but in the case of XML the actual marking up of the data is likely to be the most substantial element of the project in terms of time and cost. This has its rewards at a later stage, both in the extremely detailed data it provides, and when indices and lists of names (for example) can be generated automatically from the marked up data, rather than having to be compiled as a separate, manual, task.[12]

XML is a markup language that operates independently of software or platform. It allows data to be incorporated relatively straightforwardly into databases (via an automated conversion process), and to be interlinked with other data that has been marked up in XML. Semantically tagged data also permits researchers to design their own ways of questioning the material, thus allowing editors to present the data in the knowledge that if other scholars want to ask different questions of the material, they can do so by downloading the XML files and adding their own markup to them.[13] The researcher is therefore given a much greater choice in how they can approach the data. At the same time, the editor can display their data in multiple ways; once their material is marked up, that same information can be used to produce numerous different types of display. For example, a scholar

---

12   See G. Bodard, 'EpiDoc: Epigraphic Documents in XML for Publication and Interchange', in F. Feraudi-Gruénais, *Latin on Stone: Epigraphic Research and Electronic Archives, Roman Studies: Interdisciplinary Approaches* (forthcoming, 2010) for a detailed account of XML and its application to publishing inscribed materials.

13   Joyce Reynolds, Charlotte Roueché, Gabriel Bodard, *Inscriptions of Aphrodisias* (2007), <http://insaph.kcl.ac.uk/iaph2007> has made available its XML files to download so that the source material can be used by others for their own research needs.

publishing a corpus of inscriptions is likely to want to publish the text that can be read on the stone, the editor's version, and the translation. These can of course be published on the same page, but some editors might find it useful to be able to display these individually, particularly where different audiences are concerned. A fellow epigrapher will need all possible information on the text, including detailed comments on interpretations and previous readings of the stone. However, a student who is new to epigraphy and perhaps to the language might find that a simple display with the interpreted text and a translation is all they require. Editors who wish to give their readers a choice of displays can produce these different editions from the same source. Similarly, it might be desirable to give translations in more than one modern language, enabling collaborators or readers to select which language they wish to read.[14]

Where digital publication differs from print publication is that it is undeniably easier for the non-specialist, or even someone with little or no knowledge of a subject, to make their views known to the world. This leads to understandable concerns about the accuracy and validity of information found on the Internet. This is a situation that we are all challenged by and must find ways of navigating. Under these circumstances there is a patent need for internationally recognized standards and a commitment to peer review, both to ensure that one's own publication is taken seriously, and to inspire confidence in the reader that the information they have before them can be trusted (insofar as this can be true of any publication). In fact systems of regulation are already in place; in the case of inscribed materials, international standards of publication have already been established and the number of projects that are accepting and implementing them is increasing steadily. The EpiDoc Guidelines[15] for digital epigraphic publications provide detailed standards that are not limited by language or geographic location.[16] They have been formulated and developed by experts from a number of different countries, and are open to contributions by others working in this field (all contributions are considered by an editorial board before being approved for inclusion in the Guidelines). The EpiDoc standards also provide tools for editing

---

14   An example of where this might be useful is for projects such as the Inscriptions of Roman Cyrenaica project <http://ircyr.kcl.ac.uk>, whose material is from Libya. As this is a collaborative project between English-speaking and Arabic-speaking scholars, it would be helpful for the publication to provide Arabic as well as English translations of the inscriptions, and ideally also of their surrounding information such as description of monument, dating criteria, commentary and so forth.

15   EpiDoc = Epigraphic Documents in TEI XML <http://epidoc.sourceforge.net>. TEI = Text Encoding Initiative <http://www.tei-c.org/index.xml>, which develops and maintains standards for digital texts across the humanities and social sciences.

16   Tom Elliott et al. (eds), 'EpiDoc: Guidelines for Structured Markup of Epigraphic Texts in TEI XML' (2007) <http://www.stoa.org/epidoc/gl/5/> (accessed February 2009). The EpiDoc Guidelines are currently written in English but they apply to material that is published in any language, or indeed in any number of languages.

and publishing, as well as support through the wider EpiDoc community in the form of conferences, wikis and discussion groups.[17]

What EpiDoc cannot do, however, is guarantee the quality of the actual content of the information that has been marked up in XML. This might be enabled by a digital library such as the Scaife Digital Library,[18] which requires that its objects (including publications of inscribed materials) have received peer review; are in sustainable formats such as EpiDoc; have a long-term home separate from the producer of the object; and are available under open licensing. In terms of academic quality, it is essential that peer review of the publication has taken place. Professional digital publishers must also provide assurance to the reader that the publication conforms to a certain academic standard, just as publishers do in the medium of printed publication. A digital publication has the same legal status as a print publication and requires the same conventions of citation. It is still the case that not all countries possess evaluation bodies that give the same credit to digital publications as to print, but certainly the UK's Research Assessment Exercise (RAE) makes no differentiation between digital publication and print in terms of its value as scholarly work. Indeed the most recent RAE listed Internet publication as one of the standard output types for submission by higher education institutions (HEIs).[19]

One further concern about digital publication is that it will require more funding and more time to produce than a print publication. This is not necessarily the case: financial differences between print and digital publications are more likely to be linked to the stage of the project at which the bulk of the funding is spent, and the organizations that support the costs. To take an example of a major epigraphic digital project that published a searchable corpus of around 1,500 inscriptions, the *Inscriptions of Aphrodisias*[20] received a £300,000 grant and the project took a total of three years, employing several researchers. If it had been a print publication, it would also have taken several years, and would similarly have required several researchers during that period, including research leave. The publisher would then have spent further funds on preparing the book for publication. However, whilst a publisher would have had to sell the book to individuals or libraries at a cost of £200 or so per volume, the digital publication

---

17   For a discussion of the value of electronic publication using the EpiDoc Guidelines in publishing see *Inscriptions of Aphrodisias* (2007), <http://insaph.kcl.ac.uk/iaph2007>; also: G. Bodard, 'The Inscriptions of Aphrodisias as Electronic Publication: A User's Perspective and a Proposed Paradigm', *Digital Medievalist*, 4 (2008): on the EpiDoc Guidelines themselves, see paragraphs 4–12.

18   Christopher Blackwell and Gregory Crane, 'Cyberinfrastructure, the Scaife Digital Library and Classics in a Digital Age', in G. Crane, B. Seales, M. Terras (eds), *Changing the Centre of Gravity, Digital Humanities Quarterly* 3.1 (2009).

19   Research Assessment Exercise <http://www.rae.ac.uk/pubs/2007/c1/01/>, 'Annex B: RAE 2008: Requirements for Electronic and/or Physical Provision of Research Outputs by Output Type' (zipped PDF) (accessed May 2009).

20   Reynolds et al., *Inscriptions of Aphrodisias*.

is free to the reader: the costs of publishing digitally are met by the funding, rather than by the user.

Another difference in financial terms is that some of the *Inscriptions of Aphrodisias* funding was spent developing methodology and tools specific to the publication of inscribed materials, which was not only to the benefit of the project itself, but can also be used in the future by other projects. This means that the tools now exist to produce a similar publication more quickly and more cheaply, and in a more sophisticated manner. Whilst it has been necessary to develop a small number of specific tools for the publication of inscribed objects, the wider technologies that are required for the creation of digital publications, such as XML, are maintained and developed by international organizations.[21] Technologies that are used as extensively as XML are supported by organizations that possess far greater resources than scholars could normally access, and because these technologies are freely available, we can make use of these resources without having to draw upon our own funding to maintain them.

Contextualizing inscribed funerary materials through digital publication

Digital media provide an effective platform for displaying the contexts of archaeological evidence. In the simplest instance, plans linking an object to the cemetery or other area in which it was discovered can be produced. For example, each object will have an identifying number or name, which can be placed on the plan of findspots as a hyperlink: when the reader clicks on the link, they are taken directly to the information about that object.[22] This is not so very different from referring to a number on a map and being directed to the appropriate page of a book; however there is a distinct advantage to being able to use zoom functions: all the data can be plotted on an extremely detailed map or plan, but the reader can view this data at different levels (for instance whole site; area of site; building), thus being able to choose to see more or less detail as required. Likewise the reader can focus upon one small part of a plan if that it is the section in which their interest lies. The kind of map technologies seen perhaps most familiarly in Google Maps[23] could allow the reader to select particular objects to view; so for instance the full map might contain all the findspots of inscribed stones in that town or city, but the reader could choose to see only tombstones or altars. Alternatively the reader

---

21 The World Wide Web Consortium <http://www.w3.org/XML/>, which develops interoperable technologies including XML, is supported financially by almost four hundred companies and institutions, including software companies, communications laboratories and universities, <http://www.w3.org/Consortium/Member/List> (accessed May 2009).

22 A basic example of which can be seen in Charlotte Roueché, *Aphrodisias in Late Antiquity: The Late Roman and Byzantine Inscriptions*, 2nd rev. edn, 2004, <http://insaph.kcl.ac.uk/ala2004>, 'Plan of site' (accessed February 2009).

23 Google Maps <http://maps.google.com>.

might want to compare the distribution of civic texts with that of religious texts: this could be done simply by selecting which types of monument were required on the map, and only these monuments would be shown. In other words there is a possibility for the reader to create their own maps using their own selections of the data provided by the editor. This could prove to be a strong research tool.

Another of the fundamental uses of digital technology is the ability to display data in a customized way. Those researching changing patterns of monumental funerary commemoration at a site with a large and complex archaeological and epigraphic record, for example, might find it useful to view its monuments according to date so that variations in practice over the centuries can be identified. If the research required a clear picture of the usage of a particular type of monument over time, the user could choose to view the data on that type of monument according to date, but could exclude all other monument types. Similar visualizations could be produced for materials – monument type and material; or date and material – thus showing the use of different materials for different types of monuments and how this changed over time. All this information would be much less efficiently gathered using print publications; as inscriptions are mostly organized by location and/or monument type within print publications, the researcher would have to go through the whole volume noting down each monument's date and then process the information later. In contrast, the digital publication permits the researcher to access this data directly and to approach the material from a personally chosen perspective, rather than that chosen by the editors of the publication.

Any type or quantity of information can be included in a digital publication: the only limit is the project's own decision on what to include. When marking up an inscribed object in XML, the editor is entering factual data about that object, such as deciding upon what a decorative feature is showing, or giving a reading of a damaged letter inscribed on the stone. What it does not have to involve is the full analysis of the data that has been entered in the markup. Of course that work can be done by the editors where desired: it might be that the editors are following a particular course of enquiry, in which case they might want to ask certain questions of the data and include the results in their publication. However, where large quantities of data exist, it might be helpful to use digital tools to sort the data, and crucially, to allow the researcher consulting that publication to ask their own questions of the material. By marking up the information in XML and making that XML available, the researcher will have the same knowledge available to them as to the editors and can use it for their own purposes.

This type of digital publication also presents fewer opportunities for ambiguity, as each editorial decision is signalled in the underlying XML code. This is particularly evident in the editor's interpretation of the text itself. Whilst the conventions that are used by epigraphers to indicate editorial decisions are designed to be unambiguous, occasions still arise that can lead to uncertainty on the part of the reader. For instance, line 2 of *CIL* II 5: 812[24] reads:

24   *Corpus Inscriptionum Latinarum* II, Pars 5 (Berlin, 1998), 812.

[*vixit mensib?*]*us* . IV

The square brackets indicate text that is supplied by the editor because it has been lost from the stone.[25] However, here the editor has had to use a question mark to express his own uncertainty as to the restoration he has supplied. The problem is that it is unclear whether the question mark indicates that the editor is unsure about his whole restoration, i.e. everything within the square brackets, or that the editor is happy with his restoration of *vixit* and is only unsure about the final letters supplied, i.e. the *mensib* of *mensibus*. This is just one example of the need to make editorial decisions unambiguous, which XML requires by its very nature. In this case, the editor would have to express his editorial decision explicitly, by declaring specifically which part(s) of the restoration are uncertain. XML therefore enables clarification whilst at the same time continuing to allow the expression of *editorial* uncertainty, such as might occur with variant readings of a text (e.g. if the letters that remained on the stone were damaged, and two editors disagreed about the interpretation of those letters, so that one editor might read *is* on the stone whereas the other reads *us*).

The issue of how to integrate text and image when publishing inscriptions is, as discussed, a problem that has proved difficult to resolve. This is because in order to show how text and image operated together in a detailed way in a print publication the editor would have to find a way of displaying the findings without spending large amounts of money on printing extra photographs, which is an ultimately insurmountable problem. The issue of cost is usually the most limiting factor in a print publication: most epigraphers when encountering a stone will photograph all its aspects, and will take several photographs of specific decorative elements which they will then study before producing their publication. This is particularly true now that digital photography is so common. But in the print publication itself, if it is a corpus, it is normally only possible to publish one photograph of the inscribed face of each monument (or one photograph per inscribed face on the monument; as discussed above). Occasionally where there are particularly interesting or detailed decorative elements, an extra photograph will be included; likewise, an article might permit a greater number of photographs of a monument to be published. However the vast majority of decorative features on the sides or rears of monuments are left out of the publication except for a written description. Any editor who wants to publish a corpus of inscriptions that attempts to show links between inscribed content and decorative choice will almost certainly be prevented from doing so in any comprehensive way by the financial limits imposed by print publication.[26]

---

25   L. Robert and J. Robert, *Fouilles d'Amyzon en Carie* (Paris, 1983), pp. 9–11 on 'Signes critiques du corpus et édition'.

26   For further discussion of the scale of support and explanatory documentation that can be included in a digital publication, including photographs, see G. Bodard, 'The *Inscriptions of Aphrodisias* as Electronic Publication', paragraphs 17–19.

Digital publication, however, has an essentially unlimited capacity for publishing photographs of monuments, and is of course not limited to two-dimensional reproductions; for example, a high-resolution, dynamic-image format could allow readers to zoom in on whichever part of the photograph is of interest. At present the most practical way of representing monuments digitally is to provide a detailed set of photographs which, as noted, would usually be taken by the epigrapher anyway; it is rare for a researcher to take fewer than four or five photographs of each monument. However, three-dimensional images of archaeological objects are becoming easier and less costly to produce all the time and it is entirely feasible that we will see 3D images of monuments appearing regularly in online digital epigraphic publications within a few years, particularly as there already exists an XML-based file format for representing 3D graphics, X3D, which enables the encoding of a 3D scene using XML syntax.[27]

The possibilities of 3D imaging are not limited to individual inscribed objects; where tombstones exist in their original contexts, there is a rich quantity and quality of data that needs to be conveyed. A striking example of this is the new section of Roman cemetery discovered by the Vatican on the Via Triumphalis, in which more than two hundred tombs are well-preserved, many with their original inscriptions, frescoes and mosaics.[28] The potential for 3D visualization techniques to help to display this complex data is enormous: with an immersive environment the viewer could explore the cemetery in a way that permits all angles and viewpoints to be perceived, thus seeing how images carved onto monuments could be viewed in the contexts of the other monuments around them. This is invaluable for helping to reconstruct something of the perspective of an individual visiting a cemetery. Three-dimensional visualization would be especially useful given that cemeteries almost always consist of a jumble of monuments facing different ways and intercutting previous graves and precincts. It is rare to find a cemetery that has been in use for hundreds of years that has been carefully ordered and planned throughout that time. Using 3D technology to represent the cemetery would also allow the researcher to picture how it evolved over time; most monuments can be dated to within a century or so, and often more precisely. This means that 3D representations of a cemetery landscape could be produced for successive periods, with monuments added or altered as time progressed.

Those producing a digital publication of this type will not necessarily be part of the same team or have access to the same resources. In the case of the funerary sphere there are likely to be several teams working on data that are closely related to each other: pottery, sculpture, inscriptions and skeletal remains might all

---

27   X3D, <http://www.web3d.org/x3d/>. Richard Beacham's team at the King's Visualisation Lab is exploring visual representation for archaeology and academic research and has already produced a number of 3D representations, including the Theatre of Pompey: <http://www.kcl.ac.uk/schools/humanities/depts/cch/embedded/kvl.html>.

28   M. Steinby et al., *La necropoli della via Triumphalis: il tratto sotto l'Autoparco vaticano* (Rome, 2003).

originate in the same cemetery and be part of the same burial culture, but they are separated by us in our individual scholarly pursuits. If we are to bring these elements together there are two possibilities: either the people involved in these lines of research must be willing to work together, share their data and collaborate in practical terms as well as academic; or at a minimum they must be prepared to publish their material in a way that can be integrated with that of other projects. There appears still to be a scholarly possessiveness that, upon occasion, curtails attempts to work collaboratively; and an extension of this is anxiety over putting material online where 'anyone can use it'.[29] Ultimately, the point of research is to make information known to others, in order to study it in new ways and further our knowledge. By sharing our information and making it available for others to use, we are contributing towards greater understanding of the evidence that we possess.

Where scholars are willing to collaborate and discuss ways of integrating their data, the results can produce valuable resources. A striking example is Pleiades,[30] built upon the foundations of the *Barrington Atlas of the Greek and Roman World*,[31] itself a collaborative enterprise, which provided over a hundred maps detailing more than 50,000 sites and features of the ancient world, both cultural and geographic. Pleiades uses information provided by scholars of the ancient world including GIS data to produce a resource for geographic, bibliographic and analytical information concerning ancient places. It can be revised and updated by archaeologists and historians with new information via an editorial board to ensure accuracy and relevancy; there is, therefore, a system of peer review integrated into the process by which information is incorporated. However this resource does not stand alone, as it has been designed to be compatible with geographic references already established in other digital resources for the ancient world. Projects that collaborate with Pleiades will be able to design and obtain its maps for their own use; it is a two-way venture. It also acts as a storehouse of information about each place. Those who are running projects at a particular site can link their publication to the Pleiades information on that site, so that somebody looking up a placename or set of coordinates on Pleiades can be informed of the projects that are being undertaken at that particular location. Likewise Pleiades provides links to source materials and academic essays available online.

------

29   This possessiveness is not necessarily an objection to the Internet's potential for the democratization of knowledge ('The Democratization of Knowledge: The Group for Collaborative Inquiry', *Adult Education Quarterly*, 44:1 (1993): 43–51), but it certainly signifies an entrenched tradition of individual scholarship.

30   Pleiades Project, <http://pleiades.stoa.org> (New York University). See also T. Elliott and S. Gillies, 'Digital Geography and Classics', *Digital Humanities Quarterly*, 3:1 (2009), paragraphs 40–46.

31   R.J.A. Talbert (ed.), *University Presses of California, Columbia and Princeton* (2000).

Collaborative research and publication does not only benefit large-scale projects such as Pleiades. Smaller projects that aim to produce resources for a particular site or area should also profit if scholars are willing to work towards a common goal. The production of resources that include all the evidence that exists for burial practices at a site, rather than selected parts, will enable a much more comprehensive understanding of the material remains. Analysis by individual specialists can still be presented within that framework. This type of collaborative publication would be made significantly easier if common terms were used to identify buildings, structures and objects; it would help to alleviate ambiguity and assist with integrating data. The issue of shared taxonomies needs further discussion amongst scholars working on interdisciplinary projects.

Conclusion

The use of digital publication for inscribed materials has expanded considerably since the first EpiDoc projects were published. The existence, and the continued development and maintenance, of the EpiDoc Guidelines has been crucial in ensuring interoperability and international standards for this type of publication. The mutual support that scholars working on EpiDoc projects give each other has also been vital to the development of tools for publication and networks for discussion. Projects such as the *Inscriptions of Aphrodisias* have shown that digital publication in XML is an appropriate and more flexible medium for the publication of inscribed materials than is the printed form. The key to improving digital publication further appears to lie in the way in which scholars work together; the more interdisciplinarity can be encouraged, the better digital publications will become. This is particularly the case for the funerary sphere, whose wide-ranging archaeological materials require the attention of several different specialists. Rather than holding back from working collaboratively, we should embrace the opportunities that technological advances present, and seek new ways to further our knowledge.

Chapter 5

A Virtual Research Environment
for the Study of Documents and Manuscripts

Alan K. Bowman, Charles V. Crowther, Ruth Kirkham and John Pybus

Introduction

On a spring afternoon in March 1996, a group of papyrologists gathered around
a computer screen in the Centre for the Study of Ancient Documents (CSAD) in
Oxford to examine digital photographs taken two months earlier of a demotic
papyrus recording a barely legible population register from the Lycopolite nome.
The excitement of the moment is captured in an account by one of the participants,
Professor Dorothy Thompson:[1]

> (Willy) Clarysse and (John) Tait are together in Oxford for a conference and
> Ursula Kaplony-Heckel from Marburg is also here. It is with some trepidation
> that they call up the images on the screen in the Documents Centre. Will the
> text really be more legible than when they last worked together on the original
> and made only insignificant changes to their earlier readings? (Thompson looks
> on and listens as they start to look at the screen.) First they must locate where
> they are (that comes quickly), learn to play with the image, to zoom in and out
> on the difficult readings and to work the colour contrast that highlights the ink
> that was faded. Soon work is under way. Three people, no longer crouched and
> hunched but sitting at ease, stare across at the screen together; the adrenaline
> starts to flow. Suggestions for readings are made; a quick flip of the screen to
> two columns earlier allows a speedy check with names and elements of names
> that went before. Gods' determinatives emerge, a host of local names; the script
> comes to life. Decipherment is underway; the parts that before were illegible
> slowly take their place on the page. The transcription is transformed; the text
> grows and, though much of this damaged text is still obscure, it is significantly
> improved [Figure 5.1].
>
> I have seen the future and this future works – at least so far. Work in
> different countries on the same text at the same time can now take place without
> problem and for a long and difficult text, where the writing is small and faded,

---

1 D.J. Thompson, 'Digitising a Lycopolite Census', *CSAD Newsletter* 2 (spring 1996):
1–2, <http://www.csad.ox.ac.uk/CSAD/Newsletters/Newsletter2/Newsletter2a.html>. All
urls current at the time of writing.

the possibility of working on the image on the screen is in itself a great advance. A further lesson is clear. The human element in our work is the most important of all, and the mutual stimulation that comes from cooperative work can be greatly aided but can never be replaced.

Developments in technology and digital imaging have transformed research in the field of ancient documentary studies in the fourteen years since that spring afternoon in Oxford. Not only have texts become more legible as techniques of image capture have advanced with improvements in technology, but perennial problems of access are being significantly reduced. Large numbers of papyri and inscriptions have been digitized, delivered with metadata, and linked together by the APIS[2] and EAGLE[3] networks of projects. The Packard Humanities Institute's Searchable Greek Inscriptions resource provides online access to texts of a high proportion of published Greek inscriptions,[4] and EpiDoc has become established as a standard for the TEI XML encoding of ancient documentary texts.[5] But Dorothy Thompson's vision remains important, not least for the insistence that collaboration and interaction are central, stimulating, and sometimes decisive, in the process of recovering and deciphering written evidence from the ancient world. Simultaneous presence and sharing of ideas were vital in making progress in reading the Lycopolite census. But the collocation of scholars that made this possible was an incidental result of a conference in Oxford held for a different purpose. The possibility of reproducing that meeting of papyrologists on demand within a virtual environment has driven development of a Virtual Research Environment for the Study of Documents and Manuscripts (VRE-SDM) to enable Professor Thompson's vision of the future to become a reality: to 'work in different countries on the same text' simultaneously, allowing researchers to collaborate and form 'virtual gatherings' without being unnecessarily constrained by time or travel.

In this chapter we discuss and outline the development of the VRE-SDM project, examine its evolution and testing through a case study of the decipherment of a wooden stilus tablet, and consider the prospects and challenges for its future development and deployment.

---

2   Advanced Papyrological Information System hosted by Columbia University Libraries Digital Programme, <http://www.columbia.edu/cgi-bin/cul/resolve?ATK2059>.

3   Electronic Archive of Greek and Latin Epigraphy, <http://www.eagle-eagle.it/>.

4   Searchable Greek Inscriptions (A Scholarly Tool in Progress at the Packard Humanities Institute), <http://epigraphy.packhum.org/inscriptions/>.

5   EPIDOC: Epigraphic Documents in TEI XML, <http://epidoc.sourceforge.net/>.

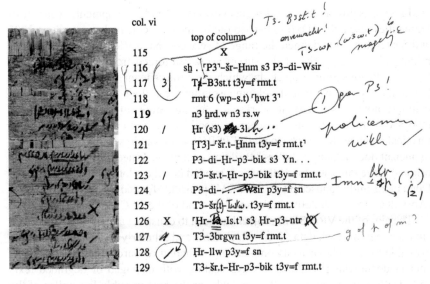

Figure 5.1   Digital photograph of Demotic census record for Lycopolite nome with manual annotations

Source: © Centre for the Study of Ancient Documents.

What is a VRE?

What is a Virtual Research Environment (VRE) and how will it help documentary scholars? The Joint Information Systems Committee (JISC) offers the following definition:[6]

> The purpose of a VRE is to help researchers in all disciplines manage the increasingly complex range of tasks involved in carrying out research. A VRE will provide a framework of resources to support the underlying processes of research on both small and large scales.

In 2005 the Humanities Division at Oxford received funding from JISC for a fifteen-month exploratory project ('Building a Virtual Research Environment for the Humanities': BVREH), led and staffed by the authors of this chapter, to examine how humanities research could most effectively be supported by VRE technologies and to construct demonstrator applications in specific fields which

---

6   JISC: Virtual Research Environment programme (Phase 2), <http://www.jisc.ac.uk/whatwedo/programmes/vre2.aspx>.

could serve as prototypes for subsequent evaluation and development.[7] A survey of humanities research in Oxford carried out by the project team between June 2005 and September 2006 defined the range of services that a VRE for the humanities might offer.[8] The results of the survey were reinforced from the experience of building demonstrator projects in which the project team worked directly with humanities researchers in developing solutions for their needs. One of these demonstrators was a Virtual Workspace for the Study of Ancient Documents (VWSAD), funded through a separate small award from the Engineering and Physical Sciences Research Council (EPSRC), which addressed the specific needs of ancient documentary scholars.[9] Building on a range of needs highlighted by the original survey this demonstrator was expanded into the pilot VRE for the Study of Documents and Manuscripts (VRE-SDM) project,[10] funded by a two-year award (April 2007 to March 2009) in the second round of the JISC VRE programme.[11]

The aim of the VRE-SDM project has been to construct a pilot of an integrated environment in which data (documents), tools and scholarly *instrumenta* could be available to the scholar as a complete and coherent resource. Scholars who edit ancient documents are almost always dealing with damaged or degraded texts and ideally require access to the originals, or the best possible facsimiles of the originals, in order to decipher and verify readings, and also to a wide range of scholarly aids and reference works (dictionaries, name-lists, editions of comparable texts, and so on) which are essential for interpretation of their texts. The originals may be in widely scattered museum and institutional collections (individual parts of archives and even single documents have suffered this fate), and the full range of scholarly tools is immediately available in only the best public and university library collections.

Although multi-spectral imaging for texts written in carbon-based ink is comparatively well known and has been used for many years,[12] there is still considerable scope for developing and refining techniques that may be applied

---

7   Building a Virtual Research Environment for the Humanities, University of Oxford, <http://bvreh.humanities.ox.ac.uk/>.

8   BVREH: Report of the User Requirements Survey, <http://bvreh.humanities.ox.ac.uk/files/User_requirementsBVREH.doc>.

9   BVREH: Virtual Workspace for the Study of Ancient Documents Demonstrator, <http://bvreh.humanities.ox.ac.uk/news/e-Science_Demonstrator/>.

10   BVREH: A VRE for the Study of Documents and Manuscripts, <http://bvreh.humanities.ox.ac.uk/VRE-SDM>.

11   JISC: Virtual Research Environments programme: Phase 2 roadmap, <http://www.jisc.ac.uk/publications/documents/pub_vreroadmap.aspx>.

12   The decipherment of the Vindolanda tablets, for example, has been based on infra-red band photography, initially using film (E. Birley, R.E. Birley and A.R. Birley, *Vindolanda Research reports, New Series, Vol. II: Reports on the Auxiliaries, the Writing Tablets, Inscriptions, Brands and Graffiti* (Hexham, 1993), pp. 103–106), but from 1996 onwards using high-resolution digital photography (*Tabulae Vindolandenses* III, p. 14, <http://vindolanda.csad.ox.ac.uk/tablets/TVdigital-2.shtml>). For a summary description

to other kinds of written material which do not yield their texts to the naked eye: texts scratched on wooden stilus tablets or incised in metals such as lead or bronze, and inscriptions on stones the top surface of which has been wholly or partly worn away. The integration of tools for image control and enhancement is a key element of the tool-kit which a VRE could potentially offer. To this end, the VRE-SDM project has been designed to complement a separate but concurrent AHRC-funded e-Science research programme into damaged and illegible documents, based at the Centre for the Study of Ancient Documents and the Oxford e-Research Centre (Image, Text, Interpretation: e-Science, Technology and Documents (eSAD)).[13] As well as developing tools to aid in the reading of damaged texts, the eSAD project is exploring how an Interpretation Support System (ISS) can be used in the day-to-day reading of ancient documents, to understand the cognitive processes involved in deciphering damaged texts and to keep track of how the documents are interpreted and read.

The design objectives set by the VRE-SDM project have been to construct a modular environment within which a researcher would be able to:

- view, manipulate and enhance digitized images of documents and manuscripts within a portal framework;
- select, store and organize items in a personal workspace;
- add annotations to these items to store comments, thoughts and responses;
- search across multiple, distributed data sets, images and texts;
- collaborate with multiple researchers in separate locations while sharing a common view of the workspace, in conjunction with real time communication via Chat, VoIP and desktop integration with Access Grid.

Although development has been driven by the requirements of researchers drawn from the papyrological and epigraphical communities, the VRE has been designed to be extensible to a wide range of humanities disciplines. The team envisaged from the beginning that a virtual workspace of this kind would be useful not only to ancient documentary scholars, but to those working with documents and manuscripts across the humanities, from specialists in medieval music manuscripts to English scholars working with digitized manuscripts of Jane Austen's work.

---

of the use of multi-spectral imaging in papyri, illustrated by interactive examples, see <http://www.papyrology.ox.ac.uk/POxy/multi/index.html>.

13   eSAD project homepage, <http://esad.classics.ox.ac.uk/>. We are very grateful to Prof. Anne Trefethen, Director of the OeRC, for her generous support.

User requirements

From the beginning, the BVREH and VRE-SDM projects have placed a strong emphasis on the process and methodology of collecting and analysing user requirements data. During 2006–2007 the BVREH team conducted a series of workshops funded by the Arts and Humanities Research Council (AHRC) entitled 'User Requirements Gathering for the Humanities'.[14] Along with recommendations to follow an iterative development cycle responsive to the feedback of researchers and to establish user champions from within humanities disciplines, one of the most important suggestions for best practice to emerge from the workshops was to encourage developers to attend meetings with researchers and to understand the nature of their research and the material with which they are working.

It was clear that the pilot VRE would only be effective if developed in constant consultation with documentary specialists (in this case, Classicists) and that a dialogue needed to be sustained between developers and researchers on a regular and continuous basis. The developers were able to form a direct understanding of user needs in collaborative sessions where they witnessed the decipherment process at first hand: simple subconscious actions such as tracing a letter in the air, or following the line of a down stroke on a digitized version of the text on a projector were observed by the project team, and made it possible to consider how these collaborative and expressive practices might be emulated in the VRE when individuals collaborate in separate locations. The digital video records made of these collaborative sessions provided an important resource for analysing and understanding user requirements.[15]

Case study

In the autumn of 2007 Professor Alan Bowman, Dr Roger Tomlin and Dr Charles Crowther began a collaboration with colleagues in Holland over a number of months to decipher a Latin text written on a wooden stilus tablet found at Tolsum in the Netherlands in the early twentieth century and now held in the Fries Museum in Leeuwarden (Figure 5.2).

The stilus tablet preserves a Latin text well known to Roman historians and experts in Roman law. The writing was transcribed, interpreted and published by the Dutch Classicist C.W. Vollgraff in 1917,[16] and his text has remained the

14   BVREH: User Requirements Gathering for the Humanities, <http://bvreh. humanities.ox.ac.uk/news/Requirements_Gathering_Workshops>.

15   See S.M. Tarte, 'Papyrological Investigations: Transferring Perception and Interpretation into the Digital World', *Literary and Linguistic Computing* 2010 (forthcoming).

16   C.W. Vollgraff, 'De tabella emptionis aetatis Traiani nuper in Frisia reperta', *Mnemosyne* 45 (1917): 341–52 (whence *AE* 1919, 51; reproduced as *FIRA* III 137).

Figure 5.2   Tolsum stilus tablet: Digital photograph of front face

Source: © Centre for the Study of Ancient Documents.

basis of understanding the document ever since. It was discussed and minimally revised in 1998 by another Dutch scholar (E. Slob),[17] who was able to conduct a carbon-dating test which supported the idea that it was written in the early Roman imperial period (probably the first century AD).

Although Vollgraff's text showed a number of peculiarities of formula, syntax and nomenclature, it has always been accepted as basically sound. One of the main reasons for this is that the subject matter, as he interpreted it, fitted very well into a known historical context. A contract for the sale of an ox is appropriate to the area and the period because we know from the historian Tacitus that in AD 29 the Frisian tribe revolted against Rome because of the heavy burden of taxation in ox-hides

---

17   E. Slob, 'De koopakte van Tolsum', *Tijdschr. v. Rechtgeschiedenis* 66 (1998): 25–52.

Figure 5.3   Tolsum stilus tablet: Enhanced digital photograph of front face
Source: © Centre for the Study of Ancient Documents.

imposed on them[18] – this was (and still is) a region famous for its Friesian cattle breed. However, there has always been some uncertainty about the exact date of the stilus tablet because the names of the consuls in the dating formula were not clearly legible; Vollgraff and later scholars thought that they might be the consuls of either AD 29 or AD 116, but the earlier date has generally been favoured simply because it makes the text fit so well into the context of the Frisian unrest described by Tacitus for the year AD 29.

At the suggestion of Professor Klaas Worp of the University of Leiden, the stilus tablet was brought to Oxford on 21–23 November 2007 by Dr Hans Laagland (Tresoar, Buma Library, Leeuwarden) and Ewert Kramer (Curator, Fries Museum, Leeuwarden) and photographed by Dr Crowther using the CSAD's equipment; a series of digital captures was made with the tablet held in a fixed position and illuminated by a focused light source moved at elevations of 10 and 15 degrees and at 45-degree intervals around an arc of 270 degrees, to replicate the shadow stereo

---

18   Tacitus, Annals IV.72 ff.

process developed in an earlier EPSRC project and documented elsewhere.[19] The images as captured were sufficiently superior to previous photographs to allow immediate progress in decipherment, but were subsequently improved further by processing by Dr Ségolène Tarte from the eSAD project team using the shadow-stereo algorithms (Figure 5.3).[20]

The VRE-SDM team decided that this collaboration would offer an excellent opportunity to refine user requirements analysis for the VRE, and filmed the researchers' collaborative meetings for use as a case study. The aim of the filming was to discover and document the inherent practices, tools and processes used to decipher ancient texts and to establish ways in which a VRE might emulate, support and advance these practices. The sessions were intended as much to gain requirements for the construction of the VRE as to test the VRE interface itself, but in the event provided a valuable instantiation and validation of the latter as well. Between February and May 2008 the VRE team filmed four collaborative meetings between the three documentary specialists. The meetings were organized to address real decipherment and research questions and the filming was designed to be as non-intrusive as possible.[21]

The initial collaborative sessions at the Oxford e-Research Centre (OeRC) were supplemented within the VRE environment through an Access Grid meeting on 21 August 2008, attended at the OeRC in Oxford by Professor Bowman, Dr Tomlin, Ms Kirkham and Mr Pybus, in Leiden by Professor Worp and Dr Laagland, and by Dr Crowther in Cirencester linking from a domestic broadband connection through an H.323-AG bridge.[22] The success of the meeting in resolving a number of outstanding areas of unclarity and uncertainty partially replicated the experience of the 1996 Oxford meeting.

The collaborative study of the stilus tablet through the VRE has produced dramatic and unexpected results. The consular date of AD 29 has been verified (although its form is somewhat unusual, with only one consul named), but major changes have been made elsewhere in the text of the tablet. Although much of Vollgraff's basic transcription turned out to be sound, the interpretation was vitiated by palaeographical uncertainties and by a number of misreadings – most notably in line four of the front face of the tablet, where a failure to identify the

---

19   Using a PhaseOne Lightphase H20 digital camera back mounted on a Hasselblad 501CM medium-format camera body with CFE 4/120 makro-planar lens. For shadow stereo and its application to writing tablets, see A.K. Bowman and R.S.O. Tomlin, 'Wooden Stilus Tablets from Roman Britain', in A.K. Bowman and J.M. Brady (eds), *Artefacts and Images of the Ancient World* (Oxford, 2004), pp. 7–14; J.M. Brady et al. 'Shadow Stereo, Image Filtering and Constraint Propagation', ibid., pp. 15–30.
20   See Tarte 2010 (forthcoming).
21   Ibid.
22   H.323 is a standard videoconferencing protocol for connectivity over the IP network; the H.323-AG bridge service allows an H.323 node (for example, a domestic user) to connect to and participate in access grid meetings; see <http://www.ja.net/services/video/agsc/services/h323andag.html>.

tail of a *q* led to the reading *l(icet) bovem* (instead of *ad quem*), from which the fictive cow and much else followed. The new text has now been published in the *Journal of Roman Studies*.[23]

The Tolsum tablet test case underlines the potential of a VRE offering access to high-resolution images, image-enhancement tools, and a collaborative environment to support the research process for ancient documentary scholars through the complete cycle from decipherment through to publication.

Technical perspective

Working in the first instance with the user requirements from the Tolsum tablet case study, the pilot VRE has adapted open source tools to enable annotation and sophisticated document viewing, making use of existing VRE tools to facilitate communication and collaboration between scholars. We have reused and repurposed tools and software wherever possible, choosing to concentrate on the user requirements of humanities scholars rather than writing proprietary software that would be specific to a local system. With this in view, we have established an instance of the uPortal framework[24] which offers interoperability with other Virtual Research and Virtual Learning Environments and allows us to reuse JSR-168 portlets from other projects whilst making our components easier for others to reuse (JSR-168 portlet containers have been used by a number of other VRE pilot projects).[25] The uPortal open source software, developed by a consortium of universities, additionally allows us to provide a framework that can be customized directly by users, who will be able to compile their own interfaces using portlets which offer the tools and services relevant to their own research. There are also newer standards for integrating components within a web environment, the most significant open effort being Google's gadget/OpenSocial initiative.[26] Future development of the VRE-SDM project is likely to include extending the VRE environment to support components built to these standards as well as JSR-168.

This means that in the long term the VRE will be able to provide tools to researchers across the humanities. Some, such as the viewing and annotation tools, will be relevant to the broadest range of scholars, while other more specialist tools can be added by individual users or groups as and when needed. For ancient documentary specialists the VRE will be an environment which emulates the current decipherment process, with the extra benefits that scholars will be

---

23   A.K. Bowman, R.S.O. Tomlin and K.A. Worp, '*Emptio bovis Frisica*: the "Frisian Ox Sale" reconsidered', *JRS* 99 (2009): 156–70.

24   uPortal, <http://www.jasig.org/uportal>.

25   JSR 168 (Java Specification Request 168 Portlet Specification) provides a specification for the development of components for Java portal servers: <http://developers.sun.com/portalserver/reference/techart/jsr168/pb_whitepaper.pdf>.

26   Google OpenSocial, <http://code.google.com/apis/opensocial/>.

able to conduct real-time meetings and to annotate digitized texts and images. Additionally, the VRE will offer an area within which other more specific tools may be deployed, such as those from the eSAD project (to aid the decipherment of degraded documentary texts through character recognition and decision support software), along with the functionality to search across specific datasets such as the *Lexicon of Greek Personal Names*, the *Vindolanda Tablets Online* texts, and other relevant resources. This approach of adding elements relevant to the individual scholar or specialism creates a customized workbench reworkable and reusable across the humanities.

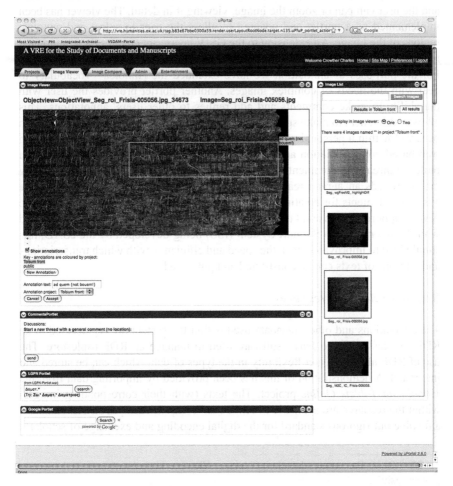

Figure 5.4   VRE interface: The Tolsum tablet with annotations

Source: © Centre for the Study of Ancient Documents.

Document viewing and annotation

One of the integral parts of the VRE for the Study of Documents and Manuscripts for all users is a superior image viewer which can handle high-resolution images and can download images at high speed over the web. The default viewer in the VRE-SDM has been developed from the Giant Scalable Image Viewer (GSIV) open source code.[27] This viewer allows large, high-resolution scans typical for digitized views of documents and manuscripts to be viewed in a web browser. By splitting the original image up into tiles and using javascript within the browser, only those parts of the image necessary to show the current view are downloaded and the user can pan or zoom the image, viewing it in detail. The viewer has been implemented as a portlet and adapted to allow the user to select and annotate regions of the image. An extension to the GSIV javascript enables these annotated regions to be displayed as a highlighted region overlaid onto the tiled image. For the purposes of annotation we have extended the Annotea[28] vocabulary to deal with the needs of complex images. Another portlet provides the user with the ability to make comments and add replies to other users' annotations. This allows researchers to make specific comments on areas of the text which can then be saved within a personal workspace or shared with other investigators through web-based communication and collaboration tools. The users of the system can build up threads of comments and annotations, recording their workings as they move towards an agreed reading. With this functionality embedded within the VRE, the elements for creating a working edition marked up in standard EpiDoc XML, supported by an audit trail of readings, are largely in place. When combined with the Interpretation Support System (ISS) being developed by the eSAD, this should lead to improvements in the speed and efficiency with which transcriptions and editions of texts can be constituted and published.

Integrating electronic resources

The annotations and other metadata used within the system are represented in an RDF format[29] with the Jena[30] software used to manage an RDF triplestore. The use of RDF allows greater flexibility in the types of data which can be stored and integrated. A demonstration of this has been provided by importing data from the *Vindolanda Tablets Online* project. The texts (with their corresponding images) within the resource are available as XML marked up to the EpiDoc TEI standard, a flexible but rigorous standard for the digital encoding and exchange of scholarly

---

27   GSIV Panoramic JavaScript Image Viewer, <http://www.mojavelinux.com/projects/gsiv/>.

28   Annotea Project, <http://www.w3.org/2001/Annotea/>.

29   Resource Description Framework, <http://www.w3.org/RDF/>.

30   Jena is a Java API for creating and manipulating RDF representations, <http://jena.sourceforge.net/>.

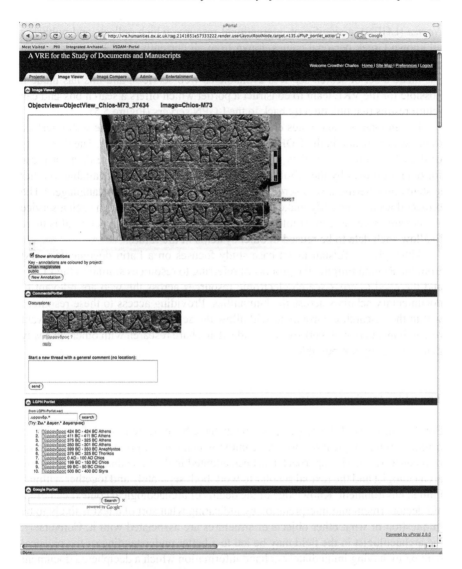

Figure 5.5   VRE interface: Annotated list of magistrates' names from Chios (SEG 27, 381) linked to an LGPN database query

Source: © Centre for the Study of Ancient Documents.

editions of ancient texts.[31] Because the texts are marked up in this way, it is a relatively simple process to extract the known readings of the images and import them into the RDF triplestore for scholars to use within the VRE. The *Lexicon of Greek Personal*

_____

31   EPIDOC Epigraphic Documents in TEI XML, <http://epidoc.sourceforge.net/>.

Names (LGPN), a significant international resource which collects and publishes all known Greek personal names drawn from all currently available sources from specific geographical regions,[32] is also now storing entries in TEI XML. The project has made a set of search services available as web services, and this has made it possible for the VRE team to construct a portlet which offers a search box and can return results that link directly back to the LGPN servers (Figure 5.5).

The annotations and notes created by users interacting with the web interface to the system reside in the RDF store on the VRE server hardware. The flexibility of the RDF store used makes it quite simple both to export these data for reuse for other purposes by the scholar and to make the data directly available to other systems by offering a web service based on the SPARQL query language.[33] The project does not currently make raw data publicly available though such a service – there are as yet no compatible systems to consume it – but the potential is there to allow such data to be reused in other systems in the future.

Although the Tolsum tablet case study focuses on a Latin documentary text from the Roman Empire, the process of referring to resources similar to the LGPN and the need to cross-search electronic resources across the web are relevant to documentary scholars across the humanities. Providing access to these resources within the research environment will allow the scholar to draw together relevant research in a personal workspace or, indeed, to share research with others in a way that is currently not possible.

The wider (ancient) world

For the purposes of the project documents have been treated as artefacts with an original archaeological or physical context which can, in principle, be recovered or reconstructed. This approach has been adopted in the hope that it will allow the archaeologist and the textual scholar to work both separately and together within a unified environment. Knowledge of the details of archaeological context can often aid decipherment and interpretation by indicating what sort of a text is likely to be in question or what other objects or structures are associated with it. Conversely, the archaeologist in the field may be led to a better understanding of the physical context by having immediately at hand information which a deciphered document can offer. The importance of this point was underlined by the experience of one of the authors as a consultant to Oxford Archaeology during the rescue excavations at Zeugma in the Euphrates valley in 2000, when digital photographs and faxes of transcriptions of inscriptions were sent from the field to the Centre for the Study of Ancient Documents in Oxford as they were found; these were sufficient to allow preliminary transcriptions and identifications to be attempted at short notice, but were only a partial substitute for direct access to the contextual record; a site

---

32   The *Lexicon of Greek Personal Names*, <http://www.lgpn.ox.ac.uk/>.
33   SPARQL Query Language for RDF, <http://www.w3.org/TR/rdf-sparql-query/>.

visit was required late in the excavation season to secure the full context and one important text was recovered only as it was about to be backfilled.[34] Provision of a full range of resources, text-and-image databases, scholarly reference works and technical tools, in a way that makes them mutually interactive and accessible to communities of documentary specialists and archaeologists, will be a significant benefit of a successful VRE implementation.

To explore the possibilities for interoperability with archaeological Virtual Research Environments, the VRE-SDM team has collaborated with the Silchester Roman Town VRE project (VERA), based at the University of Reading, which has developed a sophisticated system for registering, tracking and analysing data recorded in the field to allow efficient recovery of information on any given artefact and its original context.[35] The collaboration has resulted in the creation of a pilot system (XDB-Arch) to allow the cross-database searching of archaeological data.[36] This involves the use of the Dublin Core for Collections standard[37] to describe groups of objects held by each collaborator (Vindolanda tablets in the case of Oxford, and objects within the Integrated Archaeological Database [IADB] at Reading). A search specified in CQL (the Common Query Language, a formal language based on the semantics of Z39.50,[38] used for representing queries to information retrieval systems such as digital libraries, bibliographic catalogues and museum collections) is then distributed to each database using the Tycho middleware[39] and the results combined to return to the user in one list. For the purposes of the XDB-Arch project the VREs are focusing on objects that might be of interest both to archaeologists and ancient documentary scholars in order to demonstrate the wider potential of VRE collaboration and cross-database searching.

At the same time, the VRE-SDM team has continued to work closely with the eSAD project to build and maintain links between tools designed specifically for the decipherment of ancient documents and the VRE through which these tools can be utilized alongside communication and annotation tools by a broader base of users. Collaboration with projects such as eSAD and VERA has helped to ensure not only that the VRE is relevant to the specific research needs of humanities scholars, but also that the experience of using the VRE will be as coherent and integrated as possible.

---

34   C. Crowther, 'Inscriptions of Antiochus I of Commagene and other epigraphical finds', *Zeugma: Interim Reports, JRA Supplement*, 51 (2003): 57–67.

35   The VERA project is described in Chapter 1 of this volume.

36   XDB-Arch, <http://xdb.vera.rdg.ac.uk/>.

37   Dublin Core Metadata Initiative, <http://dublincore.org/about/>.

38   Z39.50 is a standard protocol for computer-to-computer information retrieval, <http://www.loc.gov/z3950/agency/>.

39   Mark A. Baker and Matthew Grove, 'Tycho: A Wide-area Messaging Framework with an Integrated Virtual Registry', *The Journal of Supercomputing*, 42/2 (2007): 83–106.

Future Challenges

Within the scope of the funding cycle, the VRE for the Study of Documents and Manuscripts is expected only to reach a pilot level of implementation. As a result, there are inevitably challenges to be faced to ensure and encourage user uptake and to maintain continuing development. A first priority will be to continue to broaden the scope and appeal of the service to researchers across the humanities. The project has begun to explore the potential to extend the viewing and annotation capabilities of the system to a project led by Professor Kathryn Sutherland to digitize Jane Austen's fiction manuscripts ('Jane Austen's Holograph Fiction Manuscripts: A Digital and Print Resource'). As the VRE team learns more from the XDB-Arch project and from the collaboration with the LGPN, it will be better equipped to consider similar work in fields across the humanities and to work with individual projects to meet their growing and varied needs. The work on the XDB-Arch project offers the potential to scale up and to allow the connection of multiple resources. It remains to be seen whether the current design is capable of meeting the needs of this wide range of other projects or whether it will need to be extended to do so. Even if the XDB metadata schemas are extended to cope with all of these resources, it will of course remain a challenge to gain widespread deployment among archaeological and classical resources.

It is therefore essential that the VRE provides both tools and standards that can be made use of by projects across the humanities, and also that it provides the impetus for both smaller projects and larger electronic resources to present their own tools and services for reuse within the environment. For this to be possible, projects will need to consider how they can work together to make use of compatible standards such as JSR-168 and the OpenSocial/Google gadget API. This would allow an interface to be deployed directly within the VRE framework to enable users to add these components into their workspace. It may be that other projects create separate portlet versions of their services, or they may choose to base their services on portlets in the first place, in which case they would have the opportunity to reuse VRE-SDM and other portlets within their own sites. The challenge for the VRE team, then, is to persuade others through successful demonstration and collaboration with projects such as eSAD and the LGPN that the VRE is a useful and integral part of the researcher's toolbox and as such a worthy environment through which to provide tools and services. The case study of the Tolsum tablet, described above, emphasizes that the use of these tools in such an environment is not merely a gain in efficiency of access to research resources but a real advance in our ability to improve both the quality of our data and the analysis and interpretation of our primary sources.[40] Some of the technical challenges offered by a particular set of data in a specific research field (ancient

---

40   See H. Roued Olsen et al. (2009) *Towards an Interpretation Support System for Reading Ancient Documents*, Digital Humanities Conference paper. Abstract at <http://www.mith2.umd.edu/dh09/?page_id=99> and <http://esad.classics.ox.ac.uk>.

documents) have been addressed with some success. Further opportunities for improvement will certainly continue to be offered by developing technologies and by communal recognition of the potential value of such an environment across a wide range of humanities research.

Chapter 6

One Era's Nonsense, Another's Norm: Diachronic Study of Greek and the Computer

Notis Toufexis

This chapter sets out to explore how and why digital editions of texts or text-versions could facilitate a truly diachronic study of the Greek language. It points out shortcomings of existing digital infrastructure and argues in favour of a general shift of focus towards linguistic analysis of transmitted texts with the help of electronic corpora that primarily model medieval manuscripts rather than modern editions.[1]

In April 1994 the following question was submitted to the Byzans-l mailing list:

> I'm currently performing some minor but tricky (to me at least) editing for a draft of the Psalms of Solomon. I can handle the Koine in which the Greek text was written, but the manuscript tradition ranges to the fourteenth century, and the editor/commentator wants all forms included in the index, even 'nonsense words'. Problem is, one era's nonsense is another's orthography, it would seem. Can anyone direct me to a good source for a Medieval Greek grammar and/or lexicon, especially one that accounts for changes in morphology from Classical to Medieval Greek?[2]

Many, if not all, medievalists working with Greek materials must have come across such questions when Classicists or other researchers with a Classics background, more by chance than choice presumably, have to study later texts written in registers substantially different from Classical or Koine Greek. Such questions are of course legitimate since not every Classicist can be expected to be interested in the historic development of Greek after Late Antiquity or develop an agenda of diachronic study of Greek. As in the above example most Classicists or late antique scholars will dare to enter and explore the maze of non-standardized Medieval Greek linguistic varieties only if there is some underlying reason related to the manuscript tradition of the specific text they are studying.

---

1 I am indebted to Gabriel Bodard and Simon Mahony for their suggestions in matters of style and to the reviewers for their insightful comments.

2 <http://www.uni-heidelberg.de/subject/hd/fak7/hist/o1/logs/byzans-l/log. started940401/mail-34.html> (accessed January 2008).

This comes as no surprise. 'Greek' as a linguistic label covers a span of almost three millennia. It is demanding (but not impossible) to obtain an overview of the linguistic developments of Greek in the whole period from the eighth century BC until the present day.[3] The situation becomes more complicated due to the segmentation of Greek in several periods of its history in more than one dialect with diachronically changing geographical distribution. Furthermore, literary registers of Greek always tended towards mixtures of different linguistic features, either from different dialects as in the *Kunstsprache* of the Homeric poems or from different registers (learned and vernacular) in the Medieval period.

A further difficulty in accessing the exact linguistic parameters of texts written in Greek is the existence of diglossia for long periods in the history of Greek. Diglossia is a sociolinguistic situation in which a learned variety is superposed upon the everyday vernacular and replaces it in most formal functions;[4] it has led to several puristic movements starting from the Hellenistic period right through to the nineteenth century that considered only Classical Greek (or, to be precise, what was understood as Classical Greek at each time) as 'proper' Greek worthy of being used in writing; the spoken vernacular was, as a consequence, generally neglected, especially in Medieval times.[5] During such periods Classical Greek texts are studied, copied and edited, and their linguistic style is emulated by authors who consider knowledge of Classical Greek as a constituting factor of their scholarly activity and even their own personality.[6] As Michael Jeffreys puts it:

> A breakdown in the link between spoken and written Greek was first seriously threatened around the time of Christ, when the Atticist movement introduced a *diglossia* which gradually came to dominance in writing … Through most

---

3 For such an overview see Geoffrey Horrocks, *Greek: A History of the Language and its Speakers* (Oxford, 2010). A research project at the University of Cambridge has set out to produce a 'Reference Grammar of Medieval and Early Modern Greek'. The grammar is expected to be published in 2011. For more information on the project see <http://www.mml.cam.ac.uk/greek/grammarofmedievalgreek> (accessed July 2009).

4 For diglossia in general see Alan Hudson, 'Outline of a Theory of Diglossia', *International Journal of the Sociology of Language*, 157 (2002): 1–48 and all other articles in this journal volume dedicated to the study of diglossia; for diglossia in the time of the Gospels, see Stanley E. Porter, *Diglossia and Other Topics in New Testament Linguistics* (Sheffield, 2000); for diglossia in Medieval Greek see Notis Toufexis, 'Diglossia and Register Variation in Medieval Greek', *Byzantine and Modern Greek Studies*, 32:2 (2008): 203–17.

5 For a general overview of the consequences of diglossia to the development of Greek, see Robert Browning, 'Greek Diglossia Yesterday and Today', *International Journal of the Sociology of Language*, 35 (1982): 49–68.

6 On how knowledge of Classical Greek is a defining characteristic of the group of 'literate individuals' in Late Byzantium see Franz H. Tinnefeld and Klaus Matschke, *Die Gesellschaft im späten Byzanz: Gruppen, Strukturen und Lebensformen* (Cologne-Weimar-Vienna, 2001).

Byzantine centuries the model frameworks for writing were two, the Attic dialect of the fourth century B.C. (and its textbooks) and the Biblical *Koine*. Writers positioned themselves in relation to these past forms, with more or less concessions, conscious or not, to their spoken language.[7]

Because of diglossia, already present in the Hellenistic period and throughout the Middle Ages in the Greek-speaking world, speakers of Greek developed in general an attitude of refusal towards their native language, which was not considered worth cultivating on its own. Several registers verging on Classical Greek were used for different literary purposes; a literary register closer to the vernacular appears only from the twelfth century onwards.[8] Rhetoric, education, literacy and functional literacy as well as audience design are factors that play a major role in shaping the linguistic form of most texts written in Greek in all times.[9]

Perhaps in reflection of this attitude, Medieval Greek literature is conventionally thought of as consisting of two branches: works written in learned language as opposed to works written in registers closer to the vernacular.[10] Most works considered as major literary achievements written in Greek during Medieval times are composed in registers differing substantially from what must have been the spoken language of the time and are normally full of Classical or biblical quotations and allusions.[11] For the linguistic study of such literature in learned language one relies on available handbooks for Classical and Koine Greek; on top of that, it is certainly advantageous to obtain a general awareness of idiomatic expressions and conventions developed by authors in the Medieval period, who at times follow idiosyncratic rules.[12]

---

7   Michael Jeffreys, 'The Silent Millennium: Thoughts on the Evidence for Spoken Greek between the Last Papyri and Cretan Drama', in Costas N. Constantinides (ed.), *ΦΙΛΛΕΛΗΝ. Studies in Honour of Robert Browning* (Venice, 1996), p. 133.

8   For details see Michael Jeffreys, 'The Literary Emergence of Vernacular Greek', *Mosaic*, 8:4 (1975): 171–93 and Martin Hinterberger, 'How Should We Define Vernacular Literature?', in *Unlocking the Potential of Texts: Interdisciplinary Perspectives on Medieval Greek* (Centre for Research in the Arts, Social Sciences, and Humanities, University of Cambridge, 2006), <http://www.mml.cam.ac.uk/greek/grammarofmedievalgreek/unlocking /html/Hinterberger.html> (accessed July 2009).

9   For the interplay of such factors in the development of medieval registers under diglossia, see Toufexis, 'Diglossia', 210–15; see also Erich Trapp, 'Learned and Vernacular Literature in Byzantium: Dichotomy or Symbiosis?', *Dumbarton Oaks Papers*, 47 (1993): 115–29; Hans Eideneier, *Von Rhapsodie Zu Rap: Aspekte der griechischen Sprachgeschichte von Homer bis heute* (Tübingen, 1999); Hinterberger, 'How Should We Define'.

10   See Toufexis, 'Diglossia', 203–206 with more bibliography on this issue.

11   Even those conventionally attributed to 'vernacular' literature. The distance between vernacular written literary registers and the actual spoken language is considerable and becomes smaller only towards the Early Modern period (around the sixteenth and seventeenth centuries).

12   For an argumentation towards the need of a 'genuine' grammar of Byzantine Greek see Staffan Wahlgren, 'Towards a Grammar of Byzantine Greek', *Symbolae Osloenses*, 77

One last factor that has to be taken into account when discussing issues pertaining to the study of Greek from a diachronic perspective is ideology. Ideology, in the sense of a biased interpretation of linguistic features in favour or against a predefined system of ideas, can affect choices made by scholars at all levels of their involvement with language. Editors may change the linguistic form of a text in search of readings compatible with what they consider authorial intention or for other reasons against the evidence provided by manuscript witnesses.[13] Other editors embark on a quest for an archetype in the true belief that they can reconstruct lost versions of ancient texts.[14]

The effect of ideology on the description and interpretation of linguistic facts cannot be underestimated. As a matter of fact, Greek language and (Modern Greek) national identity are, at least from the eighteenth century onwards, intertwined concepts.[15] It is not surprising, therefore, that relativism as an ideology of language has been identified as a factor that 'informs and forms collective linguistic practices' with particular reference to language debates in contemporary Greece.[16] Under such circumstances editors of texts and even linguists might find it difficult to resist following specific generalities about, for example, the language of a specific period that have been formulated under the pressure of specific dominant ideological movements. The wildly optimistic interpretation of Medieval vernacular literature as an early stage of Modern Greek literature or evidence of a Modern Greek national identity, which has been formulated in the context of the Modern Greek search for ancestry can be seen as such a characteristic example.[17]

(2002): 201–204. On how technology can assist in a collective effort to translate a Byzantine encyclopaedia written in a 'dialect somewhere between the Classical Greek of the fifth and fourth centuries BC and native language of the tenth century AD', see Anne Mahoney, 'Tachypedia Byzantina: The Suda On Line as Collaborative Encyclopaedia', *Digital Humanities Quarterly*, 3:1 (2009), paragraph 10, available: <http://www.digitalhumanities.org/dhq/vol/003/1/000025.html> (accessed March 2009).

13   For examples from the domain of Medieval Greek see Io Manolessou, 'On Historical Linguistics, Linguistic Variation and Medieval Greek', *Byzantine and Modern Greek Studies*, 32:1 (2008): 69–71.

14   For a brief but comprehensive assessment of the so-called stemmatic method, see Michael D. Reeve, 'Stemmatic Method: "Qualcosa che non funziona?"', in Peter Ganz (ed.), *The Role of the Book in Medieval Culture*, Proceedings of the Oxford International Symposium. 26 September–1 October 1982 (Turnhout 1986), pp. 57–69. See also here below, footnotes 42 and 49.

15   See Peter Mackridge, *Language and National Identity in Greece, 1766–1976* (Oxford, 2009).

16   See Spyros Moschonas, 'Relativism in Language Ideology: On Greece's Latest Language Issues', *Journal of Modern Greek Studies*, 22 (2004): 194 and Γλώσσα και Ιδεολογία (Athens, 2005).

17   For an overview of the problems associated with the study and interpretation of Medieval Greek vernacular literature see the article of Panagiotis Agapitos, 'SO Debate Genre, Structure and Poetics in the Byzantine Vernacular Romances of Love', *Symbolae*

Whatever the pitfalls might be for a truly diachronic study of the Greek language, 'Greek offers a rare opportunity, among the world's languages, to study language change over more than 3,000 years of continuous recorded tradition ...; strangely, this opportunity has often been ignored'.[18] Since especially old stages of Greek are well studied and documented, the emergence of new forms that alternate with and eventually replace older forms in later texts can easily be observed across the centuries.[19] Those studying Classical Greek thus have the rare opportunity (for a 'dead' language) to find out what happens next, 'how the story ends – although in this case it is still going on'.[20]

Because of the obvious lack of native speakers, all historical linguistic research and in our case the exploration of the development of Greek after the Classical era – this period considered as the beginning of the story also because of its cultural significance – can only be achieved through the study of available texts.[21] In a modern framework of research such study is performed optimally with the use of a controlled corpus of written texts, preferably available in electronic form.[22] In putting a corpus together one must invariably take into consideration questions drawn up in the philological tradition:

> What is a text? Which text do we choose when there are several versions of the same text? What history does a text have? How does a text relate to other texts? Is it localizable? Is it a product of a specific speech community or a discourse

---

Osloenses, 79:1 (2004): 7–101. On how Standard Modern Greek has been influenced by relativism, see Moschonas, 'Relativism', 176–7.

18   David Holton and Io Manolessou, 'Medieval and Early Modern Greek', in Willem F. Bakker (ed.), *Companion to the Ancient Greek Language* (Oxford, in print).

19   It is interesting, at least from a semiological point of view, that terminology referring to the Greek language differs from that of other European languages. The contemporary form of the language is conventionally called 'Modern', the adjective 'Old' is not used for reference to older stages of the language (as for instance in 'Old English') (see Toufexis, 'Diglossia', 206): the really old stage of Greek (compared to English or other European languages) is either not labelled at all or is called 'Classical' or 'Ancient'.

20   Holton and Manolessou, 'Medieval and Early Modern Greek'.

21   On how historical linguistics deals with the problem of the skewed nature of the data see Manolessou, 'On Historical Linguistics', 64–5.

22   For a contemporary discussion of the pros and cons of the use of electronic corpora in some aspects of historical linguistics, see Anneli Meurman-Solin, 'Structured Text Corpora in the Study of Language Variation and Change', *Literary and Linguistic Computing*, 16:1 (2001): 5–27. For a comprehensive account of the use of electronic corpora in the study of Romance languages see Claus D. Pusch, Johannes Kabatek, and Wolfgang Raible, *Romanistische Korpuslinguistik II*, 2005, <http://www.corpora-romanica. net/publications_e.htm#korpuslinguistik_2> (accessed July 2009). For a view on how philologists under the influence of technology are increasingly becoming 'corpus editors', see Greg Crane and Jeffrey A. Rydberg-Cox, 'New Technology and New Roles: The Need for "Corpus Editors"', in *Proceedings of the fifth ACM conference on Digital Libraries* (New York, 2000), pp. 252–3.

community, in other words, can it function as evidence of a dialect, or does it reflect the language use of, for instance, a professional group or a literary genre? Is it a translation? To these simple questions there are no simple answers.

In digitizing texts and including them in large databases we may multiply erroneous interpretations if we neglect careful examination of what the texts actually are.[23]

One such large database of Greek texts, the *Thesaurus Linguae Graecae* (TLG), is considered by many as 'a prime example of how a humanities discipline has changed fundamentally for the better in consequence of the acceptance of technology'.[24] The TLG's goal is 'to create a comprehensive digital library of Greek literature from antiquity to the present era'. Comprising currently more than a hundred million words, it provides access to 2,314 authors and 9,958 works and is 'constantly updated and improved with new features and texts'.[25]

The TLG was designed in 1972 as a digital library of Classical Greek texts and this legacy still dictates most aspects of its architecture and design.[26] A single modern edition is used in order to create the electronic version of each 'work' included in the TLG corpus. Newer editions of the same work merely substitute old ones, a practice reminiscent of the use of 'standard editions' in Classical studies.[27] The choice of edition invariably determines the attributes of each 'work' (as far as its linguistic form, length or any other features are concerned).

In the absence of detailed contextualization information accompanying the online version of each text, the user who wishes to check the reliability of a given edition (if, for instance, it uses all extant manuscripts of a text or not) has to refer to the printed edition or other handbooks. The same applies to any attempt to put search results obtained by the TLG within the wider context of a literary genre or a historical period. The TLG assumes in a sense that its users have a broad knowledge of Greek literature and language of all historical periods and are capable of contextualizing each search result on their own. One can assume that this must have been the case for as long as the TLG covered only Classical Greek texts: by expanding to post-Classical and Medieval periods the TLG has made more primary textual data available to its users but made, at the same time, the

---

23   Meurman-Solin, 'Structured Text Corpora', 18–19.

24   This to some extent optimistic assessment of the TLG belongs to Theodore Brunner, first director of the TLG, and is quoted by Edward Shreeves, 'Between the Visionaries and the Luddites: Collection Development and Electronic Resources in the Humanities', *Library Trends*, 40 (1992): 593.

25   <http://www.tlg.uci.edu/about> (accessed April 2009).

26   For a full account of the development of the TLG see <http://www.tlg.uci.edu/about/history.php> (accessed April 2009).

27   See Gregory Crane, David Bamman, and Alison Jones, 'ePhilology: When the Books Talk to Their Readers', in Ray Siemens and Susan Schreibman (eds), *A Companion to Digital Literary Studies* (Oxford, 2008), <http://www.digitalhumanities.org/companionDLS/> (accessed March 2009).

interpretation of search results a more demanding and time-consuming exercise for many of its users.

Nevertheless, the TLG is an everyday tool in teaching and research of invaluable importance both for Classics and all other humanities disciplines that use texts written in Greek:

> Classicists have become accustomed to scanning wide swathes of Greek and Latin literature, with full professors today who have never known a world without searchable texts. Many take for granted this core infrastructure and, when asked, admit that these tools have had far more impact upon the questions that they ask and the research that they conduct than they readily articulate. An analysis of primary source citations in the classics journals of JSTOR would give us a better appreciation of the impact which these collections have had upon published scholarship.[28]

Since in recent years the TLG has expanded considerably also in the area of Medieval Greek texts (including monastic documents from the Athos monasteries) this impact has become even more significant in other related disciplines (such as Byzantine and Medieval Greek studies). Such a large corpus of texts available online has without doubt promoted research in the domain of Greek historical linguistics. While it is true that diachronic analysis of linguistic features of Greek is much easier with the use of the TLG than without it, a large searchable database of Greek texts does not automatically solve all problems.

Put simply, historical linguistics describes, examines and evaluates the appearance of new – that is changed – linguistic forms next to old (unchanged) ones in the same text or in texts of the same date and/or geographical provenance. This interplay of old and new forms can be interpreted as evidence of language change and forms the basis of linguistic description and analysis. Let us briefly examine one particular example, the passage from the inflected Ancient Greek active participle to the uninflected Modern Greek active gerund.[29] We can already observe an established breach in the 'classical norms' for the use of participles in the Hellenistic period[30] and concrete signs of inflectional erosion with neuter nom./acc. singular forms ending in [-onta] instead of [-on] from around the fourth

---

28   Crane et al., 'ePhilology'.

29   See Io Manolessou, 'From Participles to Gerunds', in Melita Stavrou and Arhonto Terzi (eds), *Advances in Greek Generative Syntax: In Honor of Dimitra Theophanopoulou-Kontou* (Amsterdam, 2005), pp. 241–83. Manolessou's paper offers a synchronic morphological and syntactic description of this development in all periods of Greek and can be seen as a paradigmatic example of the kind of historic linguistic research that makes serious use of a diachronic corpus of Greek like the TLG.

30   For detail, see Manolessou, 'From Participles', p. 246.

century AD.[31] Innovative and 'classical' forms appear as variant readings in texts from the Late post-Classical/Early Medieval period (fourth–sixth century AD):

> the text of the critical edition of the Life of St. John the Almsgiver, 6th c. (Gelzer, 1893) prints 6 cases of the neuter participle with the new -onta ending ... and there are alternative readings in -onta in 3 more cases, to be spotted only by checking the apparatus (at 50.6, 87.22 and 97.15). However, the manuscript tradition (the 6mss., ABCDEF, used in the edition) is unanimous in none of these eight cases: three appear only in A, two only in C, one only in E, one in ACEF and one in ABCE. It is thus impossible to guess which and how many of those stood in the original text, and which are readings introduced by a later copyist.[32]

Compared to the modern edition, the linguistic picture one obtains for that particular case from medieval manuscripts is far more complicated. A scribe operating within a diglossic speech community, as described above, may unconsciously use new forms of the language and not the old forms found in the manuscript he is copying. A strong preference for old forms can also be seen as a stylistic choice, a conscious effort to elevate the register of the text. A modern editor may, however, choose to homogenize in his edition variant linguistic forms found in the manuscripts in the belief that this must have been the actual language used by the author.

It is evident, in my view, that a large corpus of Greek texts can only be used meaningfully in historical linguistic research if the following question is always kept in mind:

> How ... are we to distinguish 'variation' in Medieval Greek due to language change, from variation due to other factors? This question has been posed before by Browning as the necessity 'to distinguish between incidental imitations of purist Greek and real alternatives co-existing in the spoken tongue' and by Joseph under the guise of 'textual authenticity' (i.e., 'whether a feature found in a given text or corpus corresponds in some way to a linguistically real and linguistically significant generalization about the language and about its speakers' competence', in contrast to an inauthentic feature, 'which would have no basis in actual usage and would instead be an artificial aspect of the language of a given text').[33]

---

31   For examples and interpretation of this development see ibid., pp. 46–247.

32   Ibid., p. 247. The edition quoted here is Heinrich Gelzer (ed.), *Leontios' von Neapolis Leben des heiligen Iohannes des barmherzigen Erzbischofs von Alexandrien* (Freiburg i. B., 1893).

33   Manolessou, 'On Historical Linguistics', 72. The references quoted in this passage are Robert Browning, *Medieval and Modern Greek* (Cambridge, 1983), 11 and Brian D. Joseph, 'Textual Authenticity: Evidence from Medieval Greek', in Susan C. Herring, Pieter

Note that this dilemma does not only exist for Medieval Greek. Epigraphic and other evidence suggests that variation already existed in Classical Greek and that the rigid rules of Classical Greek morphology and syntax formulated by modern grammarians do not reflect actual language use by authors and speakers at the time. Recent linguistic research of Classical Greek registers has led to the conclusion that 'it is no longer possible to regard classical Attic as the monolithic monument of clarity, beauty and correct usage that both school grammars and much scholarly research makes of it'.[34]

Historical linguistics has developed an advanced methodology that allows researchers to formulate convincing answers to these and similar questions.[35] A central position in this methodology is occupied by the need to concentrate research and draw evidence from as many extant (manuscript) witnesses as possible. For the historical linguist

> [t]he manuscript is a concrete written speech act, a setting down of a linguistic message at a specific time in a specific place; it is the only one accessible to the linguist, and everything else is conjecture, however informed. This is especially true of cases where there is a distance between the time of supposed 'first composition' and the extant copy. This does not mean that we cannot use such texts as evidence for earlier states of language than the time they were copied; they can be so used, but only as a 'second-best' option, and only after comparative verification. And of course the above requirement, direct access to the manuscript, has as its presupposition that the linguist possesses the necessary philological skills for the 'decipherment' of an otherwise potentially confusing, misleading and incomprehensible text.[36]

Emendation, from the perspective of the critical editor, a necessary and fruitful exercise towards the aim of restoring ancient texts, is rejected by historical linguistics on the grounds that it falsifies the record and does not always depend on linguistically controlled arguments.[37] That a total refusal of emendation as a methodological practice cannot however be accepted as a general rule is evident by emendations in modern critical editions that have been confirmed by the later emergence of papyrological or other manuscript evidence.

---

van Reenen and Lene Schøsler (eds), *Textual Parameters in Older Languages* (Amsterdam, 2000): 309.

34   Jerker Blomquist, Review of Andreas Willi, *The Languages of Aristophanes. Aspects of Linguistic Variation in Classical Attic Greek* (Oxford, 2003), in *Bryn Mawr Classical Review*, 4 June 2004. Willi's book is an exemplary linguistic study of different Classical Greek registers based on available textual data.

35   For a comprehensive overview see Brian D. Joseph and Richard D. Janda (eds), *The Handbook of Historical Linguistics* (Oxford, 2003).

36   Manolessou, 'On Historical Linguistics', 67.

37   Roger Lass, *Historical Linguistics and Language Change* (Cambridge, 1997), 100.

What becomes obvious is that there exists a mismatch or a conflict of interest between the needs of the historical linguist, as described in the above passage, and those of the philologist who is primarily interested in studying all aspects of a specific text (and not only its language) and therefore is well served with a critical edition of a single text. The editor who is preparing a critical edition typically transcribes or collates all extant manuscripts of the text he is editing but presents *one* text to the reader, with variant readings in a so-called *apparatus criticus*. This conflict is strengthened by the general tendency of modern critical editing of ancient texts not to burden the apparatus 'by false and trivial reading and those useless for the constitution of the text'.[38]

A reading may of course be 'false' according to the norms governing language use of the period the text belongs to (and to the editor's understanding of how these rules apply to the text in question); what could or should not be excluded a priori is the possibility that such a 'mistake', however trivial, may also represent an intermediate stage towards a new development or an insecurity on the part of a manuscript scribe brought on by language change in his time. Since most editors of ancient texts are familiar only with the grammar of the period their text belongs to, information relevant to the study of later stages of the language may be lost if variants are concealed from the apparatus criticus, especially if the text (or the copy of the text) is dated in a period where language change has taken place.[39]

A particularly lucid example of a rather minimal but significant phonological language change that is commonly excluded from the apparatus criticus of most editions is the addition of an analogical /n/ to the original accusative singular of masculine and feminine nouns of the third declension in -a, that begun in Roman times and eventually led (together with other parallel developments) to the merger of the first and third noun declension in post-Classical times.[40] This change is documented almost exclusively with the help of evidence taken from texts like inscriptions or papyri that are normally edited diplomatically. In most critical editions of texts from relevant periods such variants are not included in the apparatus criticus (for obvious reasons of economy of space) and are only mentioned, if at all, in the introduction.

A technology-based approach can help us resolve this conflict: in a digital environment 'economy of space' is no longer an issue. By lifting the constraints

---

38   Georg Luck, 'Textual Criticism Today', *The American Journal of Philology*, 102:2 (1981): 164–94, reflecting the predominant methodology of textual criticism at the time.

39   More research is needed on the evaluation of variable readings and their relevance for the study of language change in the case of texts from the Classical era. The common hypothesis is that knowledge of Classical grammar and/or faithful copy of the source manuscript would allow most copyists to avoid such mistakes and not introduce changed forms in the text. On the other hand, most, if not all, manuscript scribes of the Medieval period are native speakers of Greek and may be influenced by their native tongue while copying a text written in Classical Greek.

40   For details of these developments see Horrocks, *Greek*, pp. 286–88.

of printed editions, a digital edition can serve the needs of both philologists and historical linguistics (or for that matter any other scholar who has an interest in approaching ancient texts).[41] A 'plural' representation of ancient texts in digital form, especially those transmitted in 'fluid' form,[42] is today a perfectly viable alternative to a printed edition. Only a few years ago such a digital endeavour seemed technologically impossible or something reserved for the very few computer-literate editors.

With the emergence of well-documented and widely used standards like the TEI (<http://www.tei-c.org>), every editor has at his disposal a versatile tool for the representation of texts in digital form. In matters of accessibility, scale, media, hypertext, updates, and iterative research and transparency digital editions are an equal if not better alternative to printed editions.[43] It is in principle now possible to create document-based digital critical editions including both main texts and their paratexts (like scholia or other annotations) as they appear in different single sources.[44]

Grid computing promises advances in the ability to store and make accessible large collections of digital items of heterogeneous nature (such as digital images of manuscripts or other witnesses, digital manuscript transcriptions and digital editions of texts based on many manuscripts); if we adopt an optimistic stance, we should be able to create a new generation of digital resources or services that adapts to the needs of users and expands accordingly.[45] Such new resources

---

41 For the use of manuscripts in the study of literature or history see Michael D. Reeve, '*Elimination codicum descriptorum:* A Methodological Problem', in John N. Grant (ed.), *Editing Greek and Latin Texts*, Papers given at the Twenty-Third Annual Conference on Editorial Problems, University of Toronto 6–7 November 1987 (New York, 1989), pp. 8–9.

42 For a discussion of fluid forms of transmission see Leighton D. Reynolds, and Nigel G. Wilson, *Scribes and Scholars. A Guide to the Transmission of Greek and Latin Literature* (Oxford, 1968), 234–7.

43 See Gabriel Bodard, 'The Inscriptions of Aphrodisias as Electronic Publication: A User's Perspective and a Proposed Paradigm', *Digital Medievalist*, 4 (2008), <http://www. digitalmedievalist.org/journal/4/bodard/> (accessed March 2009).

44 See Paolo Monella, 'Towards a Digital Model to Edit the Different Paratextuality Levels within a Textual Tradition', *Digital Medievalist*, 4 (2008), <http://www. digitalmedievalist.org/journal/4/monella/> (accessed March 2009).

45 Gregory Crane et al., 'Beyond Digital Incunabula: Modelling the Next Generation of Digital Libraries', in J. Gonzalo, C. Thanos, M.F. Verdejo and R.C. Carrasco (eds), *Research and Advanced Technology for Digital Libraries* (Berlin-Heidelberg 2006), pp. 353–66, <http://dx.doi.org/10.1007/11863878_30> (accessed March 2009); Gregory Crane, David A. Smith, and Clifford E. Wulfman, 'Building a Hypertextual Digital Library in the Humanities: A Case Study on London', in *Proceedings of the 1st ACM/IEEE-CS Joint Conference on Digital Libraries* (Roanoke, VA: 2001), pp. 426–34, available: <http:// portal.acm.org/citation.cfm?id=379437.379756> (accessed March 2009); Gregory Crane et al., 'ePhilology'.

could and should also include digital items (such as transcriptions or collations of manuscripts in digital form or even digital facsimiles of manuscripts) that are by-products of printed editions, traditionally not made available to the reader at all.[46]

The discussion until now can be aptly summarized by quoting Peter Robinson's five propositions about the nature of editorial work in the digital medium:

1. The use of computer technology in the making of a particular edition takes place in a particular research context.
2. A digital edition should be based on full-text transcription of original texts into electronic form, and this transcription should be based on explicit principles.
3. The use of computer-assisted analytic methods may restore historical criticism of large textual traditions as a central aim for scholarly editors.
4. The new technology has the power to alter both how editors edit, and how readers read.
5. Editorial projects generating substantial quantities of transcribed text in electronic form should adopt, from the beginning, an open transcription policy.[47]

Such an approach would guarantee the creation of digital editions that can be used equally well by philologists and historical linguists. Electronic editing of Greek texts should take place within the research context of diachronic linguistic research (as sketched above), providing adequate access to primary manuscript material from any period of the Greek language. Philologists and historical linguistics could benefit mutually if they would engage in interdisciplinary research without reservations and fears of contact.[48]

Even if we cannot change the way critical editors edit their texts, it is still possible to enhance 'traditional' critical editions by transposing them to the digital medium; editorial choices become transparent by linking the apparatus criticus to the electronic text and – ideally – accompanying the electronic edition with high-quality digital images of the manuscript witnesses.[49]

---

46   See Espen S. Ore, 'Monkey Business – or What is an Edition', *Literary and Linguistic Computing*, 19:1 (2004): 35–44.

47   Peter Robinson, 'The Canterbury Tales and other Medieval Texts', in John Ushworth, Katherine O'Brien O'Keeffe, and Lou Burnard (eds), *Electronic Textual Editing* (New York, 2006), p. 74, <http://www.tei-c.org/About/Archive_new/ETE/Preview/robinson.xml> (accessed March 2009).

48   For such an approach see the work done by the 'Digital Editions for Corpus Linguistics (DECL)' project at the Research Unit for Variation, Contacts and Change in English, University of Helsinki, <http://www.helsinki.fi/varieng/domains/DECL.html> (accessed March 2009).

49   For such a pilot electronic edition see Christian Brockmann (ed.), *Galen. Kommentar zu Hippokrates, Über die Gelenke. Die Einleitung und die ersten sechs Kommentarabschnitte von Buch I*, Corpus Medicorum Graecorum/Latinorum, <http://pom.

However, digital editions should not be treated as a panacea for all shortcomings of Greek historical linguistic research. Rationalizing the apparatus criticus in printed editions was not just a consequence of pragmatic but also of epistemic considerations. Separating the charting of variants, the *recensio* in traditional philological terms, from the *emendatio* (correction of these readings that are considered 'false' according to the *recensio*) is considered by contemporary textual critics as Lachmann's great contribution to textual theory.[50] Followed by generations of textual critics, this methodology has contributed, on the epistemic side, to fostering at times a scholarly attitude according to which the modern reader, assisted by the editor, is better equipped than medieval scribes to preserve the 'true' form of ancient texts;[51] the editor is allowed to introduce emendations against the manuscript tradition based solely on his command of language, style or other relevant characteristics of the texts he is editing;[52] the reader of such editions is encouraged to look down on supposedly ignorant medieval scribes.[53]

As always, the truth lies somewhere in the middle. Emendations made by sensible editors who have studied in depth the cultural context and the language of the text they are editing are valid as long as they are clearly marked as such and their rationale is explained. Editing a text is an intellectual activity and emendations can and should be enjoyed by editors and their informed readers. In a digital edition there is room for several instances of one text or multiple versions of texts; it is at the editor's discretion to let readers choose which instance of the text they prefer to read and exploit for their purposes or to restrict navigation through instances of text based on specific criteria. A pluralistic digital edition encourages readers to

---

bbaw.de/cmg/> (accessed March 2009); for an electronic edition of a corpus of inscriptions with paradigmatic character see Joyce Reynolds, Charlotte Roueché and Gabriel Bodard, *Inscriptions of Aphrodisias* (2007), <http://insaph.kcl.ac.uk/iaph2007> (accessed March 2009). For a truly 'plural' edition of the New Testament, albeit in prototype form, see the 'New Testament Transcripts Prototype', <http://nttranscripts.uni-muenster.de/> (accessed March 2009).

50   David C. Greetham, *Textual Scholarship: An Introduction* (New York, 1994), 323. For a full description of the 'lachmanian orthodox' albeit in condensed form, see Paul Maas, *Textual Criticism*, trans. from the German by Barbara Flower (Oxford, 1958).

51   For an approach to critical editing that sees in textual tradition a transformational process and not merely a deterioration see Giorgio Pasquali, *Storia della tradizione e critica del testo* (Firenze, 1952) and Reynolds and Wilson, *Scribes and Scholars*.

52   For an extreme example of such an attitude from the Medieval Greek *War of Troy* see Manolessou, 'On Historical Linguistics', 69–71. On the characteristics of what constitutes a bad critic (from the perspective of textual editing of classical texts) see Luck, 'Textual Criticism Today', 168–70.

53   For an informative account of the development of critical editing from an epistemological viewpoint see Michael D. Reeve, 'Shared Innovations, Dichotomies and Evolution', in Anna Ferrari (ed.), *Filologia Classica e Filologia Romanza; Esperienze ecdotiche a confronto*, (Spoleto, 1998), pp. 429–505.

approach all transmitted texts equally, even if one text is highlighted among the many texts included in the edition.[54]

Traditional printed critical editions represent a specific model of representation of sometimes complex relationships among different manuscript witnesses mediated by the editor; the editor's choices and the different readings of the tradition are documented in the apparatus criticus, which constitutes an organic part of the edition. They are the product of long and erudite scholarship and in many cases succeed in restoring an ancient text in remarkable detail.

Electronic dissemination of such editions *without* the apparatus criticus in a single, seemingly homogeneous, large corpus like the TLG holds the danger of a monolithic approach to the interpretation of linguistic features that relies solely on choices made by editors and nothing else. As argued above, choices made by editors can be affected by many extra-linguistic parameters and should therefore always be subjected to comparative verification. Verification should not be performed solely on the basis of authoritative textbooks or other reference material since, especially in less studied areas like Medieval Greek, the danger of erroneous literature back-referencing is quite high.[55] The conscientious researcher of linguistic issues should always check again and again the manuscript witnesses to find evidence for the validity of his arguments.[56]

Despite its limitations the TLG remains a remarkable achievement and a resource that changed for the better the way research is conducted in the field of Classics and other related disciplines.[57] Historical linguists and other scholars interested in linguistic aspects of ancient texts are better served if they do not rely solely on data retrieved from the TLG but also consult the manuscript tradition as recorded in the apparatus criticus or the introduction of critical editions. The emergence of digital critical editions in which the manuscript tradition of ancient texts is recorded in its entirety in conjunction with new, powerful electronic services will undoubtedly help us explore in detail how linguistic norms change over time, how and why such change appears or not in transmitted texts, and what are the factors shaping the linguistic properties of each era.

---

54   For the role of highlighting one instance of an edited text within a digital edition see Peter Robinson, 'The One Text and the Many Texts', *Literary and Linguistic Computing*, 15:1 (2000): 5–14.

55   Manolessou, 'On Historical Linguistics', 70.

56   For a discussion of similar issues in creating electronic tools for linguistic research see Notis Toufexis, 'Neither Ancient, nor Modern: Challenges for the Creation of a Digital Infrastructure for Medieval Greek', paper presented at the Workshop Epistemic Networks and GRID + Web 2.0 for Arts and Humanities, Internet Centre, Imperial College London, January 2008), <http://www.toufexis.info/archives/61> (accessed July 2009).

57   For a constructive criticism of the model the TLG stands for see Crane et al., 'ePhilology'.

PART III
Infrastructure
and Disciplinary Issues

Chapter 7

Digital Infrastructure and the Homer Multitext Project

Neel Smith

The Homer Multitext Project is exploring how we can exploit digital information technology to represent the historical tradition of the *Iliad*.[1] In contrast to print editions privileging the reconstruction of a particular moment in the *Iliad's* transmission, or even a conceived 'original' *Iliad*, the Multitext Project seeks to document as fully as possible a wide variety of *Iliads* ranging from Hellenistic papyri to medieval manuscripts, to early printed editions.

This chapter describes the digital infrastructure for this collaborative project. The Multitext Project explicitly aims to design an infrastructure for the study of the *Iliad* that can outlive specific software applications and survive beyond the careers of individual scholars. After a brief overview of some of the project's guiding concerns, a summary of the archival storage formats used for the project's main data types leads to a more general model for the underlying data. A simple model of citable texts and structured objects, interlinked by associated pairs of references, maps directly on to a suite of network services, on top of which higher-order functionality and end-user applications are built.

Guiding concerns and licences

While the sheer quantity of surviving material available might suggest that no matter what form our texts assume, the *Iliad* will always find an audience, the

1   This is an updated version of the work originally presented at the Digital Classicist seminar at the Institute of Classical Studies, London, in June 2007. I would like to thank the organizers for the opportunity to take part in this very stimulating series, and the audience for their interest and comments. The Homer Multitext Project is sponsored by Harvard University's Center for Hellenic Studies. I am grateful to the Center's director, Gregory Nagy, and Director of IT and Publications, Leonard Muellner, for their encouragement and support for the work described in this chapter. Among the many contributors to the Multitext Project, I especially wish to thank the project's editors, Casey Dué and Mary Ebbott, and my collaborator on the project architecture, Christopher Blackwell, for allowing me to work with them. While the opinions I offer in this chapter are my own, every step of the work has been a collaborative effort. For further information about the project, see: <http://chs.harvard.edu/chs/homer_multitext>. (All URLs were current at the time of writing.)

transformations that have accompanied changes in the media recording our *Iliads* should make us pause before assuming that just any form of digital work will serve. The shift from the scroll to the book-like form of the codex manuscript, for example, opened up new possibilities for juxtaposing text in the centre of a folio with supplementary material and commentary in the margins, in an early form of hypertext. Scribes created rich, new environments for reading the *Iliad* in manuscripts like the famous Venetus A (Greek MS Z. 458 = 841 in the Biblioteca Nazionale Marciana). But in their focus on what we might consider an end-user application – a single manuscript, neatly integrating a variety of resources for reading the *Iliad* – they neglected a crucial long-term question. Who would turn to (and therefore continue to have copied) the full text of Hellenistic scholars like Aristarchus when selections of their work were readily available in marginal scholia? The answer, unfortunately for us, was no one: not one work of Hellenistic scholarship on the *Iliad* survives today.[2]

From the outset, the Homer Multitext Project has been shaped by a sense of our generation's responsibility, as we transform the Iliadic tradition into yet another medium, to perpetuate as completely as we can the tradition we have received. We need to ensure that as we focus on the new possibilities of digital media we do not inadvertently restrict what future scholars and lovers of the *Iliad* can do with our digital material.

This means, first, that we must carefully choose the licensing terms to apply to the project's digital materials. In a world of print-only publications, it may at times have made little difference if authors granted control of their works to publishers; other scholars could not in any case directly reuse printed works except by reading them and drawing on them when writing further works for print.

But the reusability of digital resources that can be perfectly replicated and manipulated by computer programs more closely resembles software than print publications, and I would suggest that Richard Stallman's famous distinction of four kinds of freedom characterizing free software offers a helpful schema for thinking about digital scholarly resources.[3] Each of Stallman's freedoms – the freedoms to run, study, redistribute and improve software – offers a close analogy to a kind of freedom we want to preserve for our digital resources:

- The *freedom to run a program for any purpose* corresponds more generally to the freedom to use a resource unchanged for any purpose: to read a text, view an image, etc. (level 0).

---

2   I have commented briefly on examples of how our transmission of the *Iliad* has lost information in the development of new forms of text made possible by new media in Neel Smith, 'Citation in Classical Studies', in G. Crane and M. Terras (eds), *Changing the Center of Gravity: Transforming Classical Studies Through Cyberinfrastructure, DHQ,* 3.1 (2009), <http://digitalhumanities.org/dhq/vol/3/1/index.html>.

3   GNU, The Free Software Definition, <http://www.gnu.org/philosophy/free-sw.html>.

- The *freedom to study how a program works* is parallel to the freedom to study how our resources are encoded. This is an essential part of a full scholarly review process. Underlying data structures such as textual markup and code for transformation and presentation of a text must be freely accessible (level 1).
- The *freedom to redistribute copies* applies directly to any kind of digital resource, as well as to software (level 2).
- The *freedom to improve software and release your improvements* corresponds to the freedom to modify and redistribute any resource: to edit a text, resample an image, etc. (level 3).

Stallman's general observations about free software apply also equally well to our digital resources (with my additions in square brackets):

> In order for these freedoms to be real, they must be irrevocable as long as you do nothing wrong ... However, certain kinds of rules about the manner of distributing free software [or any free scholarly resource] are acceptable, when they don't conflict with the central freedoms. For example, copyleft (very simply stated) is the rule that when redistributing the program [or resource], you cannot add restrictions to deny other people the central freedoms. This rule does not conflict with the central freedoms; rather it protects them. You may have paid money to get copies of free software, or you may have obtained copies at no charge. But regardless of how you got your copies, you always have the freedom to copy and change the software [or resource], even to sell copies.[4]

Guided by these considerations, we have chosen to make all software developed for the Homer Multitext Project available under the GNU General Public License (GPL: currently, version 3).[5] Other digital resources, such as texts, images and collections of data, are licensed under the closely analogous terms of the Creative Commons (CC) Attribution-Share-Alike licence.[6] The GPL and the CC licences are our best hopes to protect scholarly use of our work from legal restrictions.

But licences alone cannot guarantee that our digital work will remain accessible to future generations: no licensing obstacles prevented medieval scribes from reproducing the work of Aristarchus. In Lawrence Lessig's memorable phrase, 'Code is law':[7] the design of a digital architecture will also determine what uses of our digital material will or will not be possible.

One essential preliminary step in planning the project's digital infrastructure is therefore to identify archival storage formats that have the most promise for long-

---

4   Ibid.

5   GNU, General Public License, <http://www.gnu.org/licenses/gpl.html>.

6   Creative Commons Attribution-Share Alike 3.0 Unported, <http://creativecommons.org/licenses/by-sa/3.0/>.

7   Lawrence Lessig, *Code and Other Laws of Cyberspace* (Basic Books, 1999).

term viability. Following widely adopted 'best practices', we use open data formats adhering to well-defined standards. The choice of storage formats described in the following section in turn points towards a very simple abstract data model that we can use flexibly in many kinds of application.

Archival material in the Homer Multitext Project

Open data formats for archival storage should capture our information as fully as possible, and be accompanied by metadata explaining the semantics associated with the format's structure. Our digital resources currently fall into one of three quite distinct categories of archival storage.

Texts (most obviously, the different texts of the *Iliad* that are at the core of the project) make up one category. In accord with the project's philosophy of reading each version synchronically as a coherent work in its own right, as well as diachronically in relation to other versions, we aim to present each text as a complete and independent document in a diplomatic edition. Comparative or critical remarks that might figure in the apparatus of a traditional edition become in the Multitext a combination of automated comparison, and separate commentary that can point unambiguously to passages in a specific version.[8] In addition to texts of the *Iliad* currently drawn from about thirty papyri and a half dozen manuscripts with extensive scholia, the project's text corpus includes the remaining contents of the manuscripts covered: scholia, and, for the Venetus A manuscript, a version of the *Chrestomathy* attributed to Proclus, and the only surviving fragment of the work *On Signs* by the Hellenistic scholar Aristonicus. Each of these works is treated as a separate document. In the case of the Venetus A and MS T (the 'Townley' manuscript = Burney 86 in the British Library), different sets of scholia located in physically distinct parts of the manuscript (such as interlinear scholia, versus marginal scholia) are also distinguished as separate texts. Each text is encoded as an Extensible Markup Language (XML) document complying with version P5 of the Text Encoding Initiative (TEI) Guidelines.[9] They validate against a RelaxNG schema that, together with the TEI Guidelines and documentation of project-specific markup conventions, define the syntax and semantics of the documents' markup.

---

8   In this respect, the Homer Multitext project stands largely outside the debate over the relation of critical editions to diplomatic editions in a digital archive. Each version of the *Iliad* in the Multitext has independent value, as a response to and interpretation of the Homeric tradition at a given moment: it is not merely a witness for reconstruction of an imagined Ur-text. See, with further references, Espen S. Ore, 'Monkey Business – or What is an Edition?', *Literary and Linguistic Computing*, 19:1 (April 2004): 35–44.

9   Text Encoding Initiative, P5 Guidelines, <http://www.tei-c.org/release/doc/tei-p5-doc/html>.

To support the project's emphasis on reading each *Iliad* in a historical framework, we need to model a variety of objects related to these texts. The Multitext Project's photography in May and June of 2007 of three manuscripts in the Biblioteca Marciana in Venice illustrates the possible range of these objects. They include tangible, physical artefacts. We maintain an inventory of the manuscripts with information about their current location, provenance and history, for example, and record in a related model information about each side of each folio in a manuscript. These folio sides are an ordered set, so that apart from further information specific to that folio side (e.g. any conservation data specific to that folio), their sequence information allows us to navigate the records of folio sides in their natural, physical order. Other objects are documentary: each of the thousands of digital images is represented by an extensive set of metadata about the instruments used in taking the photograph: photographic conditions such as lighting and exposure time, etc. Still others are purely analytical or conceptual objects, such as 'speeches' and 'speakers' in the *Iliad*. Varied as these classes of object are, each class has a common set of properties that can be readily reduced to textual data. To archive these regularly structured sets of data, we need nothing more elaborate than text files in a known character encoding with a simple tabular structure. We record metadata about the data sets in an XML document validating against a schema developed for the network service for collections of structured objects described below. This document includes Dublin Core metadata, a list of properties belonging to each object in the class with an assignment of each property to one of a very minimal set of property types, and descriptive information, so that, as with our XML texts, a specified document structure can be mapped to known semantics. Given this description of a data set, it is trivial to use the archival data source with many types of software. We have worked with some or all of our data sets in relational databases, XML databases, Joseki (an HTTP engine supporting queries of data structured in the Resource Description Framework) and the Weka data-mining package (which supports import of text data in the simple Attribute-Relation File Format), to name a few examples.

If measured in bytes, a third category of archival storage dwarfs the other two: binary image data. The original photography from Venice is archived as uncompressed TIFF files roughly 250Mb each. A set of EXIF (Exchangeable Image File Format) and IPTC (International Press Telecommunications Council) metadata is embedded in each image, including licensing information authorizing the reuse of the images, and, critically, an identifier associating the binary image with its representation in the external collection of textual data modelling images.

Underlying data models

For a project devoted to exploring the complexity of the tradition of the *Iliad*, this is a remarkably simple set of requirements for long-term archival storage. The more familiar project participants became with the project's digital resources, the more persuaded we became that the key to capturing the complexity of the Multitext in a digital model lies not in the complexity of the individual objects we work with, but in the relations among objects in the Multitext. Even the three categories suggested by our archival storage formats can be reduced to two basic models. All our binary images are after all coordinated with records in a tabular set of data about images. We could consider the binary image one further property of an 'image' class of object. It happens that this property is not easily reduced to a textual format, so for our archival storage, we keep that data in separate, coordinated files, but when we think about how to model objects in the Multitext, we only have to accommodate two fundamental types: texts, and structured objects with defined properties. I have argued elsewhere that we find a similar fundamental distinction between texts and collections of structured objects if we look at humanists' citation practice.[10] When we cite sections of a text with references to passages, we use values in a canonical reference system that serves as a kind of coordinate system to point into a continuous textual space. When we cite structured objects, on the other hand, we may refer to specific properties, but we identify the object as a discrete entity with a unique identifier. Both the way we store archival data, and the way we refer to objects, in other words, point to an ontological difference between texts and other kinds of structured object.

With Gabriel Weaver, I have proposed that canonically citable texts exhibit four essential structural properties that set them apart from other structured objects:[11] a hierarchy of versions comparable to the ontological model of the Functional Catalog of Bibliographic Records (FRBR); sequence of citable nodes; position of citable nodes in a citation hierarchy; and the possibility of mixed content within citable nodes. The choice of XML markup to represent textual content is no accident, for XML enforces two of these properties: document sequence and hierarchical organization. (In fact, the definition of XML was certainly influenced by the classic formulation of DeRose, Durand, Mylonas and Renear that text is an 'ordered hierarchy of content modules', the 'OHCO hypothesis'.[12]) But these

---

10   Smith, 'Citation in Classical Studies'.

11   D. Neel Smith and Gabriel A. Weaver, 'Applying Domain Knowledge from Structured Citation Formats to Text and Data Mining: Examples Using the CITE Architecture' 129-139 in *Text Mining Services: Building and Applying Text Mining Based Service Infrastructures in Research and Industry* (ed. Gerhard Heyer) (= Leipziger Beiträge zur Informatik, Band XIV; Leipzig: 2009). (Reprinted in Dartmouth College Computer Science Technical Report series, TR2009-649, June 2009.)

12   Originally published in Steven J. DeRose, David G. Durand, Elli Mylonas and Allen H. Renear, 'What is Text, Really?', *Journal of Computing in Higher Education*, 1:2 (1990): 3–26, full text available from <http://doi.acm.org/10.1145/264842.264843>. While some of the authors of the OHCO hypothesis later backed away from their original claims about the 'true nature' of text, the OHCO model accurately describes the ways we organize and cite texts, a point to which we will return below. See Allen Renear, Elli Mylonas and David Durand, 'Refining our Notion of What Text Really Is: The Problem of Overlapping Hierarchies', <http://www.stg.brown.edu/resources/stg/monographs/ohco.

two properties of text are the least distinctive of the four. We have already seen that some collections of structured objects, such as our model for folio sides, may have a natural sequence; and, conversely, some texts may have a completely flat hierarchy. The Homeric Hymns, for example, are cited by and organized at a single hierarchical level, the poetic line. Beyond order and hierarchy, markup languages like XML also make it possible to interleave data (simple text) and structured objects (markup elements) at the same hierarchical level, or what is referred to in the terminology of markup languages as 'mixed content models'. With mixed content models, validating XML parsers can enforce structures that are difficult or impossible to represent in many other kinds of information systems. But even the most richly marked up XML text does not capture the fourth feature distinguishing texts from other structured objects: the FRBR-like hierarchy of versions. In our archival data, therefore, we include a catalogue document, or text inventory, that documents these relations. We have many *Iliads*, all of them versions of a notional *Iliad*, and therefore representatives of the tradition of the *Iliad*.

At times, it may be useful to view an object as both a text and a structured object in a collection. A bibliographic catalogue collects similar information about each catalogued document, for example – a kind of structured object, in other words; but the textual contents of the documents in the catalogue would certainly be represented as texts, perhaps of quite varied sorts. In cases like this, a single object might appear in two distinct models capturing different aspects of the object: a record in a structured bibliographic collection, and a document in a corpus of texts. The two views of the object can be coordinated through a common set of identifiers, just as our representation of digital photographs includes coordinated tabular data and binary image data. For the Multitext Project, we are currently experimenting with multiple views of the Perseus project's Liddell–Scott–Jones Greek lexicon (LSJ). LSJ includes complex articles that are miniature texts in their own right, but the lexicon as a whole could also be viewed as a structured collection of lexical entities with similar categories of information including part of speech and morphological information, in addition to discussion of senses of the word. The fact that lexica are traditionally sorted alphabetically is no more than a convention to simplify lookup and retrieval of articles in print editions. (The readers who follow the lexicon's document order to work their way sequentially through LSJ from *alpha* to *omega* must be rare indeed.)

But whether or not we apply more than one model to a given object, we can summarize our basic dichotomy as shown in Table 7.1:

---

html>; it is described as a 'Final version, January 6, 1993', with the note that 'A slightly edited version of this paper was published in 1996 in *Research in Humanities Computing*, Oxford University Press, Nancy Ide and Susan Hockey (eds).'

Table 7.1   Models of texts and structured objects

	Texts	Structured objects in collections
Hierarchy of versions	Editions, translations, physical exemplars of a work related in a single hierarchy	Objects may include version information, but generally treated as discrete
Order of citable nodes	Document order is essential	Objects may have a natural order, but even if they do, may be sorted by other properties
Hierarchy of citable nodes	Most often organized in one or more hierarchies used for citation	Essentially flat set of properties (although these may in turn be composed of objects with their own properties)
Organization of nodes	Mixed content model normal	Structured properties

Associating objects

If we can model the objects in the Homer Multitext with two simple types of data, how can we capture the relations among objects? To read the text of the *Iliad* on a single folio of the Venetus A, we might need to know what lines of the *Iliad* the folio contains, what photographs illustrate that folio, what editorial symbols appear in the margins annotating which lines, and what scholia comment on the passage. We might also want to discover where we have other, possibly varying versions of the same lines of the *Iliad*, perhaps quoted in a source like Plato, or preserved in manuscript or papyrus copies. It is the associative web of connections like these that gives the Multitext its richness and depth.

To associate two objects, we must first be able to identify them. We can define what lines of the *Iliad* appear on a folio of a given manuscript by pairing an unambiguous reference to the passage with a reference to the folio, for example. But identification alone is not sufficient: we want to include these associations as part of our permanent project archive, so while our identifiers must be unambiguous, they must also be persistent, and defined in a standard system that makes the associations accessible to other systems, perhaps entirely unconnected with the Multitext project. Here, too, both the structure of our archival data, and the conventional practice of humanists when they cite material clarify requirements for our identification systems: texts and structured objects require different forms of reference, corresponding to the differences in citation conventions and data structures. A reference system for texts must be able to point to continuous ranges within the sequence of the document's hierarchy (just as classicists do when they cite the *Iliad* by a range of book and line numbers).

Objects like folio pages or photographs, on the other hand, are cited as discrete objects with unique identifiers.[13]

To take the simpler case first: how can we construct unique identifiers for objects so that they will be unambiguously and persistently usable over the long term? It is easy enough to create untyped strings of text that can be used in any technology – digital or other – and to guarantee that they will be unique within a collection that we manage ourselves. We can use such values in a long-term archive without worrying about either the possible longevity or the overhead of using a more complex system like Digital Object Identifiers.[14] But how do we avoid clashing identifiers across multiple projects over a long period of time?

This is analogous to the problem of identifying XML vocabularies. Since XML enables anyone to define a vocabulary conforming to some kind of schema or Document Type Definition (DTD), we need a mechanism to determine the meaning of an element when multiple schemas have elements with clashing names. The XML community's response was to use the Internet's existing Domain Name System (DNS) to create qualifying namespaces to disambiguate conflicting names. A 'title' element in the XHTML namespace is not the same element as a 'title' element in the TEI P5 namespace. Parallel to this, Domain Namespace Identifiers (DNID) use domain name qualifiers to create an unambiguous namespace – not for XML data structures, but for data identifiers. For example, '1858.1.1' is the unique inventory number of a coin in the collection of the American Numismatic Society, but it might just as well be a valid reference to some other digital object. By qualifying this identifier with the domain name 'numismatics.org', we can create a reference that is guaranteed to be unique ('numismatics.org:1858.1.1').[15] In addition to institutional domain names, the OpenID system offers one way that an individual could easily register to 'own' a domain name that could be used to define namespaces for use with DNIDs.[16]

References to texts are more complex because they need to carry information about two distinct hierarchies simultaneously. One is the organizational hierarchy that identifies passages within a work, such as the books and lines of the *Iliad*. The other hierarchy identifies the work within a conceptual model. When we cite

---

13   I provide a fuller discussion of citation in the Homer Multitext Project: Smith, 'Citation in Classical Studies'. In particular, this article provides a more detailed introduction to the CTS URNs (see below) used for references to texts in the Homer Multitext project.

14   Although sometimes mentioned as a candidate for this kind of task, Digital Object Identifiers (DOI) focus on concrete digital objects, with strong emphasis on intellectual property rights management. We require instead the ability to refer to a notional object more abstractly, even if it has no particular digital representation, or multiple digital representations. A reference to a passage of the *Iliad*, for example, should be constructed to work equally well with material in the Homer Multitext and with print editions predating the invention of digital computers. For more information about DOI, see <http://doi.org/>.

15   For more information about Domain Namespace Identifiers (DNIDs), see <http://www.dnid-community.org/>, and cf. Heath, in this volume, Chapter 2; n. 27.

16   See OpenID, <http://openid.net/>.

a passage of the *Iliad*, do we mean any version of the text? A specific translation or edition? Or even a specific individual exemplar? This is similar to the model developed in the library community for cataloguing works, as part of the Functional Requirements for Bibliographic Records (FRBR).[17]

It came as a surprise to everyone working on the Multitext when we realized that there really was no notational system currently in use for citing digital texts that explicitly expressed both of these hierarchies. A major focus of the project's technical working group has been to develop a notation for just this purpose, the Canonical Text Services Uniform Resource Name (or CTS URN).

While the CTS URN and the DNID are both simple text strings uniquely identifying a resource, they are also semantically laden. The DNID both identifies an object, and tells us a domain (identified by domain namespace) that the object belongs to. The CTS URN identifies a particular passage of text at a particular level in the notional hierarchy of a textual work. Texts are organized in groups, containing notional works. Since urn:cts:greekLit:tlg0012 refers to group tlg0012 in the greekLit namespace, namely the Homeric poems, and urn:cts:greekLit: tlg0012.tlg001 in turn refers to the *Iliad*, a reference like urn:cts:greekLit:tlg0012. tlg001:1.1 refers to the first line of the *Iliad*, without specifying a particular version, while urn:cts:greekLit:tlg0012.tlg001.msA:1.1 refers specifically to the text of the Venetus A.[18] Associating urn:cts:greekLit:tlg0012.tlg001.msA:1.1-25 with chs.harvard.edu/datans/mss/msA-012r tells us that the first 25 lines of the text in the Venetus A are connected with the object msA-012r in the CHS manuscripts namespace, that is folio twelve recto. When a link pairs two identifiers in either or both of the CTS URN and DNID reference systems, it provides a great deal of information in a simple and persistent form.

If we review the questions at the beginning of this section about what links we might want in order to read a folio of a manuscript as represented in the Multitext, they all ask about the relations between pairs of objects. We can express these relations as pairs of typed references. A CTS URN for a text passage paired with DNID for a folio relates text to folio; a DNID for an image with a DNID for a folio relates photographs and physical artefact; a CTS URN for a passage of the *Iliad* and a CTS URN for a scholion creates a commentary of one passage on another.

In addition to our two basic types of objects, then, we add a third structure to our archive, which we call a 'reference index.' Metadata about the index provides information about what kinds of references are being paired together; the index itself is nothing more than pairs of canonical references. An index of folio sides (expressed as DNIDs) to Iliadic passages (expressed as CTS URNs) provides

17 The formal description of the model is available from <http://www.ifla.org/VII/ s13/frbr/frbr.pdf>. For current information about FRBR, and ongoing activity in the very active FRBR community, see the FRBR blog at <http://www.frbr.org/>.

18 In addition to the previously cited article, current information about CTS URNs is available from <http://chs75.harvard.edu/projects/diginc/techpub/cts-urn>, mirrored at <http://katoptron.holycross.edu/cocoon/diginc/techpub/cts-urn>.

access to folios from lines of the *Iliad*, or conversely to lines of the *Iliad* from a folio reference. Texts, tabular data and reference indexes provide the archival representation of the full range of the Multitext's underlying data.

Against this background, let's return briefly to the model of text with four structural properties. The most serious objections to the unqualified OHCO model of text, discussed above, focus on the problem of overlapping hierarchies. No single hierarchical structure can contain all imaginable structures that might be desirable or necessary for some particular reading or analysis of a text. For example, a formal poetic structure, such as lines of verse, might overlap with a syntactic structure such as sentences. Since the discussion of OHCO has been in part inspired by and largely focused on how these overlapping or conflicting structures can be represented in textual markup, it is not surprising that the reaction of Renear, Mylonas and Durand tends towards *aporia*.[19] If any analysis or reading of a text that defines a new hierarchy requires a different text marked up for that analytical purpose, then each reading must create a new text that has no obvious point of contact with other versions of that text.

In the Homer Multitext, every text is instead organized by its citation hierarchy, which can be addressed by CTS URNs. An overlapping analytical structure, such as speeches in the *Iliad*, can be represented by simple tabular objects. (Our minimal model for a speech includes, in addition to a DNID for each speech, only the speaker.) Each speech is indexed to a CTS URN: this index maps a specific analytical hierarchy (in this case, speeches) to the organizing canonical hierarchy of the *Iliad*'s citation scheme. In similar fashion, any other kind of analytical scheme could be expressed by associating analytical objects with a reference to CTS URNs, so that the canonical reference of the CTS URN provides a neutral hub for converting any scheme indexed to CTS URNs to any other similarly indexed scheme. For this reason, we treat reference or citation as the fundamental organizational hierarchy of any text, and treat overlapping hierarchies as secondary in the sense that they are capable of being expressed in the terms of the fundamental hierarchy.

When we reduce the complexity of the Multitext's contents to texts and structured objects related to each other by simple indexes pairing canonical references (i.e. either a CTS URN or a DNID), we rely on the semantically laden CTS URN or a DNID to inform us about the two related objects. The final piece of the puzzle is a persistent way to refer to the relation between them. When the relation is expressed in a reference index with its associated metadata, we could refer to the relation using one more identifier: a DNID for the index. This yields a simple triplet comprising object 1 identifier, index identifier and object 2 identifier, that, in principle, should be capable of expressing in terms of persistent canonical identifiers any association we need to make between two objects. Conceptually this is very similar to the triplets used by the Resource Description Framework, or RDF, a language for describing resources on the World Wide Web, developed

---

19   Renear et al., 'Refining Our Notion'.

by the W3C consortium.[20] In RDF, a vocabulary of property names and values is associated with objects identified by URI. The relations defined by a CITE reference index (see below for an explanation of CITE) can easily be translated into RDF statements (as well as to other generic technologies), although with the loss of the CITE architecture's explanatory metadata and explicit citation semantics. Beyond individual pairs of objects, more complex networks of such associations can be modelled as object graphs with nodes representing objects, and edges representing indexes. In the following section, we will see how this abstract object model can be translated into an application architecture.

Application architecture for the Homer Multitext

The Multitext Project's overall goals influence our design of software as well as data structures. While we know that applications necessarily have short life spans, we can maintain the project's long-term focus by designing our code so that the *functionality* of Multitext applications can persist as easily as the data in our simple archival storage formats. Specific implementing code will come and go, but where our architecture relies on cleanly isolated components with well-defined interfaces, future implementations can be substituted without altering functionality, so our first architectural principle is to emphasize *APIs for distinct components* of our system. This aligns readily with a more immediate goal: to support reuse of our code. When distinct components of a system are organized so that they can be recombined, regrouped or integrated into different environments, a developer can use relevant components without having to adopt our full architecture. Our second architectural principle is therefore *independent, decoupled components*. In addition to reuse at the level of source code, we want to support interaction with running versions of our systems. This implies that our own current implementations of specific APIs should be documented and open for use by other software. In 2009, our third principle is *expose components to the Internet*. Finally, we also want to make it immediately possible for reviewers and testers to replicate and run our systems so that they can evaluate and critique them. This dictates a fourth principle: in addition to licensing our own work under a free software licence, we rely exclusively on *freely reusable software* for any linked code we depend on. Taken together, these principles lead us to an architecture built on a *suite of self-contained network services with explicit APIs, implemented in free software*.

---

20 W3C: Resource Description Framework, <http://www.w3.org/RDF/>.

The CITE suite of protocols

The simplicity of our underlying data model fits comfortably with this architecture. The most fundamental functionality we need to support is identification and retrieval of the Multitext Project's content. To decouple the different components of the Multitext Project, we expose them to the Internet in a suite of three services providing identification and retrieval of texts, of structured objects and of reference indexes associating pairs of objects. All identification and retrieval is based on canonical citation: CTS URNs for texts, DNIDs for structured objects, DNIDs to identify an index, and within an index CTS URNS and/or DNIDs for the values of each associated pair.

For these three services, we use the HyperText Transport Protocol (HTTP) for the transport mechanism, and HTTP parameters to formulate requests. (A passage of text can be retrieved, for example, by submitting a request with two parameters, the name of the request, and a URN, so the first ten lines of the *Iliad* could be retrieved by submitting a CTS request for request=GetPassage&urn=urn:cts: greekLit:tlg0012.tlg001:1.110.) All replies are formatted in XML.

To support automated service discovery, each service includes a metadata request with no further parameters named GetCapabilities (in imitation of the very useful GIS services defined by the Open Geographic Consortium). The GetCapabilities reply provides a catalogue of the service's contents, as well as indicating any optional functionality it supports. Further queries allow applications to determine what are valid identifiers for specific objects or groups of objects (e.g. what reference values are legitimate CTS URNs for a given version of a text, or what identifiers are accepted for a set of objects in a collection). A client can therefore ensure that a retrieval request includes only canonical references recognized by the service. While the full cycle of service discovery, identification of canonical references, and retrieval is necessary to guarantee that clients only submit valid requests, client applications may adopt different strategies in choosing whether to preload or batch process discovery information or requests for valid identifiers. Each service defines replies for different kinds of invalid requests (such as missing parameters, syntax errors or invalid data values), so client applications allowing end users to send requests directly to a service (e.g. by entering a text reference in a form) can react appropriately to user errors.

For each service, three coordinated formal definitions spell out the interaction between client and server. First, there is a prose specification, giving both the syntax of HTTP parameters for each request, and the meaning of each request. Second, the XML structure of each reply is defined by Relax-NG schemas, so replies from any implementation can be validated. Third, each service has a test suite composed of a test data set, and a series of requests and replies. It should be possible to load the test data into any implementation of the protocol, submit each request in turn, and check the actual reply against the expected reply provided in the test suite.

The CTS and RefIndex protocols are the most mature of the three basic services at this point. We are currently using a very basic Collections protocol, and are working on the most effective ways to allow it be extended to cover specialized kinds of data in two ways that are illustrated by images. First, just as our archival storage plans must extend the simple tabular data storage of an image collection to accommodate the special case of binary image data, so we want to permit a Collection of images to allow extensions for retrieving this binary data. Second, we want to permit an extended citation method. While we use normal DNIDs to refer to an image, our indexes often need to point more specifically to sections of an image. In the case of images, we extend the DNID with a simple rectangular region of interest, expressed in scale-independent percentage terms. Based on our experience with extending the Collections protocol to accommodate the distinctive features of images, we are trying to define a general mechanism for defining extensions of structured objects that cannot be fully represented by textual data.

To our three basic services of Collections, Indexes and Texts, we can add Extensions (and so arrive at the irresistible acronym, CITE). In a network of intercommunicating objects, these fundamental services alone are sufficient to support client applications such as text browsers, or a manuscript browser integrating (through indices) textual transcriptions and images of manuscript folios. But they can also support higher-order analytical services. To take one example: in the course of developing programs to validate a service using the test suites, it was necessary to compare the actual XML reply of a request to the expected XML of the test suite. This comparison has to be based not on literal string comparisons, but on the XML equivalence of the two document fragments (allowing, for example, for normalization of white space). This is perfectly straightforward with a code library like XMLUnit, but in running these tests on a CTS request to retrieve a passage identified by URN, it became blindingly obvious that we had, quite accidentally, almost completely written a very useful service: a URN difference service, that peforms an XML comparison of the results of retrieving two text passages identified by CTS URNs. By encapsulating the XML comparison of two passages in a service requiring just two URNs as parameters, we have abstracted a meaningful question – do these two passages differ, and if so, how? – in a form that can easily be exploited by client programs.

Current implementations

While the CITE protocols are defined independently of any specific implementation, our work on CITE has of course grown out of our experience working with running implementations. Inevitably, descriptions of software become outdated as development progresses, but because the development process must be grounded firmly on the principles described in the earlier sections of this chapter, I believe it is important to summarize briefly the status of our current implementations.

More up-to-date information, as well as downloadable code, can be found at the project's Sourceforge site.[21]

To ensure that our protocol definitions are not too closely linked to a single implementation, we have written versions of each of the three core services in two different environments. In the first environment, CTS, Collections and RefIndex services each run as a separate servlet, written in a combination of Groovy and Java. The second environment is Google's AppEngine platform: each service is a separate Google app written using Google's python library. Installing the java servlets can be as simple as dropping a .war file into a servlet container, and editing a configuration file; one option included in our build system packages the servlets in a jetty servlet container, so that instead of installing anything, they can be started by running the jetty container (on some operating systems, as straightforward as double clicking a .jar file). The servlet implementations give us the flexibility to run a CITE service anywhere we can get to a servlet container that can be easily installed and can run effectively even on an inexpensive personal computer. The AppEngine implementations give us a different kind of ubiquity. With Google's scaling and load balancing, an AppEngine installation of the CITE services can be reliably available anywhere on the Internet without requiring the service owner to worry about administering machines.[22]

In parallel with each of the three core services, we have written a java servlet that validates a service at a given URL against the test suite for that type of service. CTS3 and RefIndex pass 100 per cent of the tests in both servlet and AppEngine implementations; the servlet implementation of Collections passes 100 per cent of the tests, with the AppEngine version expected to have reached that benchmark in the spring of 2009. As we complete documentation and review of our code, we have begun to release it on the project's Sourceforge site.

With a full suite of CITE implementations in hand, we have recently begun to focus more of our attention on applications founded on material in the Homer Multitext supplied by CITE services. One example is an initial analysis of how scholia cluster in six major manuscripts of the *Iliad*.[23]

---

21   Canonical Text Services at Sourceforge, <http://cts3.sourceforge.net>.

22   As final revisions were being made to this chapter, Google announced support for the Java Virtual Machine and java servlets in AppEngine; we have begun consolidating our code so that a single code base can support compilation for either Google's AppEngine environment, or for a generic servlet environment with a relational database back end.

23   The evidence for the cluster analysis is provided solely by the URNs that are valid for each manuscript. Since the URNs show in what document scholia cited in a common citation scheme occur, we can see which scholia occur where, and identify common patterns in their distribution before we even consider their contents; Smith and Weaver, 'Applying Domain Knowledge'.

In the area of end-user applications, a publicly available example is the manuscript browser.[24] Using CITE protocols to retrieve indices mapping Iliadic references to manuscript folios, and manuscript folios to images, this javascript application uses the tiling system of Google Maps to allow fast and intuitive browsing of images at very high resolution. Images may be retrieved by references either to passages of the *Iliad*, or to specific folios in the set of manuscripts photographed by the Multitext Project.

Other end-user applications currently under development provide a browsing and editing environment for constructing and visualizing a graph of citable objects from the Multitext Project's resources, in a kind of hypermedia environment where all references are by canonical CITE identifiers. But that work is a more appropriate topic for a future work-in-progress report, or perhaps reports, including work beyond the formal boundaries of the Multitext of Homer project.

Concluding remarks

I began this chapter by suggesting that similarities between free software and digital scholarship can help us think about appropriate licensing for scholarly work. In closing, I would like to revisit the parallels between free software and digital scholarship to highlight some ways that our work to date on the Homer Multitext Project may be significant both within and beyond the field of Homeric studies.

Scholars who have, without reflection, become accustomed to proprietary software (and perhaps are even required by their university's policies to use it) may not recognize the value of free software. Among this group, one frequently encountered objection to free software purports to be pragmatic: it would be more difficult to adopt or learn new (free) software, and users already have proprietary software that 'just works'. There are many responses to this argument, but I think all of them in one way or another reject the implications of the adverb 'just'. There is no such thing as software that 'just' works. A given piece of software may work for a particular purpose, while imposing particular requirements on its users. With proprietary software, the most obvious of these requirements may be its monetary cost, but that may also be the least onerous requirement. Data formats that lock users in to a specific vendor's products, licences that restrict sharing of scholarly work, and other restrictions on the freedom of users are costs that may not figure in a university budget, but subordinate the conduct of academic research to an outside company's business strategy.

Humanists can with some justification feel that the dizzying pace of development in information technology leaves them little time to reflect on its application to

---

24 At the time of writing, this was available at <http://chs75.harvard.edu/manuscripts>.

their area of expertise. And, after all, why should they concern themselves? As long as digital scholarship 'just works' for their purposes, isn't that enough?

Here, as with software, the problem is that digital scholarship never 'just' works. The Homer Multitext Project has focused on the choice of licences, and the design of data models, archival storage formats, and an architecture for network services because those decisions determine what forms our scholarly discourse can assume in a digital environment as definitively as code determines what a piece of software can accomplish. The overwhelming majority of users of free software have never examined the source code; they still benefit from the crucial advantages of free software, however, because others – indeed, anyone – can do so. Similarly, the majority of users of end-user applications like the Homer Multitext's manuscript browser will never consider its underlying architecture; they still benefit from its advantages, because anyone can draw on the Multitext Project's resources at whatever level they choose. We hope that the architecture we have developed for the Homer Multitext will directly support a wide range of work with the project's digital material. Those who wish to work directly with the project's full archival data sets are welcome to; scholars who want to design new kinds of applications that interoperate with the Multitext Project's online services are able to do so. The variety of digital scholarship in Classics illustrated in this volume makes us optimistic that our attention to the digital infrastructure of the Homer Multitext will in the future help support Classical scholarship that we have not yet imagined ourselves.

Beyond the comparatively restricted circle of Classicists and others interested in the Homeric poems, we also hope that the Multitext Project will provide a useful model for other projects in humanities digital scholarship. By putting the design of the project's digital infrastructure in the foreground, we hope to increase humanists' awareness of the importance of this kind of scholarship. Whether or not other projects closely follow the decisions we have made about digital infrastructure, the Homer Multitext offers an explicit rationale for its choices that others can discuss or debate. The discussion should help make clear why those choices are not narrowly technological, and can only be made by technologically informed humanists. In the long run, perhaps we will reach enough of a consensus about the requirements of work on digital scholarship that a special volume like this one no longer serves a valuable purpose. In the meantime, Classicists have an important contribution to make to the maturation of this kind of thinking across the humanities, as we further clarify guiding principles and document best practices in digital scholarship.[25]

---

25   In addition to the tools released on cts3.sourceforge.net, one online source for information about the project's technological initiatives is the *Digital Incunabula* website at <http://chs75.harvard.edu/projects/diginc> (mirrored at <http://katoptron.holycross.edu/cocoon/diginc>).

Chapter 8

Ktêma es aiei: Digital Permanence from an Ancient Perspective

Hugh A. Cayless

Introduction

The Greek historian Thucydides in the introduction to his work on the Peloponnesian War discussed his motivation for writing as he did:

> καὶ ἐς μὲν ἀκρόασιν ἴσως τὸ μὴ μυθῶδες αὐτῶν ἀτερπέστερον φανεῖται· ὅσοι δὲ βουλήσονται τῶν τε γενομένων τὸ σαφὲς σκοπεῖν καὶ τῶν μελλόντων ποτὲ αὖθις κατὰ τὸ ἀνθρώπινον τοιούτων καὶ παραπλησίων ἔσεσθαι, ὠφέλιμα κρίνειν αὐτὰ ἀρκούντως ἕξει. κτῆμά τε ἐς αἰεὶ μᾶλλον ἢ ἀγώνισμα ἐς τὸ παραχρῆμα ἀκούειν ξύγκειται.

> The absence of romance in my history will, I fear, detract somewhat from its interest; but if it be judged useful by those inquirers who desire an exact knowledge of the past as an aid to the interpretation of the future, which in the course of human things must resemble if it does not reflect it, I shall be content. In fine, I have written my work, not as an essay which is to win the applause of the moment, but as a possession for all time (*ktêma es aiei*).[1]

Thucydides' remark implying the permanence of his work is interesting in several ways. First, it is not simple bravado. Statements of the immortality of an author's work (and therefore of the author also) are not uncommon in poetry, and Thucydides is responding in his introduction to a poetic tradition, but this statement is different in its form. Thucydides is talking about the permanence of his history in terms of its design. It is not written as entertainment, but as a document meant to be useful to anyone interested in the conduct of human affairs.[2]

---

1   Thucydides 1.22, trans. Richard Crawley, *Thucydides' Peloponnesian War* (London, 1903), <http://www.gutenberg.org/dirs/etext04/plpwr10.txt>. (All URLs current at the time of writing.)

2   See W. Robert Connor, *Thucydides* (Princeton, 1984), pp. 20–32 on the 'Archaeology'. See also his introduction for a discussion of Thucydides' relevance to international affairs during the Cold War.

Second, it is evidently accurate. Thucydides set the standard for historical writing and is a central text both for Greek history and for historiography in general. So how do works like this survive, and can we derive any lessons from that survival that will help with the preservation and sustainability problems we face today?

Understanding new technologies takes time. Typically, we progress in gradual stages of understanding, beginning with a metaphorical stage, in which we compare new processes to others that we already understand and ending with a thorough knowledge of the technology in itself. We know in some detail how certain works have survived from ancient times to the present day, having crossed cultural and political boundaries in both space and time, and outlasted not only the cultures that created them, but also many of the societies that passed them on. It seems reasonable then to wonder whether there are examples we can apply to digital sustainability to help us begin to understand how digital works might be preserved indefinitely.

The sustainability and permanence of electronic materials are issues much on the mind of anyone concerned with the preservation of cultural heritage in the digital age. Many granting agencies emphasize sustainability as an important component of successful applications for funding to develop new online resources.[3] The typical response to this on the part of grant applicants is to include some sort of institutional affirmation that materials created in any given project will be preserved by the institution in question. While it is laudable that these concerns for digital materials are considered important, it must be noted that no real solutions to the problem are reflected in this requirement. I hope to shed some light on how solutions, or at least strategies, might be developed by considering how certain cultural heritage materials from the ancient world have survived to the present day.

Clearly, there are important differences in both the physical nature and the modes of transmission of digital and physical objects, but it is my contention that some of the same general rules apply to both, and that an examination of the transmission or survival of truly ancient materials may provide some implementable ideas for the design of digital materials which are intended to be permanent.[4] As a basis for discussion, I will focus principally on three examples of surviving material from the ancient Mediterranean world, the works of Vergil, Sappho and the *Res Gestae Divi Augusti*, all of which have survived to the present day for different reasons.

There are four principal ways in which an artefact or text can survive for such a long period of time:

---

3   See Kevin Guthrie, Rebecca Griffiths and Nancy Maron, *Sustainability and Revenue Models for Online Academic Resource* (Ithaka, 2008), <http://www.ithaka.org/publications/sustainability> for a discussion of the importance of sustainability.

4   See James M. O'Toole, 'On the Idea of Permanence', *American Archivist*, 52 (Winter 1989) for a discussion of the idea of permanence in archives – as near forever as possible.

1. Accident: the artefact or text survives because of a fortunate (or sometimes unfortunate) chain of events.
2. Reuse: i.e. incorporation into some other entity that itself survives.
3. Republication or replication: i.e. the copying and/or re-edition of the text or artefact.
4. Durability: i.e. construction from or inscription upon some material which was capable of surviving for millennia.

The first of these does not lend itself to any sort of planning, since accidents are by definition unpredictable. Though it may be possible to minimize the chances of destruction by accident, there really is no way to maximize the chances of accidental survival. Survival by reuse may easily be argued to be a type of accident, but as we will see, there are design strategies which limit or prevent the possibility of reuse. I have chosen to mention both replication and republication because, while both imply the copying of the content of a resource, that copying may involve a degree of alteration that serves the purposes of the editor, producing an essentially new work. Finally, durability may seem to offer the best hope of the four, but it is also the hardest to attain, and is not a guarantee, some degree of fortune still being necessary.

Vergil

Vergil was widely regarded as the preeminent poet of his day. Even before it was published, posthumously, his *Aeneid* was proclaimed by his fellow poet, Propertius, to be greater than the *Iliad* of Homer. Vergil instantly became part of the Latin canon, and knowledge of his poetry would have been a necessary prerequisite to be seen as culturally literate at all periods of the Roman Empire. Indeed, his works came to be regarded as a repository for all religious knowledge and were interpreted as religious allegory by his commentators.[5] Vergil was a central component of the Roman educational curriculum and students would be expected to memorize passages from his works. His importance was not seriously diminished after the rise of Christianity, both because of his works' centrality to Roman culture and because he was regarded as a sort of 'proto-Christian'.[6] The sheer quality and great appeal of his poetry must also be acknowledged, and Christians might well be drawn to it despite the fact that its author was a pagan.

---

5 Servius's (a late fourth/early fifth century grammarian) commentary on the *Aeneid* is a gold mine of information on Roman religion and ritual because of this (see <http://www.perseus.tufts.edu//.jsp?=Perseus:text:1999.02.0053>).

6 In Vergil's fourth *Eclogue*, the birth of a miraculous child is foretold (see <http://www.perseus.tufts.edu//.jsp?=Perseus:text:1999.02.0056:poem=4>). Many Christians naturally (but mistakenly) assumed this was a prophecy of the birth of Jesus.

Naturally enough, then, there were many copies of Vergil's poems in circulation for the whole of their existence. Indeed, Vergil is the best-attested Latin author, except possibly for Terence, the comic playwright (with over six hundred surviving manuscripts).[7] We must take careful note, however, of what is meant by 'survival' in this context. The earliest complete manuscripts of Vergil's poems date from the fourth and fifth centuries CE, some four hundred years after the poet's death in 19 BCE.[8] Thus, even the earliest manuscript available is itself the product of a chain of copies of indeterminate length. This copying too, was not a mechanical process. It was done by hand, and therefore subject to human error. Even with a text like Vergil's, in relation to which, for religious and cultural reasons, there would be pressure to make the copy as exact as possible (in the early centuries of its existence at least), variants would creep in over time. Indeed, since we do not know the precise details of how the initial publication proceeded, there might have been variant versions in existence from the beginning.[9]

The popularity of Vergil's works led to their continual adaptation and reuse over the centuries. The text was put to a number of different uses both in the original and in translation. Over time, the texts acquired both a cluster of attendant works around them and also an accretion of commentary and other types of annotation that would frequently accompany an individual text when it was copied. The Vergil available to a medieval or Renaissance scholar therefore looked very different from the Vergil we find in a modern text. The history of Vergilian transmission is well understood enough that it is possible to identify different interpretive strands in that history.[10]

Sappho

Sappho's situation is very different from that of Vergil. She wrote enough lyric poetry that Alexandrian scholars compiled those poems into nine books, the first

---

7   Ronald H. Martin (ed.), Terence, *Adelphoe* (Cambridge, 1976), p. 41.

8   R.A.B. Mynors, *P. Vergili Maronis Opera* (Oxford, 1969), p. v. The Greek Bible is the only text with a better manuscript tradition.

9   *The Amores* of Ovid begins with an epigram which notes that the current publication, containing three books of poems, supercedes a previous one that contained five. Ovid appears to have been successful in replacing his first publication of the book, but other authors were less so. Galen (K xix, 8–11) complains about spurious or inaccurate texts circulated under his name that he has frequently been asked to correct. See also L.D. Reynolds and N.G. Wilson, *Scribes and Scholars: A Guide to the Transmission of Greek and Latin Literature* (Oxford, 1968), 23.

10   Christopher Baswell, *Virgil in Medieval England* (Cambridge, 1995) notes three different streams of Vergilian interpretation in Medieval England, see also Colin Burrow, 'Virgils, from Dante to Milton', in Charles Martindale (ed.), *The Cambridge Companion to Virgil* (Cambridge, 1997).

1,320 lines long.[11] Her poetry enjoyed a reputation in antiquity as the height of poetic craft, but her work survives today only in fragments, some recovered from papyrus and others quoted by later authors. The point about cultural adoption and reuse is particularly telling for Sappho in our own culture. She is once again a beloved, and much-read, poet because her work (what remains of it) resonates so well with our own sensibilities. This clearly was not the case in later antiquity, however, as Sappho ceased to be copied at some point. There are papyrus fragments containing her poems from the seventh-century CE, but no surviving manuscripts.[12]

In Vergil's day, she was clearly still very popular. Vergil's contemporary, Catullus, published a free translation of one of her poems (Fragment 31) into Latin, and Horace employs meters used by Sappho in many of his poems. But her texts were not a part of the standard curriculum, as Vergil's were, and this probably accounts for their disappearance. What does survive comes largely via quotation. Fragment 31, for example, is quoted by Longinus (10.2), in his treatise on the 'high', or grand, style in literature, περὶ ὕψους.[13] Sappho's poem is quoted as a supreme example of skill in representing the emotions felt by a lover observing her beloved. Longinus' text itself only survived through a single tenth-century manuscript and did not become popular again until the eighteenth century. The poem is still available to us because an obscure literary critic found it a useful illustration of a method that makes for high style in poetry.

The *Res Gestae*

The Roman historian Suetonius notes that one of the documents the first Roman emperor, Augustus left with the Vestal Virgins at his death, along with his will, was a narrative of his deeds, which he wished to be inscribed on bronze tablets in front of his mausoleum. The bronze tablets mentioned by Suetonius do not survive, but three copies of this document inscribed on stone have been found in the area covered by the Roman province of Galatia. One, from Ankara, contains both Latin text and Greek paraphrase, and there are fragments of a Greek translation discovered at Apollonia, and fragments of the Latin version at Antioch. There is enough text remaining for scholars to supplement and correct the Latin text and so to produce a fairly complete reconstruction of the original.

11   David A. Campbell, *Greek Lyric Poetry* (Bristol, 1994), p. 261.

12   L.D. Reynolds and N.G. Wilson, *Scribes and Scholars*, pp. 43, 46.

13   This is typically translated as On the Sublime, but as Ernst Robert Curtius, *European Literature and the Latin Middle Ages* (repr. edn, Princeton, 1991), p. 398 notes, this is somewhat misleading. We do not know who 'Longinus' was nor when he lived.

This is a text that was clearly intended to be a permanent memorial of its author. The location of the original 'engraved on two bronze pillars set up at Rome'[14] is noted at the head of the inscription. The copies, then were intended as physical representations of Augustan, and therefore Roman power and prestige, and provided a concrete link back to Rome, where the originals could be found. The copies themselves were also intended as a permanent installation, with a readable translation of the Latin original, which would have been unintelligible to most of the literate population, but nevertheless authentic. And even though the choice of medium for the originals, text inscribed on metal, was the best available, it is the copies and translations that remain, perhaps because the metal was regarded as a valuable (and reusable) commodity itself.

The nature of texts and transmission

The process of restoring the 'correct' readings of a text is called textual criticism.[15] It relies initially on the construction of a genealogical tree of relationships between manuscripts, based on the patterns of errors and variant readings contained therein. Once this recension has been constructed, manuscripts which are derived from other existing manuscripts can be eliminated from consideration as sources for reconstructing the correct version, and the intellectual process of deciding upon the best reading may proceed. This method is rarely 100 per cent successful for a variety of reasons. There may not be a clear ancestor manuscript because the existing copies may derive from multiple traditions, for example when the author made multiple editions of the work. Moreover, where there are such parallel traditions, manuscripts from different traditions may have been used by editors in the past to correct new editions, thus crossing the lines and creating a situation in which it may not be possible to reconstruct the sources. It is clear after centuries of studying the processes by which manuscripts are transmitted that precise, mechanical copying was not typically the intent of those making new editions of classical works.[16] Vergil in particular was adopted and adapted by a number of cultures for their own purposes. A new edition of an ancient work must therefore

---

14   P.A. Brunt and J.M. Moore (eds), *Res Gestae Divi Augusti: The Achievements of the Divine Augustus* (Oxford, 1989).

15   See Notis Toufexis, 'One Era's Nonsense, Another's Norm: Diachronic study of Greek and the Computer', (Chapter 6), in this volume for some useful perspective on the practices of textual criticism: the reconstruction of a single edition throws out data that are useful to historical linguists, for example.

16   Textual criticism typically aims at the reconstruction of an original version of a work, which may be impossible. The Homeric epics, for example, began as an orally transmitted tradition before they were written down. See Casey Dué and Mary Ebbott, *The Homer Multitext Project*, <http://chs.harvard.edu/chs/homer_multitext> for an attempt to use technology to represent the full sweep of Homeric textual transmission.

be examined for its rhetorical intent as well as the quality of its reproduction of its sources. As we have noted however, one of the reasons for the Vergilian corpus' success at surviving the passage of time was the ability of his editors to make their own uses of the text. Despite its limitations, textual criticism is able to produce texts which are useful to modern scholars.

The collection of difficulties that textual criticism has been developed to address consists of various kinds of copying errors. It is arguable that these may largely be mitigated in a digital environment. But the existence and success of the discipline of textual criticism shows that it is possible to do useful work on a tradition whose copying methods inherently impose a considerable degree of uncertainty on the readings of texts. These methods will have to be refined to work with digital copies and derivatives.[17]

We must also consider the question of formatting. The format in which a text of, e.g. Vergil is published today is vastly different from that in which it was originally published. At that time, the standard format for published books was the papyrus scroll. Codices, bound leaves of parchment like our own books, did not become a standard vehicle for publishing pagan literature until the second century. It seems initially to have been regarded as a low-quality, cheap medium, despite its mechanical superiority.[18] Not only was the medium different from our own, the actual placement of text on a page would also seem very unfamiliar. Words were not separated by spaces, lower-case letters were not used, nor was there any punctuation that would be familiar to us. The differences become painfully obvious when we consider that changes of speaker in drama were indicated only by a horizontal slash at the beginning of the line, or by a colon-like symbol in the middle of a line. Copying mistakes were an inevitable result.

By contrast, there is much emphasis in the modern study of digital preservation on preserving the appearance of documents, that is features like pagination, font, font size, the placement of text and figures on the page, and the like. But an overemphasis on appearance pushes one in the direction of technologies that I will argue are not the ideal vehicles for digital preservation.

Digital permanence

As we noted in the introduction, it was not uncommon for ancient authors to contend that their works would be immortal, and even that they would confer a degree of immortality upon their authors. Thucydides adapted this claim to his own, new style of writing, and we find even more explicit versions in poets like

---

17 Tools like the Versioning Machine <http://www.v-machine.org/index.php>) are the beginning of this work.

18 Reynolds and Wilson, *Scribes and Scholars*, pp. 30–31, describe the process of converting text on scrolls to codices in terms that will be familiar to anyone experienced in data migration.

Horace and Ovid.[19] What made these authors confident of their works' survival in this way, and into what sort of climate were they sending these surrogates of themselves? One answer is that they could look upon a certain continuity of culture and see that authors like themselves were still being read. They were also in many ways setting these works free. There was at the time absolutely no notion of copyright or intellectual property (IP), and no hope of royalties from book sales. Writing was thus an activity reserved for the aristocracy or for those lucky enough to acquire a patron. There was a lively book trade, mainly in cheap copies, although higher-quality editions were produced also. But an author would neither expect, nor receive any income from sales of copies of his work.

The situation is quite different today. But while the cultural circumstances surrounding modern publication are different in terms of the expectation of control over IP, and IP as a source of revenue, in the digital realm the situation is less well defined. While copyright pertains to digital objects, there are no physical barriers to copying and reuse, and the effort to develop business models for the distribution of digital material is still ongoing, with no clear winners yet. The problems with creating a revenue stream stem from the ease with which digital files may be copied and redistributed by their users. The field of digital rights management (DRM) represents one attempt to cope with this model, but the solutions presented thus far tend to be easily defeatable and/or too restrictive. DRM is an attempt to maintain control of a digital object once it has left the possession of the copyright holder. Unfortunately, this sort of control seems likely to be incompatible with long-term preservation goals, which will necessitate actions like making and distributing copies and migrating from one format to another for an indefinite period of time.

There is a growing movement to deal with the problems of digital publication by going in the opposite direction, and explicitly relinquishing some or all copying rights to the general public. The Creative Commons, for example, provides a mechanism for authors to produce licences that allow varying degrees of freedom to the consumers of their works to recopy, edit, republish, mash up or otherwise repurpose published works.[20] One objection to such licences is that they may reduce the ability of creators to profit from their work. The relationship of commerce to preservation is an important consideration, though somewhat outside the scope of this chapter. It is interesting to note that a number of authors who publish simultaneously in print and online report no adverse impact on sales. Indeed, the opposite may be the case, since open digital copies make the works much easier to discover.[21] As I noted above, to the extent that efforts to profit from digital

---

19   See Horace, *Odes* 3.30 and Ovid, *Metamorphoses* 15.871ff. for example.

20   Creative Commons, <http://creativecommons.org>.

21   See Cory Doctorow, *Ebooks: Neither E, Nor Books; Paper for the O'Reilly Emerging Technologies Conference, 2004,* <http://www.craphound.com/ebooksneitherenorbooks.txt> (2004) and Bruce Eckel, 'Why Do You Put Your Books on the Web? How Can You Make Any Money That Way?' *FAQ,* <http://web.archive.org//20041204221726/http://mindview.net/FAQ/FAQ-010>.

works involve controlling them once they have left the publisher's grasp, they reduce those works' chances of surviving long term. Creative Commons licences depend upon copyright law, and do not prevent creators from profiting from their creations, but may at the same time permit uses that improve the odds for the works' long-term survival.

It seems therefore reasonable to argue that we have returned to a situation somewhat like the one that existed in the ancient world and furthermore that perhaps some of the processes that governed the survival of ancient works might pertain to digital media. As in ancient times, a work released into the electronic environment may be copied, quoted, reused or resold without the originator's having much control over what happens to it. There are legal frameworks for controlling what happens to copies of a work, but in practice they may be hard to apply or may not be worth the trouble. Some works may be licensed in such a way that there are no legal barriers to such treatment. What we have seen from the limited survey of ancient works above is that copying often provides the most promising avenue for long-term survival.[22] We have also seen that simple mechanical copying does not represent the norm. Copies are made for a variety of reasons, but in general they reflect at least to some extent the motivations of the surrounding culture, and the copies are shaped and sometimes altered by those motivations. Copying often takes the form of reuse, or quotation, and these types of copying are by definition influenced by the motivations of the copier. Yet it is only through reuse that we have much of the Sappho that we do.

Much of the anxiety over the preservation of digital materials (particularly texts) has to do with concern over the loss of some intrinsic qualities that have to do with 'user experience'.[23] For printed materials, this means the appearance of text on the page. This has led to an effort to repurpose Adobe's Portable Document Format (PDF) as an archival digital format (PDF/A).[24] But as we noted above, there have been huge changes in the last two millennia in the ways in which written language is recorded. Modern printing methods are completely unsuited to representing the appearance of ancient texts. It wouldn't be possible to print a scroll on a modern laser printer without destroying its form. But there is absolutely no guarantee that the current standard form will be the dominant one in a hundred years. Indeed, we may be back to something more scroll-like: an 8.5 x 11-inch page does not fit well on a laptop screen. This doesn't matter yet because people in general prefer to read on paper rather than on screen, but as the technology improves, the obstacles to reading on screen will gradually be removed. Will the page as we know it make sense any longer at that point?

---

22   This is the principle behind the LOCKSS (Lots Of Copies Keep Stuff Safe) initiative, which attempts to preserve electronic content such as journals by distributing copies throughout the LOCKSS community. See <http://www.lockss.org/lockss/Home>.

23   William G. LeFurgy, 'PDF/A: Developing a File Format for Long-Term Preservation,' *RLG DigiNews*, 7:6, RLG, <http://worldcat.org/arcviewer/1/OCC/2007/08/08/0000070519/viewer/file3170.html#feature1> (15 December 2003).

24   See LeFurgy, 'PDF/A', for a summary of these efforts.

What this implies is that perhaps emphasis on technology that faithfully replicates the printed appearance of documents is misplaced. Technologies like PDF do this very well, but do so at the expense of the document's flexibility. Text-based markup technologies, on the other hand, such as XML, allow for the presentation of documents to be abstracted out to a separate set of instructions. Instead of the document being embedded in the format, the format is applied to the document. In other words, the content becomes primary again, and the appearance secondary. This type of focus is very much in keeping with the ways in which ancient documents have reached us: none of their copyists would have argued that the text's appearance was as important as its content. The appearance will have changed every time the text was copied.

O'Toole, in his seminal article on ideas of archival permanence, notes the distinction between the preservation of information and the preservation of the original documents.[25] Here we have a similar, though not identical, question to answer: whether the preservation of the precise appearance and experience of the digital original is more important than the preservation of the information it contains. As with physical preservation efforts, over the (very) long run, permanence of information seems a far more attainable goal than permanence of the originals.

Moreover, as we have seen, copies of ancient materials typically gathered additional materials in the form of commentary, glosses, and marginal notes as they progressed through history. These accretions would essentially become part of the text in many cases, because their value was recognized by those handling the text. Texts were witnesses not only of their author's words, but also of the interpretations and difficulties of their subsequent readers. It seems important to ask whether there should not be mechanisms built in to digital texts that allow for this type of annotation. In many cases there are: word processors allow for annotations and keep multiple versions of documents embedded in the same document, and PDF has a facility for this type of annotation also. What is lacking, again, is flexibility. Both are constrained by an orientation towards printed text, and in both the annotation mechanism is built in as a secondary function. Markup technologies such as XML, on the other hand, are inherently adaptable to new types of information. They also add the ability to further define and augment texts with semantic information, such as the marking and disambiguation of personal and place names as such.

Print-replicating technologies are typically argued to be preferable to others because they replicate the page structure of works, and therefore permit relatively precise citations to be made of their content.[26] Pagination is a relatively fragile construct in the digital age, however. A word-processing document will probably not retain the same pagination on two different computers. Indeed, it may change from one calculation to the next in the same program, on the same computer.

---

25   O'Toole, 'On the Idea of Permanence', 16–17.
26   LeFurgy, 'PDF/A'.

Citations by page for digital materials are thus not as helpful as they appear to be for print.[27] With the advent of full-text-searching capabilities, the need to specify the precise location of a cited thought in a monograph or article has lessened. Moreover, the digital medium provides mechanisms for very precise linking. The advantage of print-replicating technologies therefore is one based only on familiarity, not on actual usefulness. Based on these reasons, I would argue that efforts like PDF/A, while useful, are fundamentally flawed because of the way they 'freeze' the digital content.

In sum, we can see that the examination of a subset of textual transmission from the ancient world has a number of useful lessons for digital archivists.

1. We cannot predict how future generations will view or use the works in our care. The things a culture values can change radically over the course of several generations, so there is no guarantee that the intrinsic value of a work will be estimated in the same way one hundred or one thousand years from now. Therefore, while due care must be taken in preserving digital resources in our archives, their long-term survival may best be ensured by releasing copies from our control.

2. There tend to be cycles of societal interest in any work. Any long-term preservation strategy must therefore rest upon preparing the work to survive the next interval of disinterest. There were editions of Sappho's poems in the Library of Alexandria, but because they ceased to be copied, nearly all of her output is lost. Preservation decisions will be driven, at least to some extent, by the interests of the culture at large. There are no clear solutions to this problem, but a digital archivist can at least seek to inspire interest in their materials by making them generally available. The modern situation is far better than the ancient in the sense that there are fewer communication barriers and a larger audience, and so there is a higher probability of attracting an interested community around your material.

3. Self-sustaining communities of interest provide the best insurance against the ravages of time. The survival of the Vergilian corpus is in large measure due to not one but several communities that made their own uses of his texts. This suggests another possible role for the digital archivist: facilitating communication between interested users and creating communities that care about our materials.

4. Original objects typically do not survive, but their intellectual content may be preserved nevertheless. Even if there have been errors introduced into derivatives of the original work during its transmission, it is likely that the original can be reconstructed, or at least a close enough approximation to be useful. We should therefore not be overly concerned about maintaining the

---

27 Even in print, they are sometimes of dubious value: pagination changes with each new edition of a printed work, and scholars frequently have the experience of finding citations that do not actually point at the right section of text.

integrity of copies of digital resources outside our control. We especially should not over-stress the importance of preserving the original appearance of such resources.

5. The likelihood of the success of long-term preservation is higher the more copies of the work there are in existence. Digital archivists should therefore consider trying to obtain rights to reproduce digital resources without limitation. The Creative Commons licensing schemes provide a useful framework for allowing rights holders to assert those rights without hindering the reproduction or use of their materials. The sources for any access component of a digital preservation project should be made publicly available, so that they can be republished or repurposed by other projects. Publications that reuse or make partial use of archived resources are to be encouraged, because these contribute to a cultural atmosphere that values these resources.

We may conclude by returning to Thucydides' definition of his history as a possession for eternity rather than an ephemeral entertainment. This binary division suggests a strategy for digital archivists wishing to preserve cultural material: objects encumbered by restrictions on copying and reuse cannot truly be called possessions (except of the rights holder) and are therefore *ipso facto* less likely to survive and perhaps do not deserve to have limited resources used on them unless there is hope of bringing them ultimately into the public domain. This is a pessimistic view, but to the extent that this is an engineering problem, Murphy's Law can be assumed to operate: over time, anything that can go wrong, probably will. The true solution to the long-term preservation problem is to change it, as much as possible, from a technical problem to a social one. Preservation, leaving aside accidents of history, is a human enterprise, and cannot succeed without human intervention. The rise in recent years of online communities with broad adoption, such as Facebook, may point to ways of enabling digital survival by generating community interest in them.

Chapter 9

Creating a Generative Learning Object (GLO): Working in an 'Ill-Structured' Environment and Getting Students to Think

Eleanor OKell, Dejan Ljubojevic and Cary MacMahon

Introduction

UK higher education institutions (HEIs) are developing generic e-Learning strategies in response to the funding bodies' national e-Learning policy which will need to be implemented by practitioners at subject level in an awareness of Higher Education's goal of producing autonomous learners. Humanities practitioners work towards this goal through a well-established face-to-face technique – the seminar, which teaches students to evaluate multiple interpretations in order to produce the most appropriate answers from what is often incomplete evidence. A key question is whether seminar pedagogy can be computationally modelled, and if so, to what extent.

This question was addressed during an extended collaborative project (2006–2008) by the Higher Education Academy's History, Classics and Archaeology (HCA) Subject Centre and the Centre for Excellence in Teaching and Learning for Reusable Learning Objects (RLO-CETL). This project digitally modelled the seminar (as a typical instance of humanities pedagogy) in a generic form inside a software package – the Generative Learning Object (GLO) Maker software and made this available for use by practitioners in their teaching.[1]

---

1   The authors would like to thank the organizers and the audience of the Digital Classicist Seminar for the opportunity to present the prototype and their response and suggestions, which have contributed to the freely available GLO Maker software. GLO Maker, with accompanying documentation, is downloadable from <http://www.glomaker.org> and the *evaluating Multiple Interpretations* (*eMI*): *Altar of Pergamum* online interactive tutorial is available from <http://www.heacademy.ac.uk/hca/themes/e-learning/emi_glo>; along with further documentation: Eleanor R. OKell, 'e-Learning and *evaluating Multiple Interpretations* (*eMI*): The Background to the GLO Tool and Interface – A Practitioner-Developer's Perspective' and '*evaluating Multiple Interpretations* (*eMI*): The Tasks and their Pedagogical Underpinning', *HCA Work-in-Progress* (July 2007), <http://www.heacademy.ac.uk/hca/themes/e-learning/emi_glo>. (All URLs current at the time of writing.)

RLO-CETL was motivated towards collaboration by the desire to elicit pedagogical patterns from different disciplines and realize those patterns in highly user-friendly digital forms that would be adopted by practitioners. This desire means that practitioners are respected as experts in subject-specific pedagogies and the design process is practitioner-led. HCA was motivated towards collaboration by two factors. First, the pragmatic need to engage with the UK HE e-Learning agenda, in which e-Learning is seen partly as a solution to increasing student–teacher ratios and possibly as an audit tool for establishing that learning is taking place.[2] Second, the HCA disciplinary communities' desire for e-resources appropriate to their teaching practice and its goals.

The collaboration revealed that practitioner-led e-resource development can result in e-resources that can be used both to demonstrate and enhance humanities' practitioners' ability to teach students to think. This chapter outlines the background to the project, the contribution of disciplinary practitioners and the technical aspects of the development.

Background to the project

Classics, humanities and critical thinking as a learning objective

Classicists are concerned with students' use of the most widely available e-resource, the information-rich Internet:

> Classical material can be found by doing a Google search, but many searches produce a confusing plethora of mostly irrelevant hits and lead to sites for which quality assurance is lacking.[3]

Concern over students' (in)ability to judge the relevance and worth of search results is part of wider concerns about undergraduates' critical reading ability, and (in)ability to handle/grade multiple interpretations: to negotiate the multi-vocality characteristic of the historical disciplines. However:

---

2   R. Land, 'Paradigms Lost: Academic Practice and Exteriorising Technologies', *E-Learning*, 3:1 (2006): 100–10 emphasizes that the Virtual Learning Environment and the exteriorizing power of e-Learning have opened up previously hidden disciplinary and teaching processes to administrative view, making them susceptible to new managerialist auditing, assessment and criticism.

3   APA/AIA Task Force on Electronic Publications, Final Report (March 2007, updated March 2008), 5, <http://socrates.berkeley.edu/~pinax/pdfs/TaskForceFinalReport.pdf> (accessed December 2008); cf. CIBER, *Information Behaviour of the Researcher of the Future* (January 2008), <http://www.bl.uk/news/pdf/googlegen.pdf> (accessed May 2009).

You cannot say that children are intellectually lazy because they are using the Internet when academics are using search engines in their research. The difference is that [academics] have more experience of being critical about what is retrieved and whether it is authoritative. Children need to be told how to use the Internet in a critical and appropriate way.[4]

While UK HE does not deal with children, it predominantly deals with the products of an educational system in which the Internet is often the authoritative school *intra*net and success resulted from reproducing 'the answer the examiner is looking for'. Classics and modern language students have commented, 'Nobody teaches us how to read texts,' and end-of-year feedback from first years includes: 'It's all so confusing and the lecturers won't tell you the right answer.'[5] Critical awareness, therefore, does not come as standard, but is a goal for HE embodied by claims to produce autonomous learners in the Quality Assurance Agency (QAA) Subject Benchmark Statements.[6] Hence, humanities' practitioners' challenge and implicit remit is to teach students how to read and reason, not just about subject-specific material.

Thus, Humanities academics need to identify the attitudes and skills which enable students to become critical thinkers and fully-fledged exponents of their discipline and then communicate and teach these so that they motivate students to act upon them.[7] This means that academics must assist students to acquire the idea that from the same evidence base there is a range of possible

---

4   Jenny Fry of the Oxford Internet Institute, cited by Chloe Stothart, 'Web Threatens Learning Ethos', *Times Higher Education Supplement*, 22 June 2007: 2.

5   National Student Satisfaction Survey (NSSS) 2005–2006; for further evidence of student opinions, sought following NSSS 2005–2006, see A. Mortimer, A. Jasani and S. Whitmore, *University of Leeds: Assessment and Feedback in the School of Modern Languages and Cultures and the School of Classics: 'Fair, Prompt and Detailed' – Matching Staff and Student Expectations on Assessment and Feedback in Light of the National Student Survey* (Mouchel Parkman: Nottingham, April 2006), <http://www.german.leeds. ac.uk/learning/Assessment%20and%20Feedback%20Report%20FINAL%2002.05.06. htm> (accessed December 2008).

6   For 'autonomous learning' as HE study's 'endpoint' see Section 4.2.1 of QAA, 'Classics and Ancient History Benchmark Statement' (Quality Assurance Agency for Higher Education: 2000).

7   Critical thinking, according to J. Biggs, *Teaching for Quality Learning at University: what the student does* (Buckingham, 1999), only comes from a deep approach, which can be produced as a reaction to the teaching environment and is more likely to be adopted in relaxed and non-threatening learning environments, which does not mean environments lacking in challenge. See also D. Kember, 'Interpreting Student Workload and the Factors which Shape Students' Perceptions of their Workload', *Studies in Higher Education*, 29:2 (2004): 165–84, and D. Kember and D.Y.P. Leung, 'Characterising a Teaching and Learning Environment Conducive to Making Demands on Students While Not Making their Workload Excessive', *Studies in Higher Education*, 31:2 (2006): 185–98.

right answers (a 'threshold concept' for humanities), which can be differentiated because those answers: (1) depend upon evidence and disciplinary and ideological methodologies; and (2) are open to challenges in those areas.[8] For many students making the transition from seeking 'the right answer' to choosing between 'right answers', never mind advancing to formulating and defending their own 'right answers', goes against the grain of their educational experience but is necessary for progression. Successfully making that transition prepares the student to produce work that 'shows some awareness of relevant scholarly debate and the ability to engage with it intellectually; demonstrates the ability to sustain independent and rigorous argument, and shows effective powers of analysis'.[9]

The pedagogical means by which humanities disciplines have traditionally achieved this are face-to-face teaching (lectures transmitting information and demonstrating interpretative and argumentative methods and seminars), guided reading (to contextualize lectures and prepare for seminars and essay writing) and discussion in small groups (seminars, tutorials and supervisions), whereby negotiating multiple interpretations can be made challenging but not threatening, before assessing with the long essay. This is good practice because:

> Inconsistency in content and presentation can be viewed as an opportunity for effective learning – rather than as a barrier to it. These inconsistencies or dissonances can form the basis for self-directed learning as active exploration and contextualization. Providing students with a series of objects that use different vocabulary and present subject matter from different viewpoints can make the learning experience more authentic and engaging.[10]

Aligning student activities (for seminars/tutorials) with the learning outcome of becoming a critical thinker and aiming to develop and assess critical thinking skills will encourage students, even those adopting a strategic/achieving approach (who select a learning strategy to achieve their goals, e.g. passing or getting a 2:1),

---

8   'A threshold concept can be considered as akin to a portal, opening up a new and previously inaccessible way of thinking about something. It represents a transformed way of understanding, or interpreting, or viewing something without which the learner cannot progress.' E. Meyer and R. Land, 'Threshold Concepts and Troublesome Knowledge: Linkages to Ways of Thinking and Practising within the Disciplines', Occasional Report 4 of the *Enhancing Teaching-Learning Environments in Undergraduate Courses Project* (May 2003), <http://www.tla.ed.ac.uk/etl/docs/ETLreport4.pdf> (accessed December 2008).

9   Taken from the Upper 2:1 (65–69) grade descriptor, University of Durham, *Department of Classics and Ancient History Undergraduate Handbook 2007–08*, p. 32.

10   N. Friesen, 'Three Objections to Learning Objects and E-learning Standards', in R. McGreal (ed.), *Online Education Using Learning Objects* (Routledge: London, 2004), pp. 59–70.

to adopt a deep approach in order to do well.[11] Being explicit about this is essential because students' 'learning' is not directly about [subjects], but about learning how to please lecturers and gain marks'.[12] Research has shown that many students are strongly motivated by assessment. If students 'learn what they think they will be tested on', then positive results are attained by making clear what they will be tested on, and rewarding the ability to work with course content to produce a conscious, competent, well-grounded expression of a personal interpretation of the text(s) or topic(s) under consideration through assessment.[13]

Hence, a 'safe-but-challenging' learning environment facilitates, or scaffolds, the transition to critical awareness/thinking through confidence-boosting formative and summative assessment phases, linked to the knowledge of content and the ability to handle that content critically. This type of environment provides explicit explanations of the aims and objectives throughout, and develops at least deep-strategic learners and at best enthusiastic learners; both exhibit autonomy and both accept and negotiate interpretative pluralism.

Classics, humanities and e-learning

In 2005 HCA embarked on a JISC-funded scoping survey of the use of e-resources for teaching and learning in the historical disciplines in UK HE, to determine how e-resources were used and to identify opportunities for development.[14] Data analysis revealed that participating academics strongly favoured the creation of a community model enabling the sharing of both their content and the pedagogy structuring their teaching use of e-learning materials, with 76 per cent of 174

---

11   On strategic/achieving approaches, see N.J. Entwhistle and P. Ramsden, *Understanding Student Learning* (Croom Helm: London, 1983) and J. Biggs, *Student Approaches to Learning and Studying* (Australian Council for Educational Research: Hawthorn, Victoria, 1987). F. Marton and R. Säljö, 'On Qualitative Differences in Learning II: Outcome as a Function of the Learner's Conception of the Task', *British Journal of Educational Psychology*, 46 (1976): 115–27, demonstrated the positive relationship between a deep approach and success for qualitatively better learning outcomes (including critical thinking). This is confirmed in quantitative studies; see the meta-analysis of D. Watkins, 'Correlates of Approaches to Learning: A Cross-Cultural Meta-Analysis', in R.J. Sternberg and L.F. Zhang (eds), *Perspectives on Thinking, Learning and Cognitive Styles* (Mahwah, NJ, 2001), pp. 165–95, which shows the positive relationship between an achieving approach and academic achievement.

12   P. Ramsden, *Learning to Teach in Higher Education* (2nd edn, Routledge: London, 2003).

13   Biggs, *Teaching for Quality Learning*.

14   Cary MacMahon (ed.), *Using and Sharing Online Resources in History, Classics and Archaeology* (Glasgow, 2006), <http://www.heacademy.ac.uk/assets/hca/documents/UsingandSharingOnlineResourcesHCA.pdf> (accessed December 2008).

survey respondents believing their teaching could benefit from sharing e-learning resources with colleagues.

This benefit was conceptualized in terms of subject-specific knowledge and expertise as well as of enabling comparison and potential adoption/adaptation of pedagogies that successfully present general themes and address national issues, not to mention time saving. These results indicate a community desire to 'move beyond subsistence and towards a transaction economy in e-resources'.[15] Practitioners' desire, however, is not for 'plug-and-play' e-Learning resources but for e-resources customizable with particular content and for particular learning objectives and that do not require the acquisition of new skills or recourse to third-party assistance, much as they might adapt the curriculum designs, module booklets or handouts of colleagues to suit their own needs.

While practitioners may identify a handout as a Learning Object (and a reusable one), a learning technologist defines a Learning Object as something based on a single learning objective. Digital Learning Objects are comprised of a standalone collection of four web-based components:

1. *Presentation*: communication of the concept, fact, process, principle or procedure to be understood by the learner in order to support the learning objective.
2. *Activity*: something the learner must do to engage with the content in order to better understand it.
3. *Assessment*: a way in which the learner can apply their understanding and test their mastery of the content.
4. *Links*: to external resources to reinforce the message and aid understanding.

One of RLO-CETL's founding mission objectives was to address the shortcomings of Learning Object research that failed to deliver on the second of its two aims: interoperability and reusability.[16] RLO-CETL's initial work was aimed at understanding the requirements of all stakeholders in order to produce a set of Learning Objects that are reusable at curriculum level.[17] For example, one set addressed attaining study skills and these are reused in disparate disciplines to scaffold reflective writing, referencing, etc. This critical mass of curriculum-reusable Learning Objects established a collaborative design model and provided

---

15   T. Boyle, 'Design Principles for Authoring Dynamic, Reusable Learning Objects,' *Australian Journal of Educational Technology*, 19:1 (2003): 46–58.

16   See Friesen 'Three Objections' and P. Polsani, 'Use and Abuse of Reusable Learning Objects', *Journal of Digital Information*, 3:.4 (2003), <http://journals.tdl.org/jodi/article/view/89/88> (accessed May 2009).

17   Around 200 Learning Objects were created, <http://www.rlo-cetl.ac.uk/joomla/index.php>.

a data set for analysis in terms of understanding the generic properties behind the successful pedagogical design embodied in these Learning Objects.

The collaborative project followed on from this and its focus presented a suitable vehicle to explore the generic aspect behind the pedagogical design of Learning Objects because humanities curriculum reuse is atypical. In other words RLOs (as conceptualized in RLO-CETL's initial phase) had been seen as 'unsuitable' for humanities because of their initial development for/in scientific disciplines in relation to a 'core curriculum' necessary for progression, which led to a focus on presenting and testing the acquisition of facts or concepts which generate right answers (favouring linear methods of knowledge acquisition and application/problem-solving) and promoting a humanities-incompatible surface-strategic learning approach. A particular concern is that the learning design may impact adversely on the type of grounded creativity which lies at the heart of the best historical research: '[shuttering] the historical imagination, at best limiting and channeling historical thinking and at worst confining it to procedural, binary steps'.[18]

However, given the desire to share resources and pedagogy and the increased sharing enabled by RLOs and GLOs, HCA considered that it was worth discovering whether learning-technology approaches suitable for the scientific (or 'hard/applied') disciplines could be adapted for use within the 'soft/pure' humanities disciplines.

Consequently HCA adopted a fivefold plan:

1. To domesticate the Learning Object, making it relevant and responsive to disciplinary needs.
2. To subvert technology for the disciplines' ends, tailoring it to disciplinary needs rather than tailoring those needs to what e-learning resources tend to do.
3. To exteriorize the pedagogy, i.e. making the means by which the e-Learning resource teaches clear to the user (increasing relevance).
4. To illustrate that pedagogy with subject-specific examples.
5. To address a nationally, if not globally, relevant issue of teaching critical-thinking skills, by emphasizing the key threshold concept of multivocality in a manageable and accessible format, assisting students to:
   a) negotiate the reality of multiple interpretations of evidence,
   b) realize the necessity to differentiate between interpretations and the means by which this may be done,
   c) acquire/improve the ability to mediate within and contribute to this multi-vocality while retaining their own voice.

---

18   W.G. Thomas, 'Computing and the Historical Imagination', in S. Schreibman, R. Siemens and J. Unsworth (eds), *A Companion to Digital Humanities* (Blackwell, 2004), 56.

The contribution of disciplinary practitioners

With this plan in mind, HCA participated in a *Sharing the LOAD* (Learning Activities, Objects and Design) Project workshop run by Universities' Collaboration in e-Learning (UCeL) in November 2006. There HCA worked with other humanities academics, who were equally exercised about student critical evaluation skills (specifically the inability to identify the value of books other than those on the bibliography), on scaffolding students' appreciation of multiple scholarly interpretations and disciplinary difference. The resulting idea for a Learning Object was simple: take an artefact and integrate interpretations from the disciplines of Art, religion, anthropology, sociology and history/archaeology, including short bibliographies and conclude with an activity encouraging students to form their own interpretation as part of this 'Community of Learning'.

The interpretations used are up to the individual academic, as is the artefact, which could be anything from a Neolithic monument or a papyrus text, to a concept (hubris or postmodernism) or event (the Battle of Marathon). The format is that which underpins the seminar – prior research focused on an artefact is discussed to produce an opinion as part of a repeatable learning cycle, not as the endpoint of learning. The workshop participants had identified what humanities disciplines aim to do and the means by which they do it. This was achieved in a context where educational technologists keen to create the next generation of e-Learning resources could identify this aim and determine whether it could be modelled electronically.

This 'powerful pedagogical pattern',[19] which exteriorized a humanities pedagogy used to realize the learning outcome of developing a student from a 'knowledge seeker' to an 'understanding seeker', and ultimately into a thinking disciplinary exponent, was modelled as a Generative Learning Object which became known as *evaluating Multiple Interpretations* (*eMI*). The *eMI* Learning Object proof-of-concept for software development was funded by the JISC Design for Learning (DeL) Programme as part of the *Sharing the LOAD* Project and a full version of *eMI* in the GLO Maker software was funded by the Higher Education Academy Subject Centres and CETLs Collaboration initiative.

The collaboration proceeded from the premise that 'academics are not likely to adopt a teaching resource made elsewhere unless it "fits" with their assumptions about appropriate and viable methods for their content domain'.[20] Thus, academic experts were involved from the beginning to develop academic content in dialogue with learning technologists; working according to the model of distributed media

---

19   Boyle, 'Design Principles'.

20   J.D. Bain and C. McNaught, 'How academics use technology in teaching and learning: understanding the relationship between beliefs and practice', *Journal of Computer Assisted Learning* 2.2 (2006), 99–113.

development established by UCeL for RLO development, with clear divisions of responsibility being established according to expertises (see Figure 9.1).[21]

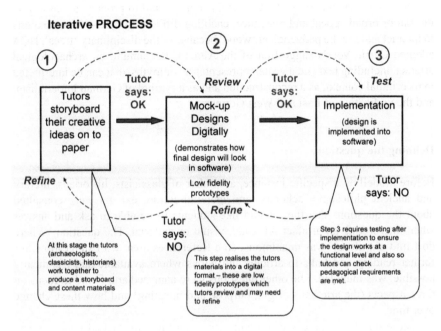

Figure 9.1   The three-stage interdisciplinary design process model

Source: Reprinted with permission from RLO-CETL, www.rlo-cetl.ac.uk.

Deciding the content

The role of practitioner-developers was to enable the learning technologists' pedagogical exteriorization by identifying the underlying discipline-specific categories which are employed during the critical interpretive process and which

---

21   For the UCeL model, see D. Leeder and R. Morales, 'Universities' Collaboration in e-Learning (UCeL): Post-Fordism in Action', *UCeL Documents* (2004), <http://www.ucel.ac.uk/documents/docs/LEEDERMORALES.pdf> (accessed December 2008), and 'Distributed Development', <http://www.ucel.ac.uk/about/development.html>; for clear divisions of responsibility, see C. Bradley and T. Boyle, 'The Design, Development, and use of Multimedia Learning Objects', *Journal of Educational Multimedia and Hypermedia*, 13:4 (2004): 371–90; also J. Struthers, *Working Models for Designing Online Courses and Materials* (York, 2002), <http://www.heacademy.ac.uk/assets/York/documents/resources/resourcedatabase/id197_Working_Models_for_Designing_Online_Courses_and_Materials.rtf> (accessed December 2008).

they use (sometimes unconsciously) in their teaching. The collaborators discovered that articulation of underlying pedagogical decisions is easiest for practitioners when working with a concrete example and that learning technologists are well-placed to identify generic patterns. For this reason, and to produce a 'showcase' tutorial of broad appeal and relevance, enabling different subject-domain experts to interact and see the pedagogical 'wood' because of the disciplinary 'trees', HCA adopted Carrie Vout's suggestion of the Altar of Pergamum: an archaeological artefact, including text and a visual representation of myths, that can be interpreted in its original context, as a reconstruction and as a symbol of German imperialism, and the unification of East and West Germany.

Defining the questions

Before modelling a specific instance, a number of classicists, historians, literary and ancient philosophy scholars, and material-culture experts were consulted about the questions that they would like students to be able to ask and answer when interpreting an artefact – textual, visual or material. The question 'Where do I find out more?' was unanimous, so a References area, with suggestions for further reading and links to articles and books where available and technically possible, was included. The other questions were analysed and found to focus on three aspects (the artefact's origin, purpose and meaning) and how these change over time.

These questions increased in complexity, starting with factual concerns and working up to self-reflexive, methodologically aware and discipline-conscious questions, culminating with disciplinary suspicion (asking, 'How do we know what we think we know?').[22] Students need exposure to each of these phases to become autonomous, and to be assessed each time for the learning outcome to be demonstrably achieved. Each phase adds to the previous one, leading to an appreciation that interpretation can affect the answers given to the initial, 'fact-seeking', questions.

In addition, the questions are frequently left implicit in interpretive activities (with the notable exception of guidance for comment questions in exams), suggesting that the questions are intrinsic to a critical approach and that identifying and appreciating the questions is part of becoming a competent disciplinary exponent. Hence, teaching the study of past cultures is not about teaching the student to interpret (teaching an explicit question set), but about developing a particular set of values, attitudes and beliefs that affect the way in

---

22   For Phase 1 questions (mainly focused on factual concerns and relating primarily to the artefact's origin), see *eMI: Altar of Pergamum* <http://www.heacademy. ac.uk/hca/themes/e-learning/emi_glo>. For Phase 1, 2 and 3 questions, see OKell, 'e-Learning and *eMI*'.

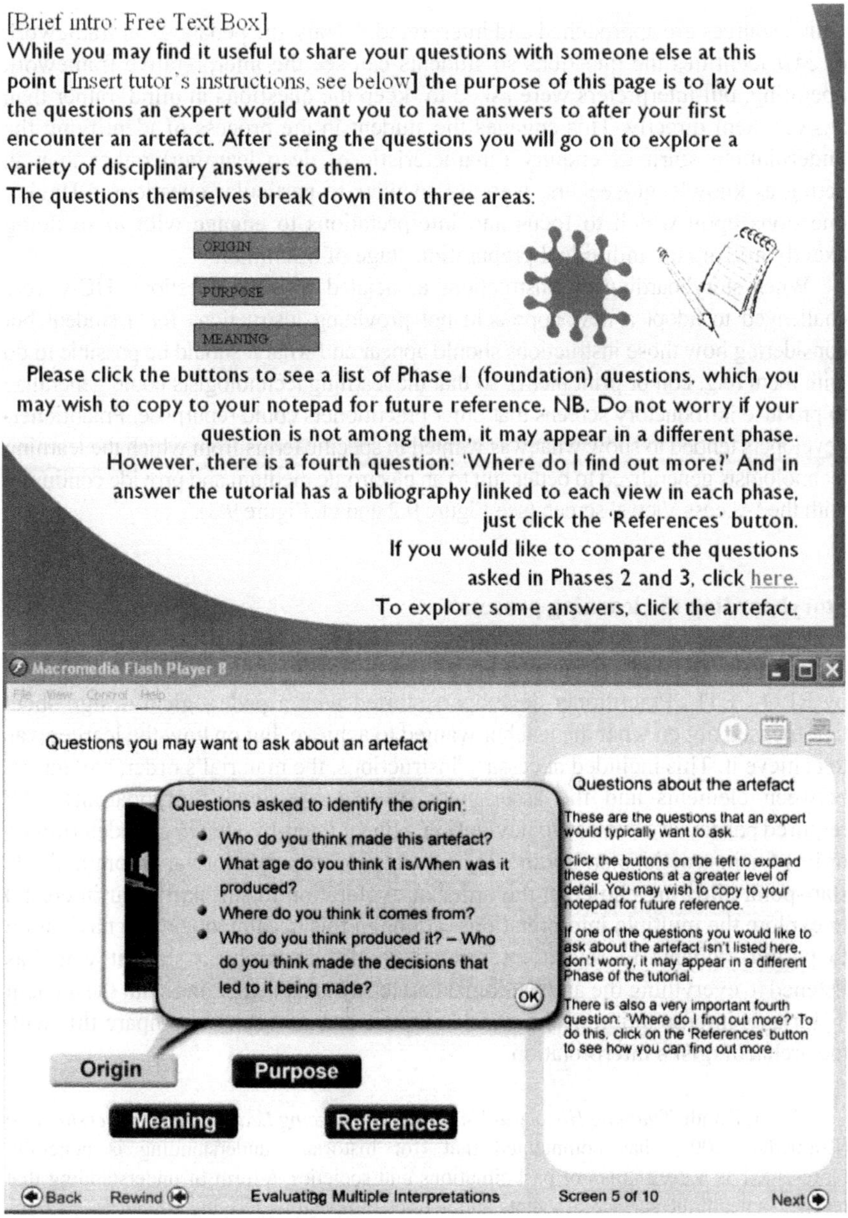

[Brief intro: Free Text Box]

While you may find it useful to share your questions with someone else at this point [Insert tutor's instructions, see below] the purpose of this page is to lay out the questions an expert would want you to have answers to after your first encounter an artefact. After seeing the questions you will go on to explore a variety of disciplinary answers to them.

The questions themselves break down into three areas:

ORIGIN

PURPOSE

MEANING

Please click the buttons to see a list of Phase I (foundation) questions, which you may wish to copy to your notepad for future reference. NB. Do not worry if your question is not among them, it may appear in a different phase. However, there is a fourth question: 'Where do I find out more?' And in answer the tutorial has a bibliography linked to each view in each phase, just click the 'References' button.

If you would like to compare the questions asked in Phases 2 and 3, click here.

To explore some answers, click the artefact.

Macromedia Flash Player 8

File View Control Help

Questions you may want to ask about an artefact

Questions asked to identify the origin:

- Who do you think made this artefact?
- What age do you think it is/When was it produced?
- Where do you think it comes from?
- Who do you think produced it? – Who do you think made the decisions that led to it being made?

(OK)

Questions about the artefact

These are the questions that an expert would typically want to ask.

Click the buttons on the left to expand these questions at a greater level of detail. You may wish to copy to your notepad for future reference.

If one of the questions you would like to ask about the artefact isn't listed here, don't worry, it may appear in a different Phase of the tutorial.

There is also a very important fourth question: 'Where do I find out more?' To do this, click on the 'References' button to see how you can find out more.

Origin   Purpose

Meaning   References

◀ Back   Rewind ◀   Evaluating Multiple Interpretations   Screen 5 of 10   Next ▶

Figure 9.2   From the 'Introducing the Questions' storyboard to the Learning Object screen

Source: Reprinted with permission from RLO-CETL, www.rlo-cetl.ac.uk.

which sources are approached and interpreted.[23] Thus, the pedagogical framework of *eMI* identifies the questions so students can see the interpretative framework operating, but interpreters were asked to 'keep the questions in mind' rather than answer them directly. This engages the student in the process of identifying the underpinning spirit of enquiry (characteristic of deep learning) rather than in acting as knowledge-seekers, wanting answers to particular questions.[24] Having questions upon which to focus and interpretations to engage with in so doing exactly mirrors the individual preparation stage of a seminar.

When storyboarding the instructions associated with the questions, HCA were challenged to adopt a new approach: not providing instructions for a student but considering how those instructions should appear and what it should be possible to do with them (e.g. edit or print them), so that the learning technologists could generalize to produce introductory screens that other practitioners could repurpose. Practitioner-developers tended to show what was wanted in specific terms from which the learning technologists generalized to better suit to an electronic medium and provide continuity with the 'Access Views' screen (see Figure 9.2 and cf. Figure 9.3).

Storyboarding the learning process

eMI's pedagogical pattern was rendered electronically using materials developed by RLO-CETL. Practitioner-developers started with a pedagogical design sheet that focused not on what the teacher wanted to achieve, but on how the learner was to achieve it. This included necessary instructions, the material's order, navigation between elements and the assessment of understanding. Storyboarding *eMI* required particular attention to navigation – linear (step-by-step in a predetermined order) for instructions and branching (a selection of ways forward from a single start-point allowing choice in the order of exploration to suit particular interests) to explore the multiple interpretations, although this became open/free navigation to permit students to revisit interpretations: for example, a student who has listened to everything the archaeologist had to say and is engaging with the ancient historian's interpretation of the altar's purpose can go back to compare this with the archaeologist's interpretation.

---

23   A. Booth, *Teaching History at University: Enhancing Learning and Understanding* (Routledge, 2003), has commented that 'for historians understanding is generally represented as a deep grasp of past situations and societies, a form of understanding that reaches beneath the surface of events and actions to reveal underlying structures, patterns and principles. In the process of deepening their understanding, students gain insight into their subject, themselves and the world around them by questioning established notions, considering diverse views and building independent judgements. Such learning is at once critical, reflective and imaginative'; see also S. Pace, 'The Roles of Challenge and Skill in the Flow Experiences of Web Users', *Issues in Informing Science and Information Technology*, 1 (2004): 341–58.

24   See further OKell 'evaluating Multiple Interpretations'.

Storyboarded screens showed the student engaging with views of the origin, purpose and meaning of the Altar of Pergamum (ever-present as an illustration) by a classicist, historian and archaeologist. These screens were reached from one emphasizing potential differences between disciplines and encouraging the student to explore one discipline at a time to reduce confusion. The learning technologists' concern at this point in the design process, given the ultimate goal of comparing disciplinary approaches as a whole, was with the learner's potential confinement within disciplinary boundaries; a confinement further implied by the sequential presentation of disciplinary interpretations. The alternative design suggestion was to enable comparison of multiple interpretations of, for example, origin alone. This suggestion was immediately taken on board by the practitioner-developers whose original preference was to enable students to make parallel comparisons at the latter (micro) level, as well as at the former (macro) level, but who had been unable to envisage appropriate navigation and had therefore reluctantly abandoned the idea. This shows how working across the disciplinary divide enables the design process to cross-compensate in a truly symbiotic fashion, whereby the *eMI* pattern's technological instantiation preserved its fitness for pedagogical purpose. For example, the GLO representation of the *eMI* pattern enables students to choose whether to engage with the interpretation of the archaeologist in its entirety or with all the disciplinary interpretations on a particular area: see Figure 9.3.

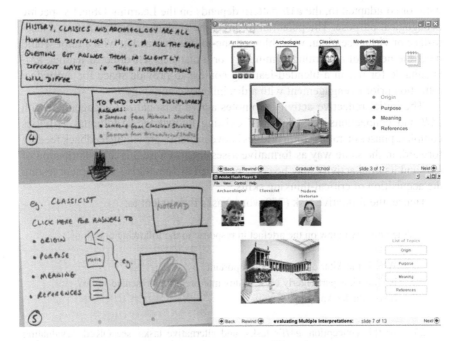

Figure 9.3   The storyboard became 'Access Views'

The layout does not privilege any particular interpretation, so the image presented on the screen reinforces one of the key points of *eMI* for the visual learner. Consider the difference if the topics appeared in a row and the interpretations in a column, which would suggest that those at the top are 'better' or should be engaged with first. Additionally, this layout permits holists (predisposed to engage with each interpretation in its entirety, and serialists (predisposed to engage with all the interpretations of a single topic) to engage with the content in the manner most suited to their own learning style.

In addition to the pedagogical benefits, computationally modelling the interpretive process allows *eMI* to be more easily repurposed, because every practitioner can insert their own artefact and interpretations, and even redefine the areas addressed, as well as varying the number of views and areas displayed.

Providing the pedagogical framework

Practitioner-developers embedded the 'Access Views' screen embodying the *eMI* pattern into a pedagogical framework that prepared students to actively engage with the interpretations. Additionally, they devised a range of exercises and quizzes aimed at encouraging students to situate themselves as interpreters within the debate by linking the process with grade criteria. The range of types of patterns (quizzes, follow-up and prerequisite exercises/tasks, etc.) that can be used in conjunction with, or co-adapted to, the *eMI* pattern depends on the Learning Object's specific pedagogical purpose. The potential to direct the student on completion to a face-to-face or virtual seminar, wiki, blog or one-to-one interaction with a tutor would meet the needs of a learning community or a distance/self-directed learner. *eMI* is suitable for use in a blended-learning context to provide space for individual reflection prior to engagement with a disciplinary community.

The initial reflective activity promotes active personalized engagement with *eMI* and connections with students' existing knowledge. Additional activities complete phases or, rather, form bridges between them – providing feedback feeding forward, in the same way as formative assessment. Phase 3 is the culmination of *eMI* and its final activity may be conceptualized as summative assessment testing the acquisition of critical-thinking skills.[25]

Hence, the formative task (750 words) asks the student to:

> Write your own view on the artefact in response to the following questions:
>
>> Why is the Altar of Pergamum important?
>> Is your view particularly close to any interpretation presented so far?
>> If so, which? And why?

---

25   For this conception, *eMI*'s tasks, and alternative tasks, see OKell, 'evaluating Multiple Interpretations'.

It then asks them to consider whether there are any areas in which their view needs expansion and which kind of interpretation they think will be most helpful.[26]

The summative task (1,500 words) is to:

> Discuss the significance of the Altar of Pergamum for our understanding of disciplinary difference.
>
> The answer should use your prior knowledge, any interpretations consulted, notes made during or after discussions, any questions raised (particularly any still unanswered) and references followed up.

However, the initial phase is focused primarily (though not exclusively) on knowledge acquisition, which it is appropriate to assess through Multiple Choice Questions (MCQs), which are a common feature of e-Learning. The electronic environment provides immediate feedback, either confirming appropriate responses and adding further information (suggesting that knowledge is a reward for good performance and affirming the expectation that knowledge should be built on) or providing guidance as to why the response is invalid, leaving the student to retry the question and prompting them to actively review their knowledge/notes.

While MCQs are generally seen as a low-level intellectual activity, their use can increase students' confidence in their command of dense explanations or challenging concepts, thereby improving the flow and standard of seminar discussions.[27] Using MCQs does not mean using single answer yes/no questions and GLO Maker offers two MCQ formats (three options with one piece of feedback or four options with four pieces, the latter of which was chosen for *eMI: Altar of Pergamum*). For example:

1) Which ruler began the construction of the Altar of Pergamum?

   a) Attalus II
   b) Eumenes
   c) Prusias II
   d) Telephus

---

26 Asking where the student thinks this information may be found leads to the kind of bibliography task outlined in OKell, 'evaluating Multiple Interpretations', Appendix A. Other possible tasks include the presentation of widely available and apparently authoritative statements for critical analysis.

27 OKell has used MCQs to build confidence with complex material on a module involving Greek tragedy and literary theory. George MacDonald Ross (Philosophy, University of Leeds) has found that HTML MCQs can contribute to developing thinking and argumentation skills leading to a reasoned critical answer, see <http://www.philosophy. leeds.ac.uk/GMR/hmp/modules/kantmcq/p19/p19frame.html>.

Feedback for a and c: He had something to do with it but he didn't begin the project. Before you try again, do you know what? If not, how would you find out?

b: Correct. Eumenes began it, Attalus II continued it (it is thought to be unfinished due to Prusias II attacking Pergamum c.156BC). Telephus is the founding hero of Pergamum and featured upon it. But who thinks that and why? And how certain are we?

Feedback for d: No, Telephus is a Greek mythological hero, not an historical monarch. Try again!

2) What is the Pergamum Altar for?

    a) Making sacrifices to Zeus
    b) Making a statement about Pergamum as a Greek city
    c) Showing the development of architectural sculpture in the Hellenistic period
    d) Showing the relationship of the German people with the classical past

Feedback: Yes, but which interpreter thought that? Why did you agree? Would the other interpreters answer differently? Are there any answers which are impossible given the evidence discussed so far?[28]

Trialling and judging the end result

As a discipline-specific example that makes the transferability of pedagogy more easily recognizable to users, *eMI* has been received positively by several disciplinary audiences who have recognized its key pedagogy, demonstrating that Learning Objects can be 'domesticated', and that learning technology can encapsulate good practice which can be transferred, modified and customized to suit specific academics' requirements. A range of *eMI* tutorials are undergoing trials in real learning environments in 2008–2009, with initial uptake in the fields of classical art, neolithic archaeology, modern history and museums outreach, with expressions of interest from theology and health sciences (to scaffold empathetic and diagnostic skills), as well as from learning technologists.[29] Evaluations of the

---

28   For the rationale and more questions, see OKell 'evaluating Multiple Interpretations'.

29   Edward Thomas (University of Durham) has secured internal 'Enhancing the Student Learning Experience' funding to integrate zoomable artefacts and slide shows to train Greek art and architecture students in critical visual skills; Karina Croucher (University of Manchester) is heading an inter-institutional team developing *eMI: Stonehenge* for archaeologists; several Historians involved in the HCA Newsfilm Online project are

pedagogical effectiveness of *eMI* may be conducted by any practitioner with the RLO-CETL Evaluation Tool-kit (<http://www.rlo-cetl.ac.uk/evaluation.htm>).

Technical aspects of the development

Technical development of the software template for the *eMI* pedagogical pattern resulted from a joint theoretical understanding of the nature of the design problem, the teaching experience (of what works and what does not), enthusiasm and dedication of the practitioner-developers, and the development team's ability to accommodate them whilst steering the process to the 'generic' conclusion. This process is best described as producing the authoring environment for the end-users (practitioners) to access generic pedagogical and technological guidance when designing Learning Objects for their local needs. Some parts of the process can be noted and replicated to ensure useful outcomes but, overall, success when designing for reuse is dependent on the working relationship between the disciplinary practitioners driving the process and the learning technologists supporting them. This relationship is aided by both parties focusing on the end-users and the learning objectives and seeking definitions of each other's terminology.[30] The value of the end product, the GLO software template, in this regard is in opening up learning design to practitioners with limited technical skills, limited access to learning technologist's support and limited time.[31]

The principled approach behind the GLO paradigm, as followed and promoted by the learning technologists, is to elucidate the 'pattern' from an already 'tried-and-tested' Learning Object, or from practice. This pattern is then coded as a software template in the GLO Maker software library. The design of the authoring features is guided by the WYSIWYG (What You See Is What You Get) principle. This approach is aimed at minimizing the opportunity for the template-creating authors (learning designers and subject-specialists) to misinterpret design features; the rationale being that the practitioner-developers can build on their knowledge and experience by interacting with the design instance before confirming its suitability for wider practitioner use/reuse.

---

embedding news footage within a structured pedagogical framework or producing related critical viewing skills training modules with GLO Maker; Janet Tatlock (Manchester Museum) is using GLO Maker both for teaching 'Values and Worth' and enabling students to record their responses.

30 See Dejan Ljubojevic, Eleanor OKell and E. Bauer, 'Not by Accident but by Design: Collaborative Design of Reusable Learning Technology', *Design Principles and Practices*, 3:3 (2009) <http://ijg.cgpublisher.com/product/pub.154/prod.234>.

31 Populating an iteration of *eMI* (including writing text and researching and recording content yourself and uploading it) is a matter of a day's work. Uploading files (text and audio) already created is a matter of ten to twenty minutes.

In the case of *eMI* this transference approach could not be closely followed, because no tried-and-tested 'blueprint' multimedia learning resource existed. Instead, the practitioner-developers produced paper-based mockups of the steps that students would take through the learning design. This part of the design process bears strong resemblance to the cognitive walkthrough (*cw*) method.[32] An important distinction of the '*eMI* cognitive walkthrough' approach from standard use of the *cw* method is the phase of the process it mediated: *cw* is commonly used with a finished software prototype to identify usability problems but in the case of the *eMI* pattern elicitation, there was only a paper prototype. What made the transference process work was the strong sense of direction and clear vision of the end functionality displayed by the practitioner-developers.

The solution to the problem of transference from a paper prototype came from learning theory and manifested itself in aggregating all the 'expert screens' (as originally designed) into 'Access Views': see Figure 9.3. The practitioners' presentation of a sequence of screens presenting 'points of view' was not only linear but could potentially create the impression that the views expressed at the start of the sequence are either more or less valid and/or date from earlier periods than the later views.

It was clear from the beginning of the design collaboration that the *eMI* pattern was especially well suited to what learning technologists define as open, ill-structured knowledge domains, such as humanities, and the learning design sought to emphasize this feature. Thus, Cognitive Flexibility Theory (CFT), with its emphasis on multiple perspectives of the concept/topic, and its focus on exposing the interrelatedness of domain concepts, was used as the guiding understanding of the design-problem space.[33] Following CFT yielded a single-screen solution for placing all the 'points of view' (represented as 'experts') before the user at the same time, to engage with and negotiate themselves. Hence, a potential design misinterpretation was avoided and a key aspect (interrelatedness) was emphasized.

GLO Maker version 1.0 was developed using Adobe Flash 9, coded with Action Script 2 (AS2). The application wrapper (the code that turns browser-based Flash into a desktop-based application) is made with MDM Zinc 2.5. Since the software is coded with AS2, so are the Flash animations (content) used in building tutorials. Other media formats that can be used with GLO Maker 1.0 include: video – Flash Video (FLV), audio (MP3), image (JPG, GIF), text (TXT, to which hyperlinks, italics, underlining, etc. can be added with HTML tags), and the

---

32   C. Wharton, J. Rieman, C. Lewis and P. Polson, 'The Cognitive Walkthrough Method: A Practitioner's Guide', in J. Nielsen and R.L. Mack (eds), *Usability Inspection Methods* (Chichester, 1994), pp. 105–40.

33   See R. Spiro and J. Jehng, 'Cognitive Flexibility and Hypertext: Theory and Technology for the Nonlinear and Multidimensional Traversal of Complex Subject Matter', in D. Nix and R. Spiro (eds), *Cognition, Education and Multimedia: Exploring Ideas in High Technology* (Hillsdale, NJ, 1990), pp. 163–205.

(interactive) animation Flash ShockWave (SWF). To create a tutorial, practitioners only need to create audio, image and text files and input them into GLO Maker 1.0 where required.

All elements input into a tutorial made with GLO Maker 1.0 are stored in a single folder package and the tutorial is accessed by means of the GLO Player SWF file. This simplifies its use: for example, a zipped folder can be uploaded into an institution's Virtual Learning Environment (VLE) as an item and set to self-extract, opening with the GLO Player SWF file. Alternatively, the SWF file may be coded into a web page, for example as an object inside an HTML table, which is particularly useful for linking the tutorial with external (prerequisite/supporting) material.

Currently (March 2009), GLO Maker 1.0 is being archived and version 2.0 is being planned and coded. Version 2.0 will allow for flexible extensions of the code base resulting in a 'plug-in' type of architecture, to meet practitioners' requirements for slideshows rather than single static images, Quicktime video enabling interaction with artefacts in 3D and short passages of text or full articles as artefacts (currently possible only by using Flash Paper). GLO Maker 2.0 is being developed in Adobe Flex 3 using Action Script 3 and will also be freely available through the GLO Maker website (see footnote 1). These planned improvements to version 2.0 will enable practitioners capable of locating pdfs or locating/producing slideshows or Quicktime videos to input these into the tutorial, thereby further reducing the requirement for a learning technologist in the production of sophisticated humanities Learning Objects.

With regards to the technical interoperability standards for developing, packaging, and delivering online learning materials, such as Shareable Content Object Reference Model (SCORM), the GLO development and packaging framework has been designed for easy integration. The GLO 'package' is designed so that all constitutive assets (animations, images, audio files, etc.) are stored separately, in a 'Media' folder, and are integrated inside the GLO at run time (by a GLO Player – GLO package interpreter software). This enables reuse of the constituents as well as the overall organizational model of the GLO tutorial. Version 2.0 of the GLO Maker software is being developed with SCORM compliance in mind.

Conclusion

RLO-CETL and UCeL, with their willingness to conceive of Learning Objects as 'dynamic micro-contexts for learning' and recognize disciplinary practitioners' contribution as experts in appropriate pedagogies as well as content, have enabled Classicists to act as pathfinders in a generic development which has the potential to increase the use of e-Learning in Humanities.[34]

---

34   Bradley and Boyle, 'Design Development, and Use'.

The *eMI* pattern in GLO Maker has exteriorized a disciplinary teaching process and rendered it electronically. The collaborative design process has taken the exteriorizing power of e-Learning and enlisted it to practitioners' advantage, showing how the high-level skills that are increasingly important to a knowledge economy are produced. The readily recognizable pedagogical pattern renders the e-Learning Object appropriate for use, opening up its potential to affect both the style and philosophy of teaching. This impact will remain whether the online multimedia tutorial approach of GLO Maker is retained or whether technologically skilled practitioners lead their students to interact with defined multiple views in a room inside Second Life, because the *eMI* pattern retains the place of the disciplinary practitioner as the creator of appropriate content to achieve the learning objectives for which and from which it has been designed.

The *eMI* pattern and GLO Maker are a concretization of the theoretical premise that innovative learning technologies need no longer be imposed upon the historical disciplines by extra-disciplinary actors, but instead can suit these disciplines' pedagogical requirements and reassert practitioners' control over teaching materials.

Chapter 10

The Digital Classicist:
Disciplinary Focus and Interdisciplinary Vision

Melissa Terras

We have moved still further from the Ancient World. In literature and the arts we have seen a startling break with tradition, and above all the technological revolution which we are witnessing is transforming our lives and insensibly affecting our outlook, encouraging us to live in the present, judging everything by the standard of technical efficiency and assuming that the latest is always the best. Descartes compared the study of antiquity to foreign travel; it was useful, he said, to know something of the manners of different nations, but when too much time was spent in travelling, men became strangers to their own country 'and the overcurious in the customs of the past are generally ignorant of those of the present'. Today, there is very little danger of living in the past.[1]

Introduction

Digital Classicists are at the forefront of digital humanities research: using, appropriating, and developing computational tools to aid in the study and exploration of Greco-Roman antiquity. Classicists were early adopters of digital technologies, identifying the potential benefits of computers to undertake their data-intensive research. Computational tools are increasingly necessary components of classical research projects, and can allow novel research which would otherwise prove impossible, occasionally benefiting computing and engineering science research as well as research in the humanities. However, undertaking research which crosses disciplinary boundaries brings with it its own logistical, practical and personal problems for the researchers involved. This chapter explores the interdisciplinary vision of the 'Digital Classicist', grounding the discussion with regard to two distinct research projects and current research on disciplinarity and cross-disciplinary team working. Understanding and predicting issues which may emerge from research projects in the Digital Classicist domain can assist those undertaking, managing and participating in future research projects.

---

1   M.L. Clarke, *Classical Education in Britain 1500–1900* (Cambridge, 1959), pp. 175–6.

Enter the Digital Classicist

The term 'Classicist' came into prominence from the mid nineteenth century with the emergence of a groundswell of scholars with a focused interest in, and increased access to primary historical evidence of, Greco-Roman antiquity.[2] Often understood as 'one who advocates the school study of the Latin and Greek classics',[3] this definition belies the complex range of sources and associated research techniques often used by academic Classicists. Varied archaeological, epigraphic, documentary, linguistic, forensic and art historical evidence can be consulted in the course of everyday research into history, linguistics, philology, literature, ethnography, anthropology, art, architecture, science, mythology, religion and beyond. Classicists have, by nature and necessity, always been working across disciplinary boundaries in a data-intensive research area, being 'interdisciplinary, rather than simply un-disciplined'.[4] The addition of advanced digital and computational tools to many a Classicist's arsenal of skills should therefore not really come as a surprise, given the efficiencies they afford in the searching, retrieval, classification, labelling, ordering, display, and visualization of data.

Indeed, Classicists were amongst the forerunners of humanities scholars willing to bear – and even create – digital tools, an endeavour which came to be known as *Humanities Computing*, or more recently *Digital Humanities*, loosely defined as 'applications of computing to research and teaching within subjects that are loosely defined as "the humanities"'.[5] Applications involving textual sources took centre stage within the early development of humanities computing with the creation of textual databases and indices. The commonly accepted first humanities computing project is the Italian Jesuit priest Father Roberto Busa's attempt to create a computational index variorum of the works of Thomas Aquinas (in medieval Latin), begun as early as the 1940s.[6] From the 1970s, fairly centralized attempts were undertaken at using computational technology to serve as a community focus and to develop electronic versions of primary source material for Classical scholars, such as David Packard's *Ibycus* system (used to process, search and

---

2   From 'the mid-sixteenth century' antiquarians had achieved 'the status of a bonafide profession and begun to establish the parameters of their discipline', P. Jacks, *The Antiquarian and the Myth of Antiquity* (Cambridge, 1993), p. 9. Classics had been taught in various forms in schools and universities from the medieval period onward, see Clarke, *Classical Education in Britain*. However, it was not until the mid-nineteenth century that new primary source material and university structure allowed 'Classics' to thrive as an independent mode of academic enquiry.

3   'Classicist', *The Oxford English Dictionary*, 2nd edn, OED Online (1989).

4   Jacks, *Antiquarian and the Myth of Antiquity*, xvi.

5   Susan Hockey, 'The History of Humanities Computing', in S. Schreibman, R.G. Siemens, J. Unsworth (eds), *A Companion to Digital Humanities* (Oxford, 2004), pp. 3–19.

6   Roberto Busa, 'The Annals of Humanities Computing: The Index Thomisticus', *Computers and the Humanities*, 14 (1980): 83–90.

browse Greek texts), the *Thesaurus Linguae Graecae* (TLG), *The Bryn Mawr Classical Review*, the *Database of Classical Bibliography*, the *Duke Databank of Documentary Papyri* and the *Perseus Projec*t.[7] The ubiquitous adoption of the personal computer in the 1990s, and the rise of the networked, Internet environment towards the close of the twentieth century encouraged a wave of decentralized, smaller digital projects. These (relatively low-cost) developments have enabled Classicists to undertake digitization of classical source material, the customization of general tools to allow searching, manipulation, and analysis of classical source material, and the sharing of a rich networked infrastructure with larger disciplines (which inevitably have greater resources than cash-strapped Classics scholars) to organize, annotate, publish and share information, and to facilitate general communication and discussion within the community.

The adoption of computing within Classical research should be seen in this wider context, not in a disciplinary vacuum:

> There should not be a history of classics and the computer, for the needs of
> classicists are simply not so distinctive as to warrant a separate 'classical
> informatics.' Disciplinary specialists learning the strengths and weaknesses
> have ... a strong tendency to exaggerate the extent to which their problems are
> unique and to call for a specialized, domain-specific infrastructure and approach
> ... For classicists to make successful use of information technology, they must
> insinuate themselves within larger groups, making allies of other disciplines and
> sharing infrastructure.[8]

Classicists must, again, work in an interdisciplinary manner: both so they can follow, understand, adopt and utilize recent computational advances to their own advantage, and to have access to computational infrastructure and resources necessary to undertake efficient and useful research in the field.

Undertaking interdisciplinary research and working in a cross-disciplinary environment is an exception from the lone, ivory-towered scholar image traditionally associated with humanities research, even within the smallest of Digital Classicist projects:

> Given that the nature of research work involves computers and a variety of skills
> and expertise, Digital Humanities researchers are working collaboratively within
> their institutions and with others nationally and internationally to undertake
> research. This work typically involves the need to coordinate efforts between
> academics, undergraduate and graduate students, research assistants, computer

---

7   Theodore Brunner, 'Classics and the Computer: The History', in J. Solomon (ed.), *Accessing Antiquity: The Computerization of Classical Databases* (Tucson, 1993), pp. 10–33; Gregory Crane, 'Classics and the Computer: An End of the History' in Schreibman, Siemens and Unsworth, *A Companion to Digital Humanities*, pp. 46–55.

8   Crane, 'Classics and the Computer', p. 47.

programmers, libraries, and other individuals as well as the need to coordinate financial and other resources.[9]

The issue becomes even more complex when software development and the writing of new, bespoke computational algorithms becomes necessary (rather than just use of existing software for, say, digitization and the creation of online resources):

> Few research centres in Digital Humanities have the staff necessary for undertaking large application development projects, and even the ones that do quickly find that cross-departmental collaborations are needed to assemble the necessary expertise ... For most Digital Humanities practitioners, amassing a team of developers almost requires that the work be distributed across institutions and among a varied group of people. Any non-trivial application requires experts from a number of different development subspecialties, including such areas as interface design, relational database management, programming, software engineering, and server administration (to name only a few).[10]

A Classicist devoting their research time to working in the digital arena will have to face both logistical and personal issues of disciplinarity, which will affect both the project, their role in the project, their own personal skills development, and perhaps their own career. Yet there has been 'minimal research on the role of teams with academic communities, particularly within the Humanities'[11] and minimal consideration of how issues of interdisciplinarity – particularly the use of new and emergent technologies within a traditional academic discipline – can affect the outcome of research projects.

The aim of this chapter is to sketch out issues of disciplinarity and the benefits of interdisciplinary research for the Digital Classicist, providing a brief overview of two successful research projects to demonstrate the varied and complex nature of interactions between Classicists, engineers, computer scientists and other interested parties. Additionally, by summarizing potential flashpoints which can arise in such projects (including disciplinary identity, developing and retaining skills sets, publication venues, administrative and management problems) this chapter highlights areas which principal investigators and managers of projects that fall within the Digital Classicist domain should be prepared to deal with successfully, should they arise within the course of their project.

---

9   Lynne Siemens, 'It's a Team if You Use "Reply All": An Exploration of Research Teams in Digital Humanities Environments', *Literary and Linguistic Computing*, 24:2 (2009): 225–33.

10   S. Ramsay, 'Rules of the Order: The Sociology of Large, Multi-Institutional Software Development Projects', presented at Digital Humanities 2008, Oulu, Finland, <http://www.ekl.oulu.fi/dh2008/Digital%20Humanities%202008%20Book%20of%20Abstracts.pdf>, 20.

11   Siemens, 'It's a Team if You Use "Reply All"'.

Disciplines and disciplinarity

Being part of a discipline gives a scholar a sense of belonging, identity and kudos. But the idea of what constitutes a discipline is muddy, and often hinges around the bricks-and-mortar proof of a university department's existence:

> [A Discipline] can be enacted and negotiated in various ways: the international 'invisible college'; individuals exchanging preprints and reprints, conferences, workshops ... But the most concrete and permanent enactment is the department; this is where a discipline becomes an institutional subject. The match between discipline and subject is always imperfect; this can cause practical difficulties when, for example, the (discipline-based) categories of research selectively do not fit the way the subject is ordered in a particular department.[12]

This notion of institutionalizing the subject would seem to give gravitas: if you can point at an academic department, the discipline exists. However, this definition of a 'discipline' is problematic, as many have specialisms and subspecialisms, which may or may not be represented in every university department, and every 'discipline' is different in character and scope from the next:

> most embrace a wide range of subspecialisms, some with one set of features and the other with different sets. There is no single method of enquiry, no standard verification procedure, no definitive set of concepts that uniquely characterises each particular discipline.[13]

Additionally, a 'discipline' is not an immutable topic of research or body of individuals: 'For nothing is more certain in the lives of the disciplines, whatever the field, whatever the institutional setting, than that they are forever changing.'[14]

The discipline gains kudos from becoming permanently established in the university subject roll-call. Academic culture can define a 'tribe' of scholars, whilst the span of disciplinary knowledge can be described as the 'territory' of the discipline.[15] 'Fields gradually develop distinctive methodological approaches,

---

12   C. Evans, 'Choosing People: Recruitment and Selection as Leverage on Subjects and Disciplines', *Studies in Higher Education*, 20:3 (1995): 253–4.

13   T. Becker and P.R. Trowler, *Academic Tribes and Territories: Intellectual Enquiry and the Culture of Disciplines*, 2nd edn (Buckingham, 2001), p. 65.

14   J. Monroe, 'Introduction: The Shapes of Fields', in *Writing and Revising the Disciplines* (Ithaca, 2002), 2.

15   Becker and Trowler, *Academic Tribes and Territories*.

conceptual and theoretical frameworks and their own sets of internal schisms,'[16] and those of Classicists are well entrenched into University culture:[17]

> Any study of European literature and thought down to at least the eighteenth century needs to begin with Greece and Rome, and the study of the classics helps to unite the modern man not only with the men of the ancient world but with all those who in later centuries learned from them.[18]

Although it is difficult to provide a definition of what a discipline may be, there are characteristics which are associated with disciplinary practice. Disciplines have identities and cultural attributes. They have measurable communities, which have public outputs, and

> can be measured by the number and types of departments in universities, the change and increase in types of HE courses, the proliferation of disciplinary associations, the explosion in the number of journals and articles published, and the multiplication of recognised research topics and clusters.[19]

Disciplines have identifiable idols in their subject,[20] heroes and mythology[21] and sometimes artefacts peculiar to the subject domain,[22] meaning that the community is defined and reinforced by being formally accepted as a university subject, but also instituting a publication record and means of output, and, more implicitly, by 'the nurturance of myth, the identification of unifying symbols, the canonisation of exemplars, and the formation of guilds'.[23] Any 'new' academic subject has gradually to be accepted into the university pantheon, with much discussion along the way regarding whether they actually are disciplines in the first place.

---

16   Ibid., p. 14
17   For an overview of the history of Classics as an academic discipline and the related quirks and approaches of the discpline, see: G. Boys-Stones, B. Graziosi and P. Vasunia (eds), *The Oxford Handbook of Hellenic Studies*, Oxford Handbooks in Classical Studies (Oxford, forthcoming); A. Barchiesi and W. Scheidel (eds) *The Oxford Handbook of Roman Studies*, Oxford Handbooks in Classical Studies, (Oxford, forthcoming); Clarke, *Classical Education in Britain*; James Morwood (ed.), *The Teaching of Classics* (Cambridge, 2003); J.P. Hallett and T. Van Nortwick, *Compromising Traditions: The Personal Voice in Classical Scholarship* (London, 1997).
18   Clarke, *Classical Education in Britain*, p. 177.
19   Becker and Trowler, *Academic Tribes and Territories*, p. 14.
20   B. Clark, *Academic Culture*, Working Paper no. 42 (Yale, 1980).
21   P.J. Taylor, 'An Interpretation of the Quantification Debate in British Geography', *Transactions of the Institute of British Geographers*, ns 1 (1976): 129–42.
22   Becker and Trowler, *Academic Tribes and Territories*.
23   D.D. Dill, 'Academic Administration', in B.R. Clark and G. Neave (eds), *Encyclopedia of Higher Education*, vol. 2 (Oxford, 1992), 1318–29.

Classics is no different from any other academic subject in this regard. Its aims: to 'know the civilizations of classical antiquity as they were, honouring the unique qualities of each' and to 'see the continuities between ancient and modern societies and their works of art' require a specialist knowledge (and investigation) of texts, artefacts, and physical sites.[24] Classics has its own defined area of source material, means of study of this material, and established modes of research output and dissemination (publishing imprints, conferences, journals). There is established behaviour associated with the classical scholar, such as specific classical writing styles.[25] The field has hierarchies and networks, with a variety of scholarly organizations and associations. There are varied and energetic discussions regarding what constitutes its curricula at both school and university levels.[26] This disciplinary behaviour has been refined and reinforced in the widespread study of Classics as a bona fide academic discipline in the past two hundred years. Computing technologies (and the scholars who bring them) are the newcomers to this established, respected, field.

The Digital Classicist, then, faces two challenges. There is that of forging an identity and gaining recognition within the established discipline of Classics itself. What are the methodological approaches of a Digital Classicist? Is there a culture that binds the scholars together? Or is the Digital Classicist community merely that – a community of practice, which shares theories of meaning and power, collectivity and subjectivity[27] but is little more than a support network for academic scholars who use outlier methods in their own individual, established, field of Classical discourse?

The second challenge, which presents both problems and opportunities for the Digital Classicist, arises for those scholars who choose to step outside the traditional Classics fold and engage with experts in data management, manipulation and visualization such as computer and engineering scientists: that is, behaving in an interdisciplinary manner. The concept of 'interdisciplinary' research, defined as 'of or pertaining to two or more disciplines or branches of learning; contributing to or benefiting from two or more disciplines',[28] became popular towards the mid twentieth century, and the use of the word has been increasing in popularity since.:

> Unlike its nearest rivals – borderlands, interdepartmental, cooperative, coordinated – 'interdisciplinary' has something to please everyone. Its base, *discipline*, is hoary and antiseptic; its prefix, *inter*, is hairy and friendly. Unlike

---

24   T. Van Nortwick, 'What is Classical Scholarship For?', in Hallett and Van Nortwick, *Compromising Traditions*, 182–90, 187.

25   Hallett and Van Nortwick, *Compromising Traditions*.

26   Morwood, *The Teaching of Classics*.

27   E. Wenger, *Communities of Practice: Learning, Meaning, and Identity* (Cambridge, 2002).

28   'Interdisciplinary', *Oxford English Dictionary*, 2nd edn, OED Online (1989).

fields, with their mud, cows, and corn, the Latinate *discipline* comes encased in stainless steel: it suggests something rigorous, aggressive, hazardous to master. *Inter* hints that knowledge is a warm, mutually developing, consultative thing ... And from the twenties on between-ness was where the action was: from interpersonal, intergroup, interreligious, interethnic, interracial, interregional and international relations to intertextuality, things coming together in the state known as inter encapsulated the greatest problems facing society in the twentieth century.[29]

Although popular, the term is often ambiguous:

It can suggest forging connections across the different disciplines; but it can also mean establishing a kind of undisciplined space in the interstices between disciplines, or even attempting to transcend disciplinary boundaries altogether.[30]

Classicists using digital technologies in their research are regularly at the forefront of research in digital humanities, given the range of primary and secondary sources consulted, and the array of tools and techniques necessary to interrogate them. However, to adopt new and developing techniques, and to adopt and adapt emergent technologies, the Digital Classicist has to work in the interdisciplinary space between Classics and computing science. What are the benefits of straddling, inhabiting or transcending the disciplinary divide, and what does this mean, both practically and theoretically, for the Digital Classicist?

Interdisciplinary vision

It is worth pausing here to consider the benefits of utilizing computational technologies to undertake Classical research, and to sketch out examples of two disparate projects which demonstrate how varied the type of work is that is undertaken in such an interdisciplinary domain, how advanced the technologies utilized can be, and how complex Classicists' research questions often are.

The benefits of digitization, the creative use of networked technologies, and the community-building elements of the Internet are obvious to those working with Classical source material:

The texts of antiquity, freed from the tyrannical limitations of expensive print publication, preserved in multiple servers across the globe, flash instantaneously

---

29   R. Frank, 'Interdisciplinary: The First Half Century', in R. Burchfield, E.G. Stanley and T.H. Hoad (eds), *Words for Robert Burchfield's Sixty-Fifth Birthday* (Woodbridge, 1988), p. 100.

30   J. Moran, *Interdisciplinarity* (Oxford, 2002).

anywhere that the Internet can reach – hundreds of millions of desktops and mobile devices. Homer, Plato, Virgil, Cicero – they all reach more of humanity than ever was conceivable in the millennia since they set down their styli for the last time and passed into dust. And it is not just physical access – we already can, with simple links between source text and its commentaries, translations, morphological analyses and dictionary entries, provide a better reading environment than was ever conceivable in print culture. We know from the readers of our web sites that texts in Greek and Latin, of many types, now fire the minds to which twenty years ago they had no access.[31]

Digital text, digital images, digital databases and digital models of both Roman and Hellenic primary evidence and related scholarship now provide the advantages routinely associated with digitization: immediate access to high-demand and frequently used items, rapid access to remotely held materials, flexibility of display, virtual reunification of dispersed collections, integration of materials into other media and teaching materials, the potential for analysis of a critical mass of materials, enhanced searchability, potential for digital enhancement and manipulation, and the potential for engaging with remote scholarly communities.[32] An example of a successful project utilizing digital media in this manner is the Perseus Digital Library at Tufts University, which for more than twenty years has been investigating how the history, literature and culture of the Greco-Roman world can be delivered, explored, expounded, questioned, analysed and researched, through collating all evidence available from this historical period and beyond.[33] Since the inception of the Perseus Project in the mid 1980s, many other classical resources have turned to digital media and networked technologies as a means to facilitate research in this data-intensive domain.

Not all projects utilizing computational technologies within Classical research need to engage on a research level with computing technologies: there are now many good guides to areas such as digitization, the provision of multimedia materials, textual processing, textual markup, database management and linguistic analysis for those establishing a Digital Classics project.[34] However, those on the cutting edge of Digital Classicist research, or working on large-scale projects,

---

31   Gregory Crane, Brent Seales and Melissa Terras, 'Cyberinfrastructure for Classical Philology', in G. Crane and M. Terras (eds), *Changing the Center of Gravity: Transforming Classical Studies Through Cyberinfrastructure, DHQ*, 3.1 (2009) <http://www.digitalhumanities.org/dhq/vol/003/1/000023.html>.

32   M. Deegan and S. Tanner, 'Digital Futures: Strategies for the Information Age', *Digital Futures Series* (Oxford, 2002), pp. 32–3.

33   Perseus Digital Library, <http://www.perseus.tufts.edu/hopper/>.

34   For an overview of the type of tools used in general humanities computing research, which are fairly accessible to new interested parties, see S. Schreibman, R. Siemens and J. Unsworth, 'The Digital Humanities and Computing: An Introduction', in *A Companion to Digital Humanities*, pp. xxiii–xxvii.

inevitably have to liaise with colleagues who are computing scientists or those who provide computational support to traditional humanities scholars. In these cases, the application of advanced computational techniques and information technology to answer Classics research questions is only useful, and indeed, possible, when there is enough knowledge and understanding regarding both the classical and computational elements of the research project by the teams of researchers. Occasionally, the research questions asked are complex or novel enough that a bespoke computational solution is required (when off-the-shelf solutions and best-practice guidelines do not cover the technological system required): the development and documentation of this solution can sometimes benefit both research within computer science and Classics, or provide infrastructure, tools and facilities for other related research projects following in the pioneer's wake. Complex Classics research questions can provide real-world issues for computer scientists to test their hypotheses on, often allowing blue-sky[35] research and development which can have positive, unforeseen outcomes radiating back into computing and engineering science themselves. Undertaking research at this level also opens up new possibilities for digital humanities in general: many projects develop technical tools and procedures which can be used in different humanities fields (is a digital image of a medieval manuscript so very different from a digital image of an ancient text?).

A brief overview of two projects carrying out novel research in both Classics and computing science is persuasive regarding the value and complexity of Digital Classics research. The author's personal experience on these, and other, projects is then used to highlight the logistical and personal issues that can face those undertaking interdisciplinary research as a Digital Classicist.

eSAD: e-Science and Ancient Documents[36]

The analysis and understanding of ancient manuscripts and texts via specifically developed technological tools can aid both the Classicist and the computer scientist, in the development of novel techniques which are applicable elsewhere. A demonstrative case is recent work done on building an intelligent image-processing and artificial intelligence based system to aid in the reading of the Roman stylus texts from Vindolanda.[37] This joint project between the Centre for the Study of Ancient Documents (CSAD) and the Department of Engineering Science at the University of Oxford between 1998 and 2002, funded by the UK's Engineering

---

35   Blue-sky research is the term given to creative or visionary research undertaken without any predefined outputs, or immediate commercial value, which can sometimes (and hopefully) lead to unexpected and novel approaches, solutions, and products.

36   e-Science and Ancient Documents, <http://esad.classics.ox.ac.uk/>.

37   M. Terras, *Image to Interpretation. An Intelligent System to Aid Historians in Reading the Vindolanda Texts*, Oxford Studies in Ancient Documents (Oxford 2006).

and Physical Science Research Council (EPSRC), resulted in a system which both aided the scholar in reading the Vindolanda texts and developed innovative image-processing algorithms, which are proving useful in a range of applications, including medical imaging analysis.[38]

Members of the original project team have since procured funding to carry on the research under the AHRC-EPSRC-JISC Arts and Humanities e-Science Initiative Programme, from September 2008 until September 2011. The project, now based between the Oxford e-Research Centre, CSAD and UCL's Department of Information Studies, will work on creating tools which can aid the reading of damaged texts like the stylus tablets from Vindolanda.[39] Furthermore, the project will explore how an Interpretation Support System (ISS) can be used in the day-to-day reading of ancient documents and keep track of how the documents are interpreted and read. A combination of image-processing tools and an ontology-based support system will be developed to facilitate experts by tracking their developing hypotheses:[40] this is founded closely on work currently being undertaken by medical imaging researchers and physicians, and systems used to track and trace medical diagnosis and treatment of colorectal cancer,[41] and is also closely linked to the system developed for the related project at CSAD, 'A Virtual Research Environment for the Study of Documents and Manuscripts'.[42]

The eSAD system will suggest alternative readings (based on linguistic and palaeographic data) to experts as they undertake the complex reading process, aiming to speed the process of understanding a text. The project also aims to investigate how the resulting images, image tools and data sets can be shared between scholars.

---

38   M. Terras and P. Robertson, 'Image and Interpretation: Using Artificial Intelligence to Read Ancient Roman Texts', *HumanIT*, 7:3 (2005); <http://www.hb.se/bhs/ith/3-7/mtpr.pdf>; N. Molton, X. Pan, M. Brady et al., 'Visual Enhancement of Incised Text', *Pattern Recognition*, 36 (2003): 1031–43; V.U.B. Schenk and M. Brady, 'Visual Identification of Fine Surface Incisions in Incised Roman Stylus Tablets' (International Conference in Advances in Pattern Recognition, 2003); M. Brady, X. Pan, M. Terras and V. Schenk, 'Shadow Stereo, Image Filtering and Constraint Propagation', in A.K. Bowman and M. Brady (eds), *Images and Artefacts of the Ancient World* (Oxford, 2005).

39   *Vindolanda Tablets Online*, <http://vindolanda.csad.ox.ac.uk/>.

40   S.M. Tarte, J.M. Brady, H. Roued Olsen, M. Terras and A.K. Bowman, 'Image Acquisition and Analysis to Enhance the Legibility of Ancient Texts', UK e-Science Programme All Hands Meeting 2008 (AHM2008), Edinburgh, September 2008; H. Roued Olsen, S. Tarte, M. Terras, M. Brady and A.K. Bowman, 'Towards an Interpretation Support System for Reading Ancient Documents', at Digital Humanities 2009, University of Maryland.

41   M. Austin, M. Kelly and M. Brady, 'The Benefits of an Ontological Patient Model in Clinical Decision-Support', *Proceedings of the 23rd AAAI Conference on Artificial Intelligence* (2008), <http://www.aaai.org/Papers/AAAI/2008/AAAI08-325.pdf>.

42   See Chapter 5 in this volume.

Necessarily, the project involves Classicists, engineering scientists, and information scientists, with close input from those with specialities in humanities computing, medical imaging analysis, papyrology, user analysis and image processing. Issues emerging include questions regarding how to model complex humanities research processes, how to facilitate the annotation of digital surrogates of primary documentary evidence, and how to encourage adoption of use of these new solutions into established papyrological method, as well as the need to create new, advanced image-processing algorithms to deal with the noisy, abraded images of ancient manuscripts utilized by the experts.

VERA: Virtual Environments for Research in Archaeology[43]

The UK Joint Information Systems Committee (JISC) funded VERA (Virtual Environments for Research in Archaeology) project is a collaboration between the University of Reading (Department of Archaeology and School of Systems Engineering), University College London (Department of Information Studies) and York Archaeological Trust. Between 2007 and 2009 the project looked at various aspects of the acquisition, management, dissemination and usability of the digital record of the large research excavation at Silchester Roman Town, Hampshire, England.[44]

VERA aimed to improve the accessibility of the digital excavation records to co-workers, particularly those such as artefact specialists who are not generally physically present on the excavation. The project centred around the IADB (Integrated Archaeological Database), which has been used as the excavation recording system at Silchester since the start of the archaeological project twelve years ago. The research approach was multifaceted, involving input from archaeologists, Roman historians, engineering scientists, information professionals and experts in humanities computing and human–computer interaction. In practical terms, this meant investigating the use of digital recording devices on site, such as hand-held tablets, digital pens and digital clipboards; the analysis of user needs; the trialling of visualization techniques to enhance the traditional archaeological representation of the excavation finds; extending the functionality of the IADB user interface; standardizing the code base of the IADB within a portal framework to improve accessibility, stability and security; and experimentation with direct publication from the IADB for scholars referencing excavation data within their research.[45]

---

43   Virtual Environment for Research in Archaeology, <http://vera.rdg.ac.uk/index. php>.
44   A full account of the excavation at Silchester can be found in Chapter 1 of this volume.
45   M. Baker, M. Grove, M. Fulford et al., 'VERA: Virtual Environment for Research in Archaeology' (4th International Conference on e-Social Science, Manchester, 18–20

Various issues have arisen throughout the course of the project – in fact one of the aims of the project was to identify the type of issues involved in such a large-scale, interdisciplinary attempt to provide a virtual research environment. These included the importance of training in new technologies, the establishment of data management, recording and data validation measures, the need for integration of users' needs in the development of new tools, the need for careful introduction of technological 'solutions' into established offline workflow, the fragility of technology (and technological infrastructure) in the trench, and issues in the use of open source architecture for providing applications such as the IADB and the verifiable maintenance of the data they contain.[46]

Project parallels

The parallels between these two very different projects are to be found in the large-scale, interdisciplinary teams they both required. Individuals involved had very different backgrounds, and understandings of both the humanities and technological dimensions to the projects. The teams were both operating across dispersed sites, meeting physically fairly regularly but by no means weekly, and utilizing online tools of communication that we come to expect from such technologically aware teams: wikis, blogs, emails, discussion lists, video conferencing, etc. The projects required individuals to take responsibility for their own tasks, and work for periods alone, within the framework of the wider project. Engagement with the wider academic community was also important, as was ascertaining of user needs, gathering community opinion regarding various issues, and involving other experts in key developments.

As representative of the type of projects a Digital Classicist may work on, these two projects also demonstrated various issues that can emerge from working in such an interdisciplinary environment. The discussion below, although informed by personal experiences within the projects detailed above and communication with related research communities, is not indicative of any particular issue within either project, nor any problem with any project team member. It serves to highlight the areas which those involved in a Digital Classicist project should consider and monitor to ensure that their own project will be a success.

June 2008); C. Fisher, C. Warwick and M. Terras, 'Integrating New Technologies into Established Systems: A Case Study from Roman Silchester', Computer Applications in Archaeology 2009, Making History Interactive. Williamsburg, Maryland, USA, 22–26 March 2009.

46 E.J. O'Riordan, M. Terras, C. Warwick et al., 'Virtual Environments for Research in Archaeology (VERA): A Roman Case Study At Silchester', Digital Resources in the Humanities and Arts, Cambridge, September 2008.

Issues in interdisciplinary research

Different academic cultures

Although many younger classical scholars are developing better computational skills and knowledge as networked technologies become more pervasive, it is often the case that projects depend on collaboration with computer scientists and engineers to develop tools, techniques and methods which may be applicable to the further understanding of classical texts (and computational algorithms). This poses many problems for both the Classicist aiming to utilize advanced computational techniques and the scientist aiming to use the Classical research question as the 'real-world' problem: not only have they to find interested collaborators, but they also have to engage with the discourse, habits and different focus of other disciplines in order to answer their own research questions.

Classics and computing science are very different beasts, and it takes conscious efforts in communication to ensure all team members both understand project developments, and are understood themselves. There can be lack of a common language, a sense of isolation on the part of some team members if there are gaps in their knowledge base, and no experience of the unconscious understanding of the way a discipline operates, leading to tensions between technical and non-technical members of a team. To function well in both disciplines, the scholar needs to understand both the subject and culture of both disciplines (which can take both time and a certain type of personality), or a larger team needs individuals who can communicate effectively across these boundaries. There is also the need to be able to meet others who may be interested in interdisciplinary work in the first place, and Digital Classicists need to be comfortable networking in both Classics and other disciplines. To have a successful team, and successful team members, depends on those involved having good communication skills.

Interdisciplinary publications

A common area of discord in interdisciplinary projects emerges when projects begin to think about publishing material. Teams which had previously happily worked together can dissolve into individuals fiercely fighting over publication territory. Interdisciplinary issues are partly the cause of this: different fields have different publication expectations, mechanisms, venues, time frames, writing styles and ways of presenting research. A Classicist used to being the sole author on academic research may find themselves somewhat far down the list of joint authors on a paper, with little or no agreement on the conventions of author name ordering.

Individuals can also face issues with the acceptance of their interdisciplinary research (and multimedia) publications by their Classical peers. Is the eSAD project described as Classics or engineering? It does not matter until the outputs are being scrutinized to decide an individual's suitability for employment (in a Classics, computing or information studies department?) or what counts as a tenure track publication. Digital outputs – such as digital editions, digital journal publications websites, etc. – are often not as respected as the traditional print based outputs of the humanities (where the single-author monograph is still viewed as the pinnacle of scholarly research, even though the publication industry sees sales of these in decline). How can a scholar working in digital media, producing digital outputs, convince their peers and superiors of their academic merit? Additionally, given that digital journal papers, digital editions, and suchlike are not well respected, or understood, how can humanities scholars working with computer code persuade other scholars that the intellectual rigours of programming are as valid as the production of scholarly textbooks?

Management

Strong communication can be fostered by good team leadership. Successful teams in digital humanities research have been defined as those who maintain a good working relationship, adopt clearly defined tasks, roles, milestones and obligations (which are to be discussed by the teams themselves), and work together to meet goals: 'it is by (un)productive working relationships that many projects live and die.'[47] There is beginning to be interest in how successful digital humanities projects function.[48] A large-scale survey project[49] has highlighted collaboration issues in digital humanities projects: in particular, there is a real need for face-to-face collaboration,[50] and strong leadership in maintaining communication links with all members of the project.

Teams are encouraged to utilize the digital communication technologies at their disposal, which can also serve as a project record, or part of the project documentation. Wikis, email, blogs, twitter and Skype can all contribute to communication within a team (although ironically, information overload from such technologies can prevent project work being carried out in the first place!) This problem can be avoided through good management and discipline, using communication technologies where necessary, not as a distraction from the business of research.

---

47   Siemens, 'It's a Team if You Use "Reply All"'.

48   S. Ramsay, S. Sinclair, J. Unsworth et al., 'Design, Coding, and Playing with Fire: Innovations in Interdisciplinary Research Project Management', Panel at Digital Humanities 2008, Oulu, Finland, <http://www.ekl.oulu.fi/dh2008/Digital%20Humanities %202008%20Book%20of%20Abstracts.pdf>, 16.

49   R. Siemens, M. Best, E. Grove-White et al., 'The Credibility of Electronic Publishing: A Report to the Humanities and Social Sciences Federation of Canada', *Text Technology*, 11:1 (2002): 1–128, <http://web.viu.ca/hssfc/Final/Credibility.htm>.

50   S. Ruecker, M. Radzikowska and S. Sinclair, 'Hackfests, Designfests, and Writingfests: The Role of Intense Periods of Face-to-Face Collaboration in International Research Teams', paper presented at Digital Humanities 2008, Oulu, Finland, <http://www. ekl.oulu.fi/dh2008/Digital%20Humanities%202008%20Book%20of%20Abstracts.pdf>, 16.

Managers may also have to do battle with administrators and administration from their university: it is relatively rare in the humanities to have cross-faculty research projects, or to have large-scale projects which involve academics from other institutions. Administrative problems can create delays in the project, affect individual staff, and impinge on available research time, if not carefully managed and monitored.

Finding funding

Administrative issues can also be present when applying for, or trying to find, funding for Digital Classicist projects. Research which involves a computational element often requires much higher levels of funding than simple sabbatical funding for traditional, lone-scholar, humanities endeavours, given the facilities, staff and technologies required. The funding required is often 'blue-sky': with defined project outcomes sometimes hard to gauge, which is not attractive to funding councils in the current climate of accountability, where evidence of impact and value are application requirements. Additionally, those using computing in their research are often 'too technical' to be eligible for funding from the humanities sector, and 'not technical enough' to secure funding through engineering and computing science channels. As computing becomes more pervasive, there are signs that this is changing. In the UK, USA and Canada, various joint-funding council calls have recently been issued to provide funding for advanced computer techniques to be employed for the benefits of the arts, humanities, cultural and heritage sectors. For example, the eSAD project, detailed above, is funded by a joint funding programme, the Arts and Humanities Research Council, Engineering and Physical Sciences Research Council, and Joint Information Systems Committee Arts and Humanities e-Science Initiative.[51] The UK's Joint Information Systems Committee and the USA's National Endowment for the Humanities have recently embarked on a transatlantic digitizsation programme.[52] However, an interdisciplinary scholar is often too busy battling different cultures and regimes to succeed in either, or both, disciplines, and requires temerity and dedication to succeed in these highly competitive funding calls.

Recruitment and training

Many young Classics scholars have been immersed in IT, but this does not mean that they are computationally literate. Finding a PhD student or research assistant with the prerequisite subject expertise and good knowledge of digital techniques is difficult as individuals 'with the adequate combination of research in a humanities

---

51 e-Science Research Grant and Postgraduate Studentship Awards (2007), <http://www.ahrcict.rdg.ac.uk/activities/e-science/awards_2007.htm>.

52 JISC/NEH transatlantic digitisation collaboration grants, <http://www.jisc.ac.uk/fundingopportunities/funding_calls/2007/09/circular0307>.

discipline and technical expertise are rare and valuable'.[53] An extensive training budget is often required for individuals working on digital humanities projects: ironically, once they are trained, it can be hard to retain qualified and experienced staff for future projects given the short-term nature of project-based grant funding and the emerging demand for computer-literate humanities scholars. However, individuals involved in such projects often benefit whether or not they stay in academic research: the skills and experience accrued in a successful interdisciplinary research projects are not just useful for academia, but can stand both humanities and science students and researchers in good stead by indicating their improved range of competencies, especially in a competitive job market.

Project charters

To counteract many of these problems, and to overcome cultural issues positively, it has been suggested that at the start of a project a 'charter' is drawn up between all project stakeholders, stipulating modes of communication, expected roles, expected means of conduct, and expected means and modes of publication.[54] Making such issues explicit at the start of a project can foster openness of communication, and alleviate any doubt for team members or managers regarding their individual roles, duties or expectations in the interdisciplinary environment.

Promoting Digital Classics

Given these issues and difficulties, but the latent intellectual and social potential waiting to be explored through such interdisciplinary endeavours, how can Digital Classical research be encouraged? What can be done to increase collaboration between those in computing and engineering science and Classics? How can Classical research questions be made more interesting to computing science? How are funding agencies coping with cross-disciplinary research proposals? Interdisciplinary research can be consciously fostered at individual, community, institution and funding council level, although this requires effort (and courage) from all stakeholders.

Individuals working in the area of Digital Classics have to become self-publicists, taking part in the wider Classics community, institution and beyond. By being intellectually and socially brave enough to establish dialogues with those in computing-based disciplines, both in person and in online forums, the

53   Claire Warwick, Isabel Galina, Melissa Terras et al., 'The Master Builders: LAIRAH Research on Good Practice in the Construction of Digital Humanities Projects', *Literary and Linguistic Computing* (2009).

54   S. Ruecker and M. Radzikowska, 'The Iterative Design of a Project Charter for INTERDISCIPLINARY research', paper presented at DIS 2008, Cape Town, South Africa.

profile of Digital Classics will be raised, as will the chance of meeting like-minded collaborators, hearing about relevant funding schemes, and developing computational skills and knowledge. Individuals can also encourage the establishment of, and take part in, teaching programmes, summer schools, and workshops to encourage both the traditional humanities scholar, and the younger generation of Classicists, in the understanding that using computational methods within Classical research is entirely feasible, useful and increasingly normal. Individuals must also document the contribution they make to digital projects on their CVs, and consistently demonstrate to colleagues and superiors that digital outputs are worthwhile. It will take some time to change the culture regarding academic acceptance of digital media: but individuals can be proactive in their attempts to encourage its recognition as bona fide academic endeavour.

The activities of the Digital Classicist community are part of the solution: encouraging discussion via email, wiki, discussion lists and presentations from interested individuals at Classics, digital humanities, e-Science and computing conferences, and generally highlighting the rich research area which exists in the intersection between Classics and computational technology.[55] The Digital Classicist also provides a supportive community in which to share ideas, ask questions, point to other relevant sources and engage with Digital Classics in a disciplinary manner. This can both encourage and aid individuals in undertaking their research (on a professional and personal level), and foster the idea that Digital Classics operates as an academic discipline (which is important, again, for the acceptance and understanding of a scholar's activities when applying for jobs, funding, etc.).

Research councils have recently begun to encourage interdisciplinary research. Academic institutions can foster cross-disciplinary networking by establishing events, research centres, and employing individuals who can respond at speed to these calls, encouraging disparate scholars to work together. Given the wide range of sources of funding, many institutions are becoming aware that it can be useful for someone in a research services role to highlight funding possibilities to scholars and teams who may not have come across the funding streams in their day-to-day academic duties, and to encourage or 'matchmake' interdisciplinary academic teams within the context of their wider institution.

Funding councils can promote and encourage interdisciplinary research by providing adequate funding for multidisciplinary projects, and by not being too prescriptive regarding the type of 'added value' they expect from 'blue-sky' research. Cross-funding council schemes, such as those run jointly by the UK's Arts and Humanities Research Council, Engineering and Physical Science Research Council, and Joint Information Systems Committee, would seem the best opportunity for those undertaking novel computational research in the humanities, although humanities research councils themselves should not shy away from providing adequate funding to help humanities scholars engage in the increasingly pervasive networked research environment.

---

55   The Digital Classicist, <http://www.digitalclassicist.org>.

Conclusion

> The greatest barrier that we now face is cultural rather than technological. We
> have all the tools that we need to rebuild our field, but the professional activities
> of the field, which evolved in the print world, have only begun to adapt to the
> needs of the digital world in which we live – hardly surprising, given the speed
> of change in the past two decades and the conservatism of the academy.[56]

Computational technologies can provide the scholar of Greco-Roman culture with
an array of tools for creating, searching, manipulating, accessing, analysing and
publishing the disparate types of information routinely utilized by the discipline.
Engaging constructively with these tools requires that the Classics scholar embrace
computing techniques, often extending their own skill set beyond the usual Classical
domain, or working (however formally) in large-scale interdisciplinary teams with
individuals from the computing, engineering and information sciences. Working
in a cross-disciplinary fashion can raise personal and professional issues for the
Digital Classicist. The same, of course, is true of the integration of computational
resources into other humanities disciplines, but the range and span of information
resources routinely consulted by Classicists, and the early adoption and creation
of computational tools and techniques by the Digital Classicist community, places
it at the frontline of interdisciplinary complications. This chapter has attempted
to expound the problems, and highlight issues, which can face those choosing to
work at the forefront of digital technologies in Classical research.

By understanding issues of interdisciplinarity, and being aware of both the
pressures and rewards in operating in such a domain, those undertaking Digital
Classicist research should be better placed to undertake successful projects. After
all, given the increasingly pervasive nature of technology within general society
and academic research, what other choice do we have, other than to engage and
tackle bravely the cultural divide to raise the voice of Classics in the computational
environment?

---

56   Crane, Seales and Terras, 'Cyberinfrastructure for Classical Philology'.

Bibliography

Agapitos, P., 'SO Debate Genre, Structure and Poetics in the Byzantine Vernacular Romances of Love', *Symbolae Osloenses*, 79/1 (2004): 7–101.

American Council of Learned Societies, *Report of the Commission on the Humanities* (New York: American Council of Learned Societies, 1964).

American Council of Learned Societies, *Our Cultural Commonwealth* (New York: American Council of Learned Societies, 2006).

Anderson, S., 'Past Indiscretions: Digital Archives and Recombinant History', in Marsha Kinder and Tara McPherson (eds), *Interactive Frictions* (Berkeley: University of California Press, forthcoming).

APA/AIA Task Force on Electronic Publications, *Final Report* (March 2007, updated March 2008), <http://socrates.berkeley.edu/~pinax/pdfs/TaskForceFinalReport.pdf>.

Austin, M., Kelly, M. and Brady, M., 'The Benefits of an Ontological Patient Model in Clinical Decision-Support', *Proceedings of the 23rd AAAI Conference on Artificial Intelligence* (2008), <http://www.aaai.org/Papers/AAAI/2008/AAAI08-325.pdf>.

Bailey, H., Hewison, J. and Turner, M., 'Choreographic Morphologies: Digital Visualization and Spatio-Temporal Structure in Dance and the Implications for Performance and Documentation', in Stuart Dunn, Suzanne Keene, George Mallen and Jonathan Bowen (eds), *EVA London 2008: Conference Proceedings* (London, 2008), pp. 9–18.

Bain, J.D. and McNaught, C., 'How Academics Use Technology in Teaching and Learning: Understanding the Relationship between Beliefs and Practice', *Journal of Computer Assisted Learning*, 2/2 (2006): 99–113.

Baker, M.A. and Grove, M., 'Tycho: A Wide-Area Messaging Framework with an Integrated Virtual Registry', *Journal of Supercomputing*, 42/2 (2007): 83–106.

Baker, M., Grove, M., Fulford, M. et al., 'VERA: Virtual Environment for Research in Archaeology', paper presented at the 4th International Conference on e-Social Science, Manchester, 18–20 June 2008.

Barchiesi, A. and Scheidel, W. (eds), *The Oxford Handbook of Roman Studies*, Oxford Handbooks in Classical Studies (Oxford University Press, forthcoming).

Baswell, C., *Virgil in Medieval England* (Cambridge: Cambridge University Press, 1995).

Becker, T. and Trowler, P.R., *Academic Tribes and Territories*, 2nd edn (Buckingham: Society for Research into Higher Education/Open University Press, 2001).

Bergman, M., *The Deep Web: Surfacing Hidden Value* (2001), <http://dx.doi.org/10.3998/3336451.0007.104>.

Berners-Lee, T., *Cool URIs Don't Change* (W3.org, 1998), <http://www.w3.org/Provider/Style/URI>.

Biggs, J., *Student Approaches to Learning and Studying* (Hawthorn, Victoria: Australian Council for Educational Research, 1987).

Biggs, J., *Teaching for Quality Learning at University: What the Student Does* (Buckingham: Society for Research into Higher Education/Open University Press, 1999; 2nd edn, 2003).

Bintliff, J., 'Time, Structure and Agency: The Annales, Emergent Complexity, and Archaeology', in John Bintliff (ed.), *A Companion to Archaeology* (Oxford: Blackwell, 2004), pp. 174–94.

Birley, E., Birley, R.E. and Birley, A.R., *Vindolanda Research Reports, New Series, Vol. II: Reports on the Auxiliaries, the Writing Tablets, Inscriptions, Brands and Graffiti* (Hexham: Vindolanda Trust, 1993).

Blackwell, C. and Crane, G., 'Cyberinfrastructure, the Scaife Digital Library and Classics in a Digital Age', in G. Crane and M. Terras (eds), *Changing the Center of Gravity: Transforming Classical Studies Through Cyberinfrastructure*, *DHQ*, 3/1 (2009), <http://www.digitalhumanities.org/dhq/vol/3/1/000035.html>.

Blomqvist, J., 'Review of: Willi, Andreas, *The Languages of Aristophanes. Aspects of Linguistic Variation in Classical Attic Greek* (Oxford: Oxford University Press, 2003)', *Bryn Mawr Classical Review*, 4 June (2004), <http://ccat.sas.upenn.edu/bmcr/2004/2004-06-04.html>.

Bodard, G., 'The Inscriptions of Aphrodisias as Electronic Publication: A User's Perspective and a Proposed Paradigm', *Digital Medievalist*, 4 (2008), available: <http://www.digitalmedievalist.org/journal/4/bodard/>.

Bodard, G., 'EpiDoc: Epigraphic Documents in XML for Publication and Interchange', in F. Feraudi-Gruénais, *Latin on Stone: Epigraphic Research and Electronic Archives* (Roman Studies: Interdisciplinary Approaches, 2009).

Bodard, G. and Garcés, J., 'Open Source Critical Editions: A Rationale', in M. Deegan and K. Sutherland (eds) *Text Editing, Print and the Digital World* (Farnham: Ashgate, 2009), pp. 83–98.

Bodel, J., 'Epigraphy and the Ancient Historian', in J. Bodel (ed.), *Epigraphic Evidence: Ancient History from Inscriptions* (London and New York: Routledge, 2001), pp. 1–56.

Booth, A., *Teaching History at University: Enhancing Learning and Understanding* (London and New York: Routledge, 2003).

Boyle, T., 'Design Principles for Authoring Dynamic, Reusable Learning Objects', *Australian Journal of Educational Technology*, 19/1 (2003): 46–58.

Boys-Stones, G., Graziosi, B. and Vasunia, P. (eds), *The Oxford Handbook of Hellenic Studies*, Oxford Handbooks in Classical Studies (Oxford University Press, forthcoming).

Bowman, A.K. and Brady, J.M. (eds), *Artefacts and Images of the Ancient World* (Oxford: Oxford University Press, 2004).

Bowman, A.K. and Tomlin, R.S.O., 'Wooden Stilus Tablets from Roman Britain', in A.K. Bowman and J.M. Brady (eds), *Artefacts and Images of the Ancient World* (Oxford: Oxford University Press, 2004), pp. 7–14.

Bowman, A.K., Tomlin, R.S.O. and Worp, K.A., 'Emptio bovis Frisica: The "Frisian Ox Sale" reconsidered', *Journal of Roman Studies*, 99 (forthcoming).

Bradley, C. and Boyle, T., 'The Design, Development, and Use of Multimedia Learning Objects', *Journal of Educational Multimedia and Hypermedia*, 13/4 (2004): 371–90.

Brady, J.M., Pan, X., Terras, M. and Schenk, V., 'Shadow Stereo, Image Filtering and Constraint Propagation', in A.K. Bowman and J.M. Brady (eds), *Artefacts and Images of the Ancient World* (Oxford: Oxford University Press, 2004), pp. 15–30.

Brockmann, C. (ed.), *Galen. Kommentar zu Hippokrates, Über die Gelenke. Die Einleitung und die ersten sechs Kommentarabschnitte von Buch I*, Corpus Medicorum Graecorum/Latinorum, <http://pom.bbaw.de/cmg/>.

Brodie, N., Doole, J. and Watson, P., *Stealing History: The Illicit Trade in Cultural Material* (Cambridge: The McDonald Institute for Archaeological Research, 2000).

Browning, R., 'Greek Diglossia Yesterday and Today', *International Journal of the Sociology of Language*, 35 (1982): 49–68.

Browning, R., *Medieval and Modern Greek* (Cambridge: Cambridge University Press, 1983).

Brunner, T., 'Classics and the Computer: The History', in J. Solomon (ed.), *Accessing Antiquity: The Computerization of Classical Databases* (Tuscon: University of Arizona Press, 1993), pp. 10–33.

Brunt, P.A. and Moore, J.M. (eds), *Res Gestae Divi Augusti: The Achievements of the Divine Augustus* (Oxford: Oxford University Press, 1989).

Burnet, A., Amandry, M. and Ripollès, P., *Roman Provincial Coinage: From the Death of Caesar to the Death of Vitellius (44 BC–AD 69)* (2 vols, London: British Museum Press, 1998).

Burrow, C., 'Virgils, from Dante to Milton', in Charles Martindale (ed.), *The Cambridge Companion to Virgil* (Cambridge: Cambridge University Press, 1997).

Busa, R., 'The Annals of Humanities Computing: The Index Thomisticus', *Computers and the Humanities* 14 (1980): 83–90.

Campbell, D.A., *Greek Lyric Poetry* (Bristol: Bristol Classical Press, 1994).

CIBER, *Information Behaviour of the Researcher of the Future* (January 2008), <http://www.bl.uk/news/pdf/googlegen.pdf>.

Claburn, T., 'Google Search Share Slips', *Information Week*, 14 January 2009, available: <http://www.informationweek.com/news/internet/reporting/show Article.jhtml?articleID=212900619>.

Clark, B., *Academic Culture*, Working Paper number 42 (New Haven: Yale University Higher Education Research Group, 1980).

Clarke, A. and Fulford, M., 'The Excavation of Insula IX, Silchester: The First Five Years of the "Town Life" Project, 1997–2001', *Britannia* 33 (2002): 129–66.

Clarke, A., Fulford, M. and Rains, M., 'Nothing to Hide: Online Database Publication and the Silchester Town Life Project', in M. Doerr and A. Sarris (eds), *CAA 2002. The Digital Heritage of Archaeology. Computer Applications and Quantitative Methods in Archaeology. Proceedings of the 30th Conference, Heraklion, Crete, April 2002*. (Archive of Monuments and Publications Hellenic Ministry of Culture, Greece, 2003), pp. 401–404.

Clarke, A., Fulford, M. and Rains, M., 'Silchester Roman Town Insula IX: The Development of an Urban Property c. AD 40–50–c. AD 250' (Archaeology Data Service, 2007), <http://ads.ahds.ac.uk/catalogue/archive/silchester_ahrc_2007>.

Clarke, A., Fulford, M., Rains, M. and Tootell, K., 'Silchester Roman Town Insula IX: The Development of an Urban Property c. AD 40–50–c. AD 250', *Internet Archaeology* 21, <http://intarch.ac.uk/journal/issue21/silchester_index.html>.

Clarke, A., Fulford, M. et al., *Silchester Insula IX: The Town Life Project: The First Six Years 1997–2002* (Reading: University of Reading Department of Archaeology, 2002).

Clarke, M.L., *Classical Education in Britain 1500–1900* (Cambridge: Cambridge University Press, 1959).

Condron, F., Richards, J., Robinson, D. and Wise, A., 'Strategies for Digital Data: A Survey of User Needs' (York: Archaeology Data Service, 1999), <http://ads.ahds.ac.uk/project/strategies/>.

Connor, W.R., *Thucydides* (Princeton: Princeton University Press, 1984).

Crane, G., 'Classics and the Computer: An End of the History', in S. Schreibman, R. Siemens and J. Unsworth (eds), *A Companion to Digital Humanities* (Oxford: Blackwell Publishing, 2004), pp. 46–55.

Crane, G. and Rydberg-Cox, J.A., 'New Technology and New Roles: The Need for "Corpus Editors"', in *Proceedings of the Fifth ACM Conference on Digital Libraries* (New York: ACM, 2000), pp. 252–3.

Crane, G. and Terras, M., 'Changing the Center of Gravity: Transforming Classical Studies Through Cyberinfrastructure', *Digital Humanities Quarterly*, 3/1 (2009).

Crane, G., Bamman, D. and Jones, A., 'ePhilology: When the Books Talk to Their Readers', in Ray Siemens and Susan Schreibman (eds), *A Companion to Digital Literary Studies* (Oxford: Blackwell, 2008), <http://www.digitalhumanities.org/companionDLS/>.

Crane, G., Seales, B. and Terras, M., 'Cyberinfrastructure for Classical Philology', in G. Crane and M. Terras (eds), *Changing the Center of Gravity: Transforming Classical Studies Through Cyberinfrastructure, Digital Humanities Quarterly*, 3/1 (2009), <http://www.digitalhumanities.org/dhq/vol/003/1/000023.html>.

Crane, G., Smith, D.A. and Wulfman, C.E., 'Building a Hypertextual Digital Library in the Humanities: A Case Study on London', in *Proceedings of the 1st ACM/IEEE-CS Joint Conference on Digital Libraries* (Roanoke, Virginia: ACM, 2001), <http://portal.acm.org/citation.cfm?id=379437.379756>.

Crane, G., Bamman, D., Cerrato, L. et al., 'Beyond Digital Incunabula: Modelling the Next Generation of Digital Libraries', in J. Gonzalo, C. Thanos, M.F. Verdejo and R.C. Carrasco (eds), *Research and Advanced Technology for Digital Libraries* (Berlin-Heidelberg: Springer, 2006), <http://dx.doi.org/10.1007/11863878_30>.

Crowther, C., 'Inscriptions of Antiochus I of Commagene and Other Epigraphical Finds', *Zeugma: Interim Reports*, JRA Supplement 51 (2003): 57–67.

Crawley, R., *Thucydides' Peloponnesian War* (London: J.M. Dent, 1903); reproduced in Project Gutenberg, <http://www.gutenberg.org/dirs/etext04/plpwr10.txt>.

Crumley, C., 'Sacred Landscapes, Constructed and Conceptualized', in B.A. Knapp and W. Ashmore (eds), *Archaeology of Landscape: Contemporary Perspectives* (Oxford: Blackwell Press, 1999), pp. 269–76.

Curtius, E.R., *European Literature and the Latin Middle Ages* (reprint, Princeton: Princeton University Press, 1991).

Deegan, M. and Tanner, S., 'Digital Futures: Strategies for the Information Age', *Digital Futures Series* (Library Association Publishing, 2002).

DeRose, S.J., Durand, D.G., Mylonas, E. and Renear, A.H., 'What is Text, Really?' *Journal of Computing in Higher Education*, 1/2 (1990): 3–26, <http://doi.acm.org/10.1145/264842.264843>.

Dickinson, O.T.P.K., 'Comments on a Popular Model of Minoan Religion', *Oxford Journal of Archaeology*, 13/2 (1994): 173–84.

Dill, D.D., 'Academic Administration', in B.R. Clark and G. Neave (eds), *Encyclopedia of Higher Education*, vol. 2 (Oxford: Pergamon Press, 1992), pp. 1318–29.

Dimitrova, N.M., *Theoroi and Initiates in Samothrace: The Epigraphical Evidence* (Princeton: Hesperia Supplement 37, 2008).

Doctorow, C., 'Ebooks: Neither E, Nor Books', paper presented at the O'Reilly Emerging Technologies Conference, 2004, <http://www.craphound.com/ebooksneitherenorbooks.txt>.

Dornan, J.L., 'Agency in Archaeology: Past, Present and Future Directions', *Journal of Archaeological Method and Theory*, 9/4 (2002): 303–29.

Dué, C. and Ebbott, M. (eds), *The Homer Multitext Project*, Harvard Center for Hellenic Studies, <http://chs.harvard.edu/chs/homer_multitext>.

Dunn, S. and Blanke, T., 'Next Steps for e-Science, the Textual Humanities and VREs', *D-Lib Magazine*, 14/12 (January/February 2008), <http://www.dlib.org/dlib/january08/dunn/01dunn.html>.

Dunn, S. and Isaksen, L., 'Space and Time: Methods in Geospatial Computing for Mapping the Past', AHRC ICT Methods Network workshop report 2007, <http://www.methodsnetwork.ac.uk/redist/pdf/act24report.pdf>.

Eckel, B., 'Why Do You Put Your Books on the Web? How Can You Make Any Money that Way?', *FAQ*, <http://web.archive.org/web/20041204221726/http://mindview.net/FAQ/FAQ-010>.

Eideneier, H., *Von Rhapsodie Zu Rap: Aspekte der griechischen Sprachgeschichte von Homer bis heute* (Tübingen: Günther Narr, 1999).

Eiteljorg, H., *Archaeological Computing* (2nd edn, Centre for the Study of Architecture: Bryn Mawr, 2008), <http://archcomp.csanet.org/>.

Elliott, T. et al., (eds), *EpiDoc: Guidelines for Structured Markup of Epigraphic Texts in TEI XML* (2007) <http://www.stoa.org/epidoc/gl/5/>.

Elliott, T. and Gillies, S., 'Digital Geography and Classics', in G. Crane and M. Terras (eds), *Changing the Center of Gravity: Transforming Classical Studies Through Cyberinfrastructure*, *Digital Humanities Quarterly*, 3/1 (2009), <http://www.digitalhumanities.org/dhq/vol/3/1/000031.html>.

Emmett, K., *Alexandrian Coins* (Lodi: Clio's Cabinet, 2001).

Emmett, K., 'An Unpublished Alexandrian Coin of Augustus', *The Celator* 17/8 (2003).

Entwhistle, N.J., 'Contrasting Perspectives on Learning', in F. Marton, D. Hounsell and N.J. Entwhistle (eds), *The Experience of Learning* (Edinburgh: Scottish Academic Press, 1984), pp. 3–23.

Entwhistle N.J. and Ramsden, P., *Understanding Student Learning* (London: Croom Helm, 1983).

Evans, C., 'Choosing People: Recruitment and Selection as Leverage on Subjects and Disciplines', *Studies in Higher Education* 20/3 (1995): 253–65.

Fabre, G., Mayer, M. and Rodà, I., *Inscriptions Romaines de Catalogne IV. Barcino* (Paris, 1997).

Fisher, C., Warwick, C. and Terras, M., 'Integrating New Technologies into Established Systems: A Case Study from Roman Silchester', *Computer Applications in Archaeology (2009), Making History Interactive* (Williamsburg, MD, 22–6 March 2009).

Frank, R., 'Interdisciplinary: The First Half Century', in R. Burchfield, E.G. Stanley and T.H. Hoad (eds), *Words for Robert Burchfield's Sixty-Fifth Birthday* (Woodbridge: Boydell and Brewer, 1988).

Friesen, N., 'Three Objections to Learning Objects and E-learning Standards', in R. McGreal (ed.), *Online Education Using Learning Objects* (London: Routledge, 2004), pp. 59–70.

Fulford, M.G. and Clarke, A., 'Victorian Excavation Methodology: The Society of Antiquaries at Silchester in 1893', *Antiquaries Journal* 82 (2002): 285–306.

Fulford, M.G. and Timby, J., 'Late Iron Age and Roman Silchester: Excavations on the Site of the Forum-Basilica, 1977, 1980–86', *Britannia Monograph* 15 (London: Society for the Promotion of Roman Studies, 2000).

Fulford, M.G., Clarke, A. and Eckardt, H., *Life and Labour in Late Roman Silchester: Excavations in Insula IX since 1997*, Britannia Monograph 22 (London: Society for the Promotion of Roman Studies, 2006).

Gaffney, V. and Fletcher, R.P., 'Always the Bridesmaid and Never the Bride! Arts, Archaeology and the e-Science Agenda', in P. Clarke, C. Davenhall, C. Greenwood and M. Strong (eds), *Proceedings of Lighting the Blue Touchpaper for UK e-Science – Closing Conference of ESLEA Project* (Edinburgh, 2007), <http://adsabs.harvard.edu/abs/2007lbtu.conf...31G>.

Gallo, I., *Greek and Latin Papyrology*, trans. M. Falivene and J. March, Classical Handbook 1 (London: Institute of Classical Studies, 1986).

Gelzer, H. (ed.), *Leontios' von Neapolis Leben des heiligen Iohannes des barmherzigen Erzbischofs von Alexandrien* (Freiburg i. B., 1893).

Gibin, M., Singleton, A., Milton, R., Mateos, P. and Longley, P., 'An Exploratory Cartographic Visualisation of London through the Google Maps API', *Applied Spatial Analysis and Policy*, 1/2 (July 2008): 85–97.

Goodchild, M.F., 'Citizens as Voluntary Sensors: Spatial Data Infrastructure in the World of Web 2.0', *International Journal of Spatial Data Infrastructures Research*, vol. 2 (2007): 24–32.

Gore, A., 'The Digital Earth: Understanding our Planet in the 21st Century', speech given at the California Science Center, Los Angeles, California, 31 January 1998, <http://www.isde5.org/al_gore_speech.htm>.

Gorman, G.E., 'Editorial: Is the Wiki Concept Really so Wonderful?', *Online Information Review*, 29/3 (2005): 225–6.

Greetham, D.C., *Textual Scholarship: An Introduction* (New York: Routledge, 1994).

Griffiths, J. and Brophy, P., 'Student Searching Behavior and the Web: Use of Academic Resources and Google', *Library Trends*, Spring (2005): 539–54.

Group for Collaborative Inquiry, 'The Democratization of Knowledge', *Adult Education Quarterly*, 44/1 (1993): 43–51.

Guess, A., 'Research Methods "Beyond Google"', *Inside Higher Ed* (2008), <http://www.insidehighered.com/news/2008/06/17/institute>.

Guthrie, K., Griffiths, R. and Maron, N., *Sustainability and Revenue Models for Online Academic Resources* (Ithaka, 2008), <http://www.ithaka.org/publications/sustainability>.

Hallett, J.P. and Van Nortwick, T., *Compromising Traditions: The Personal Voice in Classical Scholarship* (London: Routledge, 1997).

Hayes, B., 'Cloud Computing', *Communications of the ACM*, 51/7 (2008): 9–11.

Hayes, J., *Late Roman Pottery* (London: British School at Rome, 1972).

Heath, S. and Tekkök, B., *Greek, Roman and Byzantine Pottery and Ilion (Troia)* <http://classics.uc.edu/troy/grbpottery>.

Hill, L.L., *Georeferencing: The Geographic Associations of Information* (Cambridge, MA: MIT Press, 2006).

Hinterberger, M., 'How Should We Define Vernacular Literature?', in *Unlocking the Potential of Texts: Interdisciplinary Perspectives on Medieval Greek* (Cambridge: Centre for Research in the Arts, Social Sciences, and Humanities, University of Cambridge, 2006), <http://www.mml.cam.ac.uk/greek/grammarofmedievalgreek/unlocking/html/Hinterberger.html>.

Hockey, S., 'The History of Humanities Computing', in S. Schreibman, R. Siemens, J. Unsworth (eds), *A Companion to Digital Humanities* (Oxford: Blackwell, 2004), pp. 3–19.

Hodder, I., '"Always Momentary, Fluid and Flexible": Towards a Reflexive Excavation Methodology', *Antiquity*, 71 (1997): 691–700.

Holton, D. and Manolessou, I., 'Medieval and Early Modern Greek', in W.F. Bakker (ed.), *Companion to the Ancient Greek Language* (Oxford: Wiley-Blackwell, in print).

Hopkins, H., 'Britannica 2.0: Wikipedia Gets 97% of Encyclopedia Visits', *Hitwise Intelligence*, 1 (2009), <http://weblogs.hitwise.com/us-heather-hopkins/2009/01/britannica_20_wikipedia_gets_9.html>.

Horrocks, G., *Greek: A History of the Language and its Speakers* (2nd edn, Oxford: Wiley-Blackwell, 2010).

Hudson, A., 'Outline of a Theory of Diglossia', *International Journal of the Sociology of Language*, 157 (2002): 1–48.

Isaksen, L., *Pandora's Box: The Future of Cultural Heritage on the World Wide Web*, unpublished conference paper, <http://leifuss.files.wordpress.com/2009/04/pandorasboxrev1.pdf>.

Iyer, A., 'The Present Past: Towards an Archaeology of Dance', in S. Jordan (ed.), *Preservation Politics: Dance Revived, Reconstructed, Remade* (London: Dance Books, 2000), 141–5.

Jacks, P., *The Antiquarian and the Myth of Antiquity* (Cambridge: Cambridge University Press, 1993).

Jeffreys, M., 'The Literary Emergence of Vernacular Greek', *Mosaic*, 8/4 (1975): 171–93.

Jeffreys, M., 'The Silent Millennium: Thoughts on the Evidence for Spoken Greek between the Last Papyri and Cretan Drama', in C.N. Constantinides (ed.), *ΦΙΛΛΕΛΗΝ. Studies in Honour of Robert Browning* (Venice: Istituto Ellenico di Studi Bizantini e Postbizantini di Venezia, 1996), pp. 133–49.

Johnsen, H. and Olsen, B., 'Hermeneutics and Archaeology: On the Philosophy of Contextual Archaeology', in J. Thomas (ed.), *Interpretive Archaeology* (Leicester: Leicester University Press, 2000), pp. 97–117.

Joseph, B.D., 'Textual Authenticity: Evidence from Medieval Greek', in S.C. Herring, P. van Reenen and L. Schøsler (eds), *Textual Parameters in Older Languages* (Amsterdam: Benjamins, 2000), pp. 309–28.

Joseph, B.D. and Janda, R.D. (eds), *The Handbook of Historical Linguistics* (Oxford: Blackwell, 2003).

Keay, S. and Williams, D., *Roman Amphorae: A Digital Resource* (2005–2009), <http://ads.ahds.ac.uk/catalogue/resources.html?amphora2005>.

Kember, D., 'Interpreting Student Workload and the Factors which Shape Students' Perceptions of their Workload', *Studies in Higher Education*, 29/2 (2004): 165–84.

Kember, D. and Leung, D.Y.P., 'Characterising a Teaching and Learning Environment Conducive to Making Demands on Students while not Making their Workload Excessive', *Studies in Higher Education*, 31/2 (2006): 185–98.

Kenney, E.J., *The Classical Text: Aspects of Editing in the Age of the Printed Book* (Berkeley: University of California Press, 1974).

Koortbojian, M., '*In commemorationem mortuorum*: Text and Image along the "Streets of Tombs"', in J. Elsner (ed.), *Art and Text in Roman Culture* (Cambridge: Cambridge University Press, 1996), pp. 210–33.

Koppi, T., Bogle, L. and Bogle, M., 'Learning Objects, Repositories, Sharing and Resusability', *Open Learning*, 20/1 (2005): 83–91.

Koppi, T., Bogle, L. and Lavitt, N., 'Institutional Use of Learning Objects: Lessons Learned and Future Directions', *Journal of Educational Multimedia and Hypermedia*, 13/4 (2004): 449–64.

Land, R., 'Paradigms Lost: Academic Practice and Exteriorising Technologies', *E-Learning*, 3/1 (2006): 100–10.

Lass, R., *Historical Linguistics and Language Change* (Cambridge: Cambridge University Press, 1997).

Laurillard, D., 'Design Tools for e-Learning' (Conference Keynote ASCILITE, 2002), <http://www.ascilite.org.au/conferences/auckland20/proceedings/papers/key_laurillard.pdf>.

Leeder, D. and Morales, R., 'Universities' Collaboration in e-Learning (UCeL): Post-Fordism in Action', *UCeL Documents* (2004), <http://www.ucel.ac.uk/documents/docs/LEEDERMORALES.pdf>.

LeFurgy, W.G., 'PDF/A: Developing a File Format for Long-Term Preservation,' *RLG DigiNews*, (2003) 7/6, RLG, <http://worldcat.org/arcviewer/1/OCC/200 7/08/08/0000070519/viewer/file3170.html#feature1>.

Lessig, L., *Code and Other Laws of Cyberspace* (New York: Basic Books, 1999).

Lesure, R.G., 'Archaeologists and the Site', in J.K. Papadopoulos and R.M. Levanthal (eds), *Theory and Practice in Mediterranean Archaeology: Old World and New Perspectives* (Los Angeles: Costen Institute of Archaeology, 2003), pp. 199–202.

Ljubojevic, D., OKell, E. and Bauer, E., 'Not by Accident but by Design: Collaborative Design of Reusable Learning Technology', *Design Principles and Practices*, 3/3 (2009) <http://ijg.cgpublisher.com/product/pub.154/prod.234>.

Lock, G., *Using Computers in Archaeology: Towards Virtual Pasts* (London: Routledge, 2003).

Lock, G. and Brown, K. (eds), *On the Theory and Practice of Archaeological Computing* (Oxford University Committee for Archaeology/Oxbow Books, 2000).

Luck, G., 'Textual Criticism Today', *The American Journal of Philology*, 102/2 (1981): 164–94.

Maas, P., *Textual Criticism*, trans. from the German by Barbara Flower (Oxford: Clarendon Press, 1958).

Macal, C.M. and North, M.J., 'Tutorial on Agent-based Modeling and Simulation', *Proceedings of the 37th Conference on Winter Simulation*, Orlando, Florida (2005): 1–15.

Mackridge, P., *Language and National Identity in Greece, 1766–1976* (Oxford: Oxford University Press, 2009).

MacMahon, C. (ed.), *Using and Sharing Online Resources in History, Classics and Archaeology* (Glasgow: History, Classics and Archaeology Subject Centre, 2006),<http://www.heacademy.ac.uk/assets/hca/documents/UsingandSharing-OnlineResourcesHCA.pdf>.

Mahoney, A., 'Tachypedia Byzantina: The Suda On Line as Collaborative Encyclopaedia', *Digital Humanities Quarterly*, 3/1 (2009), <http://www.digitalhumanities.org/dhq/vol/003/1/000025.html>.

Manolessou, I., 'From Participles to Gerunds', in M. Stavrou and A. Terzi (eds), *Advances in Greek Generative Syntax: In Honor of Dimitra Theophanopoulou-Kontou* (Amsterdam: Benjamins, 2005) pp. 241–83.

Manolessou, I., 'On Historical Linguistics, Linguistic Variation and Medieval Greek', *Byzantine and Modern Greek Studies*, 32/1 (2008): 69–71.

Martin, R.H. (ed.), *Terence: Adelphoe* (Cambridge: Cambridge University Press, 1976).

Marton, F. and Säljö, R., 'On Qualitative Differences in Learning II: Outcome as a Function of the Learner's Conception of the Task', *British Journal of Educational Psychology*, 46 (1976): 115–27.

Meurman-Solin, A., 'Structured Text Corpora in the Study of Language Variation and Change', *Literary and Linguistic Computing*, 16/1 (2001): 5–27.

Meyer, E. and Land, R., 'Threshold Concepts and Troublesome Knowledge: Linkages to Ways of Thinking and Practising within the Disciplines', Occasional Report 4 of the *Enhancing Teaching-Learning Environments in Undergraduate Courses Project* (May 2003), <http://www.tla.ed.ac.uk/etl/docs/ETLreport4.pdf>.

Molton, N., Pan, X., Brady, M. et al., 'Visual Enhancement of Incised Text', *Pattern Recognition*, 36 (2003): 1031–43.

Monella, P., 'Towards a Digital Model to Edit the Different Paratextuality Levels within a Textual Tradition', *Digital Medievalist*, 4 (2008), <http://www.digitalmedievalist.org/journal/4/monella/>.

Monroe, J., 'Introduction: The Shapes of Fields', in *Writing and Revising the Disciplines* (Ithaca: Cornell University Press, 2002), pp. 1–12.

Morris, I., *Death-Ritual and Social Structure in Classical Antiquity* (Cambridge: Cambridge University Press, 1992).

Mortimer, A., Jasani, A. and Whitmore, S., *University of Leeds: Assessment and Feedback in the School of Modern Languages and Cultures and the School of Classics: 'Fair, Prompt and Detailed' – Matching Staff and Student Expectations on Assessment and Feedback in Light of the National Student Survey* (Mouchel Parkman: Nottingham, April 2006), <http://www.german.leeds.ac.uk/learning/ Assessment and Feedback Report FINAL 02.05.06.htm>.

Morwood, J. (ed.), *The Teaching of Classics* (Cambridge: Cambridge University Press, 2003).

Moschonas, S., 'Relativism in Language Ideology: On Greece's Latest Language Issues', *Journal of Modern Greek Studies*, 22 (2004): 173–205.

Moschonas, S., Γλώσσα και Ιδεολογία, (Athens: Patakis, 2005).

Mynors, R.A.B., *P. Vergili Maronis Opera* (Oxford: Oxford University Press, 1969).

National Endowment for the Humanities, *Preservation and Access: Humanities Collections and Resources*, <http://www.neh.gov/grants/guidelines/ Collections_and_resources.html>.

Newby, Z. and Leader-Newby, R. (eds), *Art and Inscriptions in the Ancient World* (Cambridge: Cambridge University Press, 2006).

Nogales Basarrate, T., Edmondson, J. and Trillmich, W., *Imagen y Memoria: Monumentos Funerarios con Retratos en la Colonia Augusta Emerita* (Madrid: Real Academia de la Historia, 2001).

OKell, E.R., 'e-Learning and *evaluating Multiple Interpretations (eMI)*: The Background to the GLO Tool and Interface – a practitioner-developer's perspective', *HCA Work-in-Progress* (July 2007), <http://www.heacademy. ac.uk/hca/themes/e-learning/emi_glo>.

OKell, E.R., '*evaluating Multiple Interpretations (eMI)*: The Tasks and their Pedagogical Underpinning', *HCA Work-in-Progress* (July 2007), <http://www. heacademy.ac.uk/hca/themes/e-learning/emi_glo>.

Oliver, G.J. (ed.), *The Epigraphy of Death* (Liverpool: Liverpool University Press, 2000).

Ore, E.S., 'Monkey Business – or What is an Edition?' *Literary and Linguistic Computing*, 19/1 (2004): 35–44.

O'Riordan, E.J., Baker, M., Clarke, A., Fisher, C., Fulford, M.G., Rains, M., Terras, M. and Warwick, C., 'Virtual Environments for Research in Archaeology (VERA): A Roman Case Study At Silchester', paper presented at Digital Resources in the Humanities and Arts, Cambridge, September 2008.

O'Toole, J.M., 'On the Idea of Permanence', *American Archivist*, 52 (1989): 10–25.

Pace, S., 'The Roles of Challenge and Skill in the Flow Experiences of Web Users', *Issues in Informing Science and Information Technology*, 1 (2004): 341–58.

Pasquali, G., *Storia della tradizione e critica del testo* (2nd edn, Florence: F. Le Monnier, 1952).

Pearce, J., Millett, M. and Struck, M. (eds), *Burial, Society and Context in the Roman World* (Oxford: Oxbow Books, 2000).

Pearson, M. and Shanks, M., *Theatre/Archaeology* (London: Routledge, 2001).

Peatfield, A., 'The Topography of Minoan Peak Sanctuaries', *Annual of the British School at Athens*, 78 (1983): 273–80.

Polsani, P., 'Use and Abuse of Reusable Learning Objects', *Journal of Digital Information*, 3/4 (2003), <http://journals.tdl.org/jodi/article/view/89/88>.

Porter, S.E., *Diglossia and Other Topics in New Testament Linguistics* (Sheffield: Sheffield Academic Press, 2000).

Pusch, C.D., Kabatek, J. and Raible, W., *Romanistische Korpuslinguistik II* (2005), <http://www.corpora-romanica.net/publications_e.htm#korpuslinguistik_2>.

QAA, 'Classics and Ancient History Benchmark Statement' (Gloucester: Quality Assurance Agency for Higher Education, 2000), <http://www.qaa.ac.uk/academicinfrastructure/benchmark/honours/classics.pdf>.

Ramsay, S., 'Rules of the Order: The Sociology of Large, Multi-Institutional Software Development Projects', presented at Digital Humanities conference 2008, Oulu, Finland, abstract <http://www.ekl.oulu.fi/dh2008/Digital%20Humanities%202008%20Book%20of%20Abstracts.pdf>.

Ramsay, S., Sinclair, S., Unsworth, J., Radzikowska, M. and Ruecker, S., 'Design, Coding, and Playing with Fire: Innovations in Interdisciplinary Research Project Management', panel at Digital Humanities 2008, Oulu, Finland, abstract <http://www.ekl.oulu.fi/dh2008/Digital%20Humanities%202008%20Book%20of%20Abstracts.pdf>.

Ramsden, P., *Learning to Teach in Higher Education* (2nd edn, London and New York: Routledge Falmer, 2003).

Reeve, M.D., 'Stemmatic Method: "Qualcosa che non funziona"?', in P. Ganz (ed.), *The Role of the Book in Medieval Culture*, proceedings of the Oxford International Symposium, 26 September–1 October 1982 (Turhhout: Brepols, 1986), pp. 57–69.

Reeve, M.D., '*Elimination codicum descriptorum:* A Methodological Problem', in J.N. Grant (ed.), *Editing Greek and Latin Texts. Papers given at the Twenty-Third Annual Conference on Editorial Problems, University of Toronto 6–7 November 1987* (New York: AMS Press, 1989), pp. 1–35.

Reeve, M.D., 'Shared Innovations, Dichotomies and Evolution', in A. Ferrari (ed.), *Filologia Classica e Filologia Romanza; Esperienze ecdotiche a confronto,* (Spoleto: Centro Italiano di Studi sull'Alto Medioevo, 1998), pp. 429–505.

Reilly, P. and Rahtz, S. (eds), *Archaeology and the Information Age: A Global Perspective*, One World Archaeology 21 (London: Routledge, 1992).

Renear, A., Mylonas, E. and Durand, D., 'Refining our Notion of What Text Really Is: The Problem of Overlapping Hierarchies', <http://www.stg.brown.edu/resources/stg/monographs/ohco.html>.

Renfrew, C., 'Geography, Archaeology, Environment: 1. Archaeology', *Geographical Journal*, 149/3 (1983): 316–33.

Reynolds, J.M., Roueché, C. and Bodard, G., *Inscriptions of Aphrodisias* (2007), <http://insaph.kcl.ac.uk/iaph2007>.

Reynolds, L.D. and Wilson, N.G., *Scribes and Scholars: A Guide to the Transmission of Greek and Latin Literature* (Oxford: Oxford University Press, 1968).

Rivett, P., 'Conceptual Data Modelling in an Archaeological GIS', *Proceedings of GeoComputation '97 and SIRC '97* (1997), pp. 15–26.

Robert, J. and Robert, L., *Fouilles d'Amyzon en Carie* (Paris: De Boccard, 1983).

Robinson, J.M. and Zubrow, E.B., 'Between Spaces: Interpolation in Archaeology' in M. Gilling, D. Mattingly and J. Van Dalen (eds), *Geographic Information Systems and Landscape Archaeology* (Oxford, 2000), pp. 65–84.

Robinson, P., 'The One Text and the Many Texts', *Literary and Linguistic Computing*, 15/1 (2000): 5–14.

Robinson, P., 'The Canterbury Tales and Other Medieval Texts', in J. Unsworth, K. O'Brien O'Keeffe and L. Burnard (eds), *Electronic Textual Editing* (New York: Modern Languages Association, 2006).

Ross, S., Moffett, J. and Henderson, J. (eds), *Computing for Archaeologists*, Oxford University Committee for Archaeology Monograph 18 (Oxford: Oxford University Committee for Archaeology, 1991).

Roth, P., *The Plot Against America* (London: Vintage, 2005).

Roueché, C., *Aphrodisias in Late Antiquity: The Late Roman and Byzantine Inscriptions* (rev. 2nd edn, 2004) <http://insaph.kcl.ac.uk/ala2004>.

Roued Olsen, H., Tarte, S., Terras, M., Brady, M. and Bowman, A., 'Towards an Interpretation Support System for Reading Ancient Documents', paper presented at Digital Humanities conference 2009, University of Maryland, abstract <http://www.mith2.umd.edu/dh09/?page_id=99>.

Rouse, L.R., Bergeron, S.J. and Harris, T.M., 'Participating the Geospatial Web: Collaborative Mapping, Social Software and Participatory GIS', in Arno Scharl and Klaus Tochtermann (eds), *The Geospatial Web* (Berlin: Springer, 2007), pp. 153–8.

Ruecker, S. and Radzikowska, M. 'The Iterative Design of a Project Charter for Interdisciplinary Research', paper presented at DIS 2008, Cape Town, South Africa.

Ruecker, S., Radzikowska, M. and Sinclair, S., 'Hackfests, Designfests, and Writingfests: The Role of Intense Periods of Face-to-Face Collaboration in International Research Teams', paper presented at Digital Humanities conference 2008, Oulu, Finland, abstract <http://www.ekl.oulu.fi/dh2008/Digi tal%20Humanities%202008%20Book%20of%20Abstracts.pdf>.

Rutkowski, B., *The Minoan Peak Sanctuaries: The Topography and Architecture* (Liège, 1988).

Sauerman, L. and Cyaniak, R., *Cool URIs for the Semantic Web* (2008), <http:// www.w3.org/TR/cooluris/>.

Scharl, A. and Tochtermann, K. (eds), *The Geospatial Web* (Berlin: Springer, 2007).

Schenk, V.U.B. and Brady, M., 'Visual Identification of Fine Surface Incisions in Incised Roman Stylus Tablets', paper presented at International Conference in Advances in Pattern Recognition, 2003.

Schreibman, S., Siemens, R. and Unsworth, J., 'The Digital Humanities and Computing: An Introduction', in S. Schreibman, R. Siemens and J. Unsworth (eds), *A Companion to Digital Humanities* (Oxford: Blackwell, 2008).

Shadbolt, N., Hall, W. and Berners-Lee, T., 'The Semantic Web Revisited' (2006), *IEEE Intelligent Systems*, <http://eprints.ecs.soton.ac.uk/12614/1/Semantic_Web_Revisted.pdf>.

Shreeves, E., 'Between the Visionaries and the Luddites: Collection Development and Electronic Resources in the Humanities', *Library Trends*, 40 (1992): 579–95.

Siemens, L., '"It's a Team if You Use 'Reply All'": An Exploration of Research Teams in Digital Humanities Environments', *Literary and Linguistic Computing*, 24/2 (2009): 225–33.

Siemens, R., Best, M., Grove-White, E. et al., 'The Credibility of Electronic Publishing: A Report to the Humanities and Social Sciences Federation of Canada', *Text Technology*, 11/1 (2002): 1–128, <http://web.viu.ca/hssfc/Final/Credibility.htm>.

Slob, E., 'De koopakte van Tolsum', *Tijdschr. v. Rechtgeschiedenis* 66 (1998): 25–52.

Smith, D.N., 'Citation in Classical Studies', in G. Crane and M. Terras (eds), *Changing the Center of Gravity: Transforming Classical Studies Through Cyberinfrastructure*, *Digital Humanities Quarterly*, 3/1 (2009), <http://www.digitalhumanities.org/dhq/vol/3/1/000028.html>.

Smith, D.N. and Weaver, G.A., 'Applying Domain Knowledge from Structured Citation Formats to Text and Data Mining: Examples Using the CITE Architecture', in Gerhard Heyer (ed), *Text Mining Services: Building and Applying Text Mining Based Service Infrastructures in Research and Industry* (Leipziger Beiträge zur Informatik, Band XIV; Leipzig: 2009), pp. 129–139. (Reprinted in Dartmouth College Computer Science Technical Report series, TR2009-649, June 2009.)

Solomon, J., *Accessing Antiquity: The Computerization of Classical Studies* (Tucson: University of Arizona Press, 1993).

Spinella, M., 'JSTOR and the Changing Digital Landscape', *Interlending and Document Supply*, 36/2 (2009): pp. 79–85.

Spiro, R. and Jehng, J., 'Cognitive Flexibility and Hypertext: Theory and Technology for the Nonlinear and Multidimensional Traversal of Complex Subject Matter', in D. Nix and R. Spiro (eds), *Cognition, Education and Multimedia: Exploring Ideas in High Technology* (Hillsdale, NJ: Lawrence Erlbaum, 1990), pp. 163–205.

Steinby, M. et al., *La necropoli della via Triumphalis: il tratto sotto l'Autoparco vaticano* (Rome: 'L'Erma' di Bretschneider, 2003).

Stothart, C., 'Web Threatens Learning Ethos', *Times Higher Education Supplement*, 22 June 2007: 2.

Struthers, J., *Working Models for Designing Online Courses and Materials* (York: LTSN Generic Centre, 2002), <http://www.heacademy.ac.uk/assets/York/documents/resources/resourcedatabase/id197_Working_Models_for_Designing_Online_Courses_and_Materials.rtf>.

Talbert, R.J.A. (ed.), *Barrington Atlas of the Greek and Roman World* (Princeton: University Presses of California, Columbia and Princeton, 2000).

Tarte, S., Brady, J.M., Roued Olsen, H., Terras, M. and Bowman, A.K., 'Image Acquisition and Analysis to Enhance the Legibility of Ancient Texts', UK e-Science Programme All Hands Meeting 2008 (AHM2008), Edinburgh, September 2008.

Tarte, S.M., 'Papyrological Investigations: Transferring Perception and Interpretation into the Digital World', *Literary and Linguistic Computing* (2010, forthcoming).

Taylor, P.J., 'An Interpretation of the Quantification Debate in British Geography', *Transactions of the Institute of British Geographers*, ns 1 (1976): 129–42.

Terras, M., *Image to Interpretation. An Intelligent System to Aid Historians in Reading the Vindolanda Texts*, Oxford Studies in Ancient Documents (Oxford: Oxford University Press, 2006).

Terras, M. and Robertson, P., 'Image and Interpretation: Using Artificial Intelligence to Read Ancient Roman Texts', *HumanIT*, 7/3 (2005), <http://www.hb.se/bhs/ith/3-7/mtpr.pdf>.

Thomas, W.G., 'Computing and the Historical Imagination', in S. Schreibman, R. Siemens and J. Unsworth (eds), *A Companion to Digital Humanities* (Oxford: Blackwell, 2004), pp. 56–68.

Thompson, D.J., 'Digitising a Lycopolite Census', CSAD Newsletter 2, Spring (1996), pp. 1–2, <http://www.csad.ox.ac.uk/CSAD/Newsletters/Newsletter2/Newsletter2a.html>.

Timpanaro, S., *Die Entstehung der Lachmannschen Methode* (2nd edn, Hamburg: H. Buske, 1971).

Tinnefeld, F.H. and Matschke, K.P., *Die Gesellschaft im späten Byzanz: Gruppen, Strukturen und Lebensformen* (Cologne-Weimar-Vienna: Böhlau, 2001).

Toufexis, N., 'Diglossia and Register Variation in Medieval Greek', *Byzantine and Modern Greek Studies*, 32/2 (2008): 203–17.

Trapp, E., 'Learned and Vernacular Literature in Byzantium: Dichotomy or Symbiosis?', *Dumbarton Oaks Papers*, 47 (1993): 115–29.

Tringham, R., Ashley, M. and Mills, S., 'Senses of Places: Remediations from Text to Digital Performance', (California 2008), <http://chimeraspider.wordpress.com/2007/03/01/beyond-etext-remediated-places-draft-1/>.

UK Government, *The Location Strategy for the United Kingdom. Geographic Information Panel* (2008), <http://www.communities.gov.uk/publications/communities/locationstrategy>.

Ullmann, L. and Gorokhovich, L., 'Google Earth and Some Practical Applications for the Field of Archaeology', *CSA Newsletter*, 18/3 (2006), <http://csanet.org/newsletter/winter06/nlw0604.html>.

Unsworth, J.M., *Our Cultural Commonwealth: The Report of the ACLS Commission on Cyberinfrastructure for the Humanities and Social Sciences* (American Council of Learned Societies, 2006).

Vollgraff, C.W., 'De tabella emptionis aetatis Traiani nuper in Frisia reperta', *Mnemosyne* 45 (1917): 341–52.

Wahlgren, S., 'Towards a Grammar of Byzantine Greek', *Symbolae Osloenses*, 77 (2002): 201–204.

Warwick, C., Galina, I., Terras, M., Huntington, P. and Pappa, N., 'The Master Builders: LAIRAH Research on Good Practice in the Construction of Digital Humanities Projects', in *Literary and Linguistic Computing* (2009).

Warwick, C., Terras, M., Fisher, C. et al., 'iTrench: A Study of the Use of IT in Field Archaeology', *Literary and Linguistic Computing*, 24/2 (2009): 211–23.

Watkins, D., 'Correlates of Approaches to Learning: A Cross-Cultural Meta-Analysis', in R.J. Sternberg and L.F. Zhang (eds), *Perspectives on Thinking, Learning and Cognitive Styles* (Mahwah, NJ: Lawrence Erlbaum, 2001), pp. 165–95.

Wenger, E., *Communities of Practice: Learning, Meaning, and Identity* (Cambridge: Cambridge University Press, 2002).

Wharton, C., Rieman, J., Lewis, C. and Polson, P., 'The Cognitive Walkthrough Method: A Practitioner's Guide', in J. Nielsen and R.L. Mack (eds), *Usability Inspection Methods* (Chichester: John Wiley and Sons, 1994), pp. 105–40.

Wheatley, D. and Gillings, M., *Spatial Technology and Archaeology: Archaeological Applications of GIS* (New York: Taylor and Francis, 2002).

Willetts, R.F., *The Law Code of Gortyn* (Berlin: de Gruyter, 1967).

Willi, A., *The Languages of Aristophanes. Aspects of Linguistic Variation in Classical Attic Greek* (Oxford: Oxford University Press, 2003).

Willis, S., *National Research Framework Document* (Study Group for Roman Pottery, 1997), <http://www.sgrp.org.uk/07/Doc/2.htm>.

Zorich, D., *A Survey of Digital Cultural Heritage Initiatives and Their Sustainability Concerns* (Washington, DC: Council on Library and Information Resources, 2003).

Index

For Product Safety Concerns and Information please contact our
EU representative GPSR@taylorandfrancis.com
Taylor & Francis
Verlag GmbH, Kaufingerstraße 21, 80331 München, Germany.